EVERY LIVING THING

HOW POPE FRANCIS, EVANGELICALS AND
OTHER CHRISTIAN LEADERS ARE INSPIRING
ALL OF US TO CARE FOR ANIMALS

General Editor,
Christine Gutleben

Contributing Editors,
Antonia Gorman and Karen Allanach

The Humane Society of The United States

For more information and further discussion, visit
http://www.humanesociety.org/faith

ISBN: 978-1-942011-09-5

Cover Design: Christen Quakenbush

Version 1.0

Published By Front Edge Publishing

42807 Ford Rd., Suite 234

Canton, Michigan, USA

For information about customized editions, bulk purchases or permissions, contact Front Edge Publishing, LLC at admin@FrontEdgePublishing.com.

For the life of every living thing is in his hand,
and the breath of every human being.
—Job 12:10 New Living Translation (NLT)

Contents

ACKNOWLEDGEMENTS

THIS PROJECT WOULD not have materialized without the commitment of The Humane Society of the United States' leadership who believe in the essential collaboration between faith communities and animal advocates. Their vision led to the creation of our Faith Outreach program, and their support allowed us to strengthen and expand the program through the years.

My deepest gratitude goes to Karen Allanach, my longtime colleague and friend, who oversaw the creation of The HSUS online library of religious statements on animals, the source for much of the content of this book, and helped guide the project from online library to book with her characteristic creativity and enthusiasm. I am very grateful to my talented colleagues for their helpful and wise feedback, especially Reasa Currier, Deanne Thomsen, Bernard Unti, Rachel Querry, Kelly Williams and Elizabeth Bagley. I am also indebted to my former supervisors, Heidi Prescott and Joe Maxwell, whose guidance and ongoing encouragement brought this project into focus. Jennifer Hillman, my current supervisor, also enabled this project in countless ways and I am thankful for her ability to inspire our team.

A huge thanks to Dr. Antonia Gorman for her critical role in the creation of this book as well as providing expert counsel and assistance on this project over many years. Many thanks to Dr. Karen Swallow Prior and Dr. Charles Camosy for contributing the forwards and for their ongoing support and critical insight. Special thanks go to David Crumm and the staff at Read the Spirit and at Front Edge Publishing who paved the way for this important opportunity, shared their knowledge and experience, and kept us on track. I am also blessed to work with Mark Rodgers, Abby Skeans and Molly Connolly at the The Clapham Group. Learning from them has been one of my greatest joys as an advocate.

And most of all, thanks to my incredible family, especially Carl, Colten and Kenny Becker, who bring such happiness and love to my life.

FOREWORD

IN EIGHTEENTH- AND nineteenth-century England, leaders from my own Christian tradition, Evangelicalism, viewed the fight against cruel treatment of animals as part of their fight against cruel treatment of humans, both of which were widely accepted in their day. In fighting barbarity of all kinds, these Christian visionaries (who represented a variety of denominations, from Anglican to Nonconformist) sought to cultivate throughout all of society an attitude of universal benevolence which, as the eighteenth-century playwright Oliver Goldsmith pointed out, is allied to all the virtues.

Benevolence toward the lower creatures has been, in fact, a feature of the Evangelical movement from the start, beginning with John Wesley, who argued movingly in his *Compendium of Natural Philosophy, Being a Survey of the Wisdom of God in the Creation* that animals "that want the help of man have a thousand engaging ways, which, like the voice of God speaking to his heart, command him to preserve and cherish them." William Cowper, coauthor with John Newton of the *Olney Hymns*, linked love of man and love of animals in his 1785 poem *The Task*, declaring that he would not count among his friends "the man who needlessly sets foot upon a worm." Toward the end of the eighteenth century, Sarah Trimmer, a founder of the Sunday school movement, put animal welfare at the forefront of her program for moral education. And in the nineteenth century, William Wilberforce, most known for his leading role in the Evangelical crusade against slavery, played a central part in the campaign against animal cruelty. Indeed for the group of believers of which Wilberforce formed a part, known as the Clapham Sect, the abolition of slavery was only one of many issues they embraced in their program for the moral improvement of nineteenth-century England. Among other causes they championed were the abolition of the lottery, dueling, and public hangings; and the promotion of Sabbath Day observance, popular education, and penal reform. But many today have forgotten that these Evangelicals were at the forefront of the establishment of England's first animal welfare laws.

Like their fight against slavery, victory for animal welfare was not without tremendous opposition. The first legislation against bullbaiting (a cruel "sport," not unlike that with which Michael Vick was charged, that sets a tethered bull against a vicious dog) was introduced, with Wilberforce's support, in 1800. But the first legislative victory did not come until 1822.

Two years later, at an 1824 coffeehouse gathering, the Society for the Prevention of Cruelty to Animals (which would under Queen Victoria become the Royal Society for the Prevention of Cruelty to Animals) was formed, largely under the leadership of activist Christians. Wilberforce was appointed, along with fellow Members of Parliament and several clergymen, to superintend the publication of sermons and tracts on animal welfare in hopes of influencing public opinion toward their unpopular position.

From its beginnings, then, the modern animal welfare movement was a movement of moral, Christian reformers who recognized the link between one form of barbarism and another. For, as theologian Albert Schweitzer argued, all ethics are rooted in compassion. The animal welfare movement led by my Evangelical ancestors was rooted in a call to compassion and benevolence, as well as in the Christian's duty to God's creation.

Ample biblical support from the moral laws of Exodus to the wisdom of the Proverbs can be cited to advocate compassionate care for animals rather than exploitative domination. But perhaps the most compelling evidence of the implicit assumption in Scripture of the nature of man's relationship to animals is found in the picture God provides of His relationship to us: namely, that of the Good Shepherd "who lays down his life for the sheep" (John 10:11).

Adapted with permission from "Animals and Evangelicals," *Liberty Journal*. October 2007

—***Karen Swallow Prior***, *Professor of English at Liberty University in Lynchburg, VA, earned her Ph.D. and M.A. at the State University of New York at Buffalo and her B.A. at Daemen College.*

She is a member of the graduate faculty and teaches British literature primarily, with a specialty in eighteenth century British literature, which she loves for its emphasis on philosophy, ethics, aesthetics, community, and the "middle way."

Her books include Fierce Convictions: The Extraordinary Life of Hannah More: Poet, Reformer, Abolitionist *(Thomas Nelson, 2014) and a literary and spiritual memoir,* Booked: Literature in the Soul of Me *(T. S. Poetry Press, 2012). She is a contributing writer for* Christianity Today, The Atlantic, In Touch, *and* Think Christian. *Her writing has also appeared at* Comment, Relevant, Books and Culture, Fieldnotes, The Well, *and* Salvo. *She has spoken at numerous writing conferences including the Festival of Faith and Writing and the Roanoke Regional Writers Conference and Q Ideas.*

Prior is a member of the Faith Advisory Council of The Humane Society of the United States and a research fellow with the Ethics & Religious Liberty Commission of the Southern Baptist Convention. She lives in rural Virginia with her husband along with sundry dogs, horses, and chickens.

FOREWORD

CHRISTIANITY, AS UNDERSTOOD and interpreted by my faith tradition, has always had a strong sense of the non-human. Before the dis-enchanted world of the secular Enlightenment came to dominate the developed Western world, it was taken for granted that non-human spiritual beings were all around us. Scripture reveals, for instance, that angels played special roles in revealing God's will to humanity—and, indeed, were the non-human persons who announced the incarnation of the Word Made Flesh and the Resurrection. Jesus himself speaks of angels being deeply connected to the lives of little children. Evil non-human forces are also present in the form of demons and devils, bringing with them disease and other disasters.

Some view Pope Francis as a thoroughly modern and progressive Pope, but this is a mistake. The Holy Father—a product of the developing world—radically affirms a traditional, pre-modern, enchanted view of the world—one which is thoroughly aware of the non-human powers in our world, including (much to the bewilderment of those who cover him) the Devil.

It is no accident that Pope Francis has also resisted the modern view of the human person as the dominant center of creation, with everything else understood as so much window dressing. It is no accident that he chose to focus his first encyclical on ecology—*Laudato Si'*—lifting up the value of all of God's creation over and against the domination of human concerns at every turn.

The Pope, time and time again, makes special mention of non-human animals—insisting that their value is not merely as "resources" but rather insisting that they "have value in themselves." Indeed, when a particular species is damaged or destroyed, Francis describes the damage as "incalculable." The encyclical even makes clear that animals are part of Paradise at the end of time.

In teaching this, of course, the Holy Father is not coming up with something new. Sacred Scripture tells us that the end times will bring with them a new earth in which all things are made new. Indeed, we are given a vision of God's will for animals in the stories of pre-fall Genesis in which animals are pronounced "good" by God, independent of human beings. This peaceable Kingdom is free of violence, including the kind of violence which comes with animals and humans eating each other. Animals are brought to Adam by God, not to eat, but because it is not good man should be alone.

This tradition of concern for the non-instrumental value of animals was found in the Church Fathers (many of whom considered refusing to eat meat as a way of getting closer to God), the scholastics of the Middle Ages (St. Albert the Great was, among other things, a great zoologist), and of course St. Francis—the most famous animal-lover of all time.

It could be argued, however, that the Church's theology after the secular Enlightenment—and particularly after in the 1960s—took a dramatic modern inward turn to focus almost exclusively on the human person. Indeed, non-human animals are not even mentioned in the great Dogmatic Constitution on the Church which came out of the Second Vatican Council. With *Laudato Si'*, however, Pope Francis has steadied the Church in refocusing on the traditional position in favor of the intrinsic value of all creation.

What this wonderful book demonstrates, however, is that this movement is happening throughout the Christian Churches. What an incredibly hopeful moment! Without a strong counter-culture to resist it, the seemingly all-powerful secular consumerism of the developed West will continue to dominate. For most of the developing world, it is the efficient consuming of the human person which is the center of our moral universe. Everything else—including the billions of animals tortured and killed in factory farms each year—is understood to be at the service of this goal.

When the early Church debated about what aspects of the Jewish law should bind Christian converts, the eventual resolution included the prohibition of eating animals which had been sacrificed to idols. But the meat produced by today's factory farms comes from animals who have been sacrificed to the idol of consumerism. And as first toward rediscovering our ancient traditions, therefore, let me propose that Christians refuse to eat such meat.

There is much which needs to be done for the Church to fully reflect our teachings on the value of God's creation, and the overwhelming changes which need to take place may seem overwhelming. But resisting the sin social structure of factory farms is a good place to start, and the pages which follow will no doubt lead to reader to consider other important ideas as well.

But the bottom line is this: Christians have deep resources on non-human animal in our tradition, and it is high time we time begin engaging them seriously. This book is a fantastic tool for doing precisely this.

—***Charles C. Camosy*** *is Associate Professor of Theology at Fordham University. He is the author of several books, including* For Love of Animals: Christian Ethics, Consistent Action. *He was co-editor of a special issue of the* Journal of Moral Theology *devoted to concern for animals, and is co-convener of the animal ethics interest group with the Society of Christian Ethics. You can follow him on Twitter @nohiddenmagenta.*

Introduction

What are religious statements on animals?

At The Humane Society of the United States (HSUS), we work to highlight the rich history of compassion and concern for animals among people of faith. This tradition is no more apparent than in the statements on animals issued by faith leaders and the governing bodies of denominations. These statements are theological expressions rooted in concern for God's creatures, and can help to define a faith community's set of beliefs around animals. Religious statements on animals establish accountability for the welfare of animals and their protection, and can authorize action on behalf of its followers. In some cases, statements define a denomination's official position on specific animal welfare issues. Most of the statements are crafted by committees of theologians, clergy and lay leaders and come from a process of extensive reflection and review. Many statements receive final approval at national church-wide assemblies and leadership gatherings.

While nearly every major religious tradition has a history of concern for animals, this book will focus on the Christian traditions in the United States. For more information on statements on animals from traditions outside of the scope of this book, we have compiled a list of sources in Appendix 2.

According to a Pew Research Center 2014 survey, "the United States remains home to more Christians than any other country in the world, and a large majority of Americans—roughly 7 in 10—continue to identify with some branch of the Christian faith." The Christian faith is a powerful source of discernment for many Americans. It has much to give in the way of guiding and cultivating a movement of faithful adherents towards a more consistent ethic of concern for God's creatures.

Religious statements on animals reveal animal protection as a natural part of the matrix of concerns addressed by faith communities and leaders. They root an understanding of the issues in biblical exegesis, serve as a catalyst for collaboration between faith communities and animal advocates and provide an authentic, theological basis for human responsibility towards animals.

STATEMENTS IN ACTION

There are countless examples of how religious statements on animals have influenced public policy, campaigns and public opinion related to them.

In 2007, The HSUS was involved in an unprecedented ballot measure campaign to improve the living conditions of farm animals in California. Proposition 2 required that, for the majority of the day, egg-laying hens, gestating pigs and veal calves would have enough room to stand up, lie down, turn around and extend their limbs and wings. The Faith Outreach program provided faith leaders in the state with information on their traditions' statements about animals. In the case of the United Methodist Church and the Episcopal Church, there were clear mandates about the treatment of farm animals. These statements opened the door for constructive conversations about the issue with bishops, faith leaders and religious institutions, which ultimately led to well over 100 public endorsements from faith leaders across the state.

The Rt. Rev. Marc Andrus, Bishop of the Episcopal Diocese of California, provided the following endorsement: "The Prevention of Farm Animal Cruelty Act is a modest but important measure that will simply give veal calves, breeding pigs and egg-laying hens enough room to engage in basic movements. God entrusts animals to our care, denying them the ability even to turn around is surely not an example of faithful stewardship." Bishop Andrus was inspired by the Episcopal Church's 2003 Convention resolution entitled, "Support Ethical Care of Animals," which states that, "The Episcopal Church encourages its members to ensure that husbandry methods for captive and domestic animals would prohibit suffering in such conditions as puppy mills, and factory farms." Denominational statements on animals played a key role in the active and public support from faith communities and leaders in California for Proposition 2. Due to the overwhelming support from faith leaders and a broad range of coalitions, the ballot measure won by a landslide with the biggest margin in the history of the state.

Religious statements on animals have also led to faith community involvement in a variety of programs that help animals. The HSUS's Fill the Bowl Project encourages church communities to collect pet food and supplies for local food banks and animal shelters. Church committees and their governing bodies are inspired when they learn that church doctrine supports this work. For instance, The United Methodist Church's Social Principles states, "We support regulations that protect the life and health of animals, including those ensuring the humane treatment of pets and other domestic animals..." As a result, we have had several Methodist churches participate in the program.

Throughout the years, The HSUS has enjoyed the partnership and support of many religious leaders on a range of issues—many of these collaborations are a direct result of a denomination's statements on animals. From increased penalties for animal fighting to participation in programs that provide critical support for families and pets in need, faith leaders and communities have referenced their church doctrine and statements as the context for their support.

THE BEGINNING OF THE EVANGELICAL STATEMENT ON THE RESPONSIBLE CARE OF ANIMALS

In 2011, The HSUS hosted a Religious Leaders Summit in Washington, D.C. Faith leaders from across the country met with HSUS executives and staff for two days to discuss animal welfare issues. During this meeting, we presented our online database of religious statements on animals. Dr. Barrett Duke, vice president of the Ethics and Public Policy Center for the Southern Baptist Convention, pointed out that evangelicals were the only major faith tradition in the United States that did not have a statement on animals. It was at that moment that he and others at the meeting began conversations around drafting such a statement. Michael Cromartie, vice president of the Ethics and Public Policy Center and Mark Rodgers, principal of The Clapham Group and former chief of staff to Senator Rick Santorum, agreed to draft the document with Dr. Duke. For three years, the document underwent a series of revisions as the drafters sought feedback from evangelical theologians nationwide. During this time, the statement garnered critical involvement and support from a range of evangelical leaders and theologians. Although theologically and operationally independent, the evangelical statement project was also done in cooperation with the Faith Outreach program of The Humane Society of the United States.

Laudato si': POPE FRANCIS' ENCYCLICAL LETTER "ON CARE FOR OUR COMMON HOME"

On June 18, 2015, Pope Francis, who chose Saint Francis of Assisi, the patron saint of animals and the environment as his "guide and inspiration," released the first encyclical in the history of the Vatican on environmental concerns. *Laudato si'* is translated, "Praise be to you" in honor of his namesake's prayer, "Canticle of the Sun," written in 1224, in praise of God's creation: "Be praised, my Lord, through all Your creatures." Pope Francis effectively defines environmental issues as moral issues and calls upon people of faith to take definitive action on behalf of God's creation. Throughout the encyclical, Pope Francis highlights the connection between human and animal flourishing. We are reminded over and over again, "all creatures are connected, each must be cherished with love and respect, for all of us as living creatures are dependent on one another." Many of the statements on animals in *Laudato si'* are referenced in the section on the Roman Catholic Church.

The providential timing of this encyclical, just months before the release of the evangelical statement on animals, provides people of faith with a more comprehensive and explicit set of responses to animal welfare issues and reflections on their value as God's creatures.

ORGANIZATION OF THIS BOOK

Due to the very recent launch of the Evangelical Statement on Responsible Care for Animals, this statement and the explanatory essay are presented at the beginning of the Statements section later in this book. Denominational statements are then listed in alphabetical order according to denomination.

Information on The Humane Society of the United States and the Faith Outreach program follow the Statements section, as well.

Appendices 1 and 2 include information on key resources for further reflection and how to become involved.

REFLECTIONS

Working with faith leaders and faith community members on animal welfare issues has given me the privilege to witness the unlimited human capacity for kindness, mercy and compassion. Despite full schedules and much to do, countless pastors and faith leaders willingly incorporate animal welfare issues into the scope of their priorities. Likewise, I have colleagues at The HSUS who have adopted children and others who volunteer at homeless shelters and spend their weekends mentoring inner-city kids. The HSUS works with hundreds of volunteers, many of whom juggle multiple responsibilities while also donating their time and talents to helping animals. I see constant examples of people heeding a call to help both animals and people and feeling a natural inclination towards both.

Pastor Randy Craighead, Sr. Pastor at Church of the King in New Orleans, noted, "Helping animals helps people." Pastor Craighead said this after he witnessed the work of his parishioner, Dr. John Mauterer, who routinely offered free veterinary services to people in underserved areas. Pastor Craighead saw how much it meant to people to provide care for their beloved companions. Church of the King permanently integrated Dr. Mauterer's veterinary services alongside the medical services they were providing for people during their monthly community service events. This holistic approach to serving people, recognizing the integral place of animals in our lives, is catching on in communities across the country. Thousands of churches nationwide now provide either annual or ongoing events that recognize animals as worthy of our attention and concern.

I believe more than ever that kindness begets kindness and as we work for compassion, no matter the cause—it opens our hearts to more. Caring for animals does not equate to prioritizing animals over people. More than anything it's an acknowledgement that everything matters, including animals.

—*Christine Gutleben* *is senior director of The HSUS Faith Outreach program. Since joining The HSUS in 2007, Ms. Gutleben has drawn together and worked with hundreds of religious leaders and individuals around the cause of animal protection, facilitating gatherings for religious leaders across the country to form partnerships that address the widespread abuse of animals. Ms. Gutleben received her master's degree from the Graduate Theological Union and its affiliate, The Dominican School of Philosophy and Theology, in Berkeley, California where she studied theology and the interplay between food and faith.*

HISTORY AND STRUCTURE OF THIS BOOK

IN 2008, I began working with the Humane Society of the United States Faith Outreach program on an online library of religious statements on animals. Insights from the largest Christian denominations in the country were gathered together, divided by denomination, and organized into three sections of quotes: official, historical, and contemporary. Initially, these quotes were given no additional context or comment, under the premise that this structure would allow denominations to "speak for themselves" about animals without any unintentional bias imposed by commentary. It soon became clear, however, that an un-annotated collection of quotes presented a number of problems for readers, the most serious of which was the difficulty inherent in plodding, unaided, through dense material originating from a wide range of documents expressing widely divergent viewpoints. In order to help readers navigate the terrain, the organizational structure of the online material was altered in 2010. The newer structure has been adapted for this book and the resource material has been updated.

Denominations have been selected solely because of their membership size and not because of their position on animals (except to the extent that their literature must contain *some* reference to animals or to creation as a whole). Each denomination is presented using an identical format: general information about the denomination and its membership size is presented briefly, followed by quotes on animals, when these could be found, or quotes on creation as a whole, when statements concerning animals could not be located or when these statements required a larger context in order to be fully appreciated. The quotes are then divided into three main sections—official, historical (when available), and contemporary—and then further divided into thematic units. Each unit is given a single-line subheading encapsulating the theme that runs through the unit, followed by a paragraph explaining the theme in more detail. Original material is indented to distinguish it from subheadings and explanatory paragraphs. Each new original quote is identified with a bullet point and a footnote identifying its source. Subheadings and explanatory paragraphs confine themselves to summaries of the material quoted, refraining from comment except when incidental facts, such as dates or events surrounding the material's original release, have been deemed useful. The words chosen for the subheadings and explanatory paragraphs are taken largely from the quotes themselves and word choices (for instance, the use of the word "man" versus "humanity") attempt to reflect the choices made within the original documents so as not to color reader perception unduly. Although certain themes appear across several denominations (for instance, the importance to God of human beings versus animals), all themes arise organically out of the original material and have not been artificially superimposed on it.

The "Official," "Historical," and "Contemporary" sections represent different source material and different degrees of authority. Material within the "Official Statements" section has been obtained, as the title implies, from the denomination's official documents and are the only quotes that represent the denomination's official position on animals. In general, these statements tend to have a theological focus (e.g., human account-ability to God for our treatment of animals) but occasionally address specific issues impacting animals (e.g., species extinction and habitat loss). More often, however, specific issues appear, when they appear, in the "Contemporary Reflections" section. Quotes within the contemporary section have been drawn from a variety of sources, including departments within the denomination, well-known members of the church, articles published by the denomination's magazines and/or website, and, on one rare occasion when little else could be found, from documents signed by members of the church hierarchy but not produced or published by the church. Quotes in the Historical References on Animals section are drawn from saints, founders, seminal thinkers or members of the denomination who were influential during its formative years. Conflicting opinions are sometimes expressed between and within the Official, Contemporary, and Historical sections, but, as already stated, only the statements that appear within the "Official Statements on Animals" section represent official church doctrine, although quotes from other sections may reflect unofficial church policy.

In 2012, after the online library was updated and completed, each denomination was contacted, asked to review their information, and given the opportunity to make suggestions and to request revisions. While not every denomination responded to this initial invitation, nine of the twelve churches did reply: the Assemblies of God, the Church of God in Christ, The Church of Jesus Christ of Latter-day Saints, The Episcopal Church, the Evangelical Lutheran Church in America, The Lutheran Church – Missouri Synod, the Presbyterian Church (U.S.A.), the Southern Baptist Convention, and the United Methodist Church. In 2015, as material was being further updated in preparation for print, denominations were contacted again, this time with copyright requests and with an opportunity to offer additional suggestions and/or comments. Responses were received from three new sources: the United Church of Christ, the Libreria Editrice Vaticana (the publishing arm of The Roman Catholic Church) and the Ellen G. White Estates (the repository of the writings of one of the founders of the Seventh-day Adventist Church). Many of the people and institutions that responded, both in 2012 and today, were generous with their time, insights, corrections, suggestions for overlooked or incorrectly placed material, and information regarding upcoming events or resolutions that had relevance to this project. All of these individuals, denominations, and organizations have my sincerest thanks.

I hope this brief explanation of the structure of this book, the sources of its information and the process behind its creation will help you enjoy, evaluate and apply its insights to your own relationships with animals. As you will see when you read further, religious values have much to say about our engagement with animals and our obligation to treat all God's creatures with kindness, compassion and mercy. These values have the capacity to touch our hearts and inspire our actions when we are open to them.

*—**Antonia Gorman, Ph.D.** received a doctorate in Theological and Religious Studies from Drew University, where she was a Will Herberg scholar and the winner of the Mulder Prize for academic excellence. Her doctoral dissertation,* The Blood of Goats and Bulls: An Eco-Spiritual Response to the Sacrifice of Creation, *was a constructive theology of salvation that brought together feminist, process, and ecological theologies with insights from the animal protection movement. Dr. Gorman has presented papers at both regional and national conferences of the American Academy of Religion. She has written for* The Berkshire Encyclopedia of Sustainability Vol. 1, EcoSpirit: Religions and Philosophies for the Earth, *and* The Way of Compassion: Survival Strategies for a World in Crisis *as well as for the journals* Ecotheology *(recently renamed* Journal for the Study of Religion, Nature and Culture) *and* Satya: Vegetarianism, Environmentalism, Animal Advocacy, Social Justice. *She has been a consultant with* The HSUS's Faith Outreach *program since 2008.*

An Evangelical Statement on Responsible Care for Animals

Preface

Jesus Christ is Lord, and "By Him all things were created, both in the heavens and on the earth, visible and invisible, whether thrones or dominions or rulers or authorities—all things have been created through Him and for Him." (Col. 1:16) As such we hold that our view of all living creatures, as our view of everything, must be thoroughly shaped, informed and tested against Scripture.

The following then aspires to be a holistic Biblical approach to an understanding of how we treat an especially vulnerable subset of all God's creatures: animals. While we recognize that all living creatures deserve respect as part of God's creation, we want to help focus attention on animals, as these creatures can be most subject to irresponsible and cruel treatment by humans.

We Believe

We believe that God created the heavens and the earth; that He created a multitude of living creatures, each after their own kind, including animals; that he gave them the breath of life; and that he declared all of this "good."

(Gn. 1:1, 20-25, 30; 6:17; 7:15, 22; Ps. 104:29-30)

We believe God uniquely created humankind in his own image and likeness, in contrast to creatures, including animals, who are created after their own kind; that He appointed humankind to rule over all living creatures, including animals; that God blessed Adam and Eve and commanded them to be fruitful and multiply and to fill the earth; that God instructed them to subdue the earth; that He gave them every seed bearing plant for food; and that God declared all that He had made, "very good."

(Gn. 1:26-31; Ps. 8:4-8; 1 Cor. 15:39; Jam. 3:9)

We believe that when sin entered the world through human rebellion it corrupted all relationships, firstly between humanity and God, but also relationships between people and between humankind and animals.

(Gn. 3:14, 4:8, 6:12-13, 49:6; Ex. 23:4-5; Prv. 12:10; Hos. 4:1-3; Hb. 2:17; Rom. 5:12, 8:20-21)

We believe that after the flood God caused all animals to fear humankind and gave them into our hand and for food; that God included animals in the covenant he made after the flood and commands us to show the same respect and concern for the life and welfare of animals that He does.

(Gn. 3:21, 6:19, 8:1, 8:9, 9:1-17; Ex. 23:4-5, 12, 19, 34:26; Dt. 25:4; Jon. 4:11; Acts 10:13-15)

We believe that all animals ultimately belong to God, are sustained by Him, and exist to bring Him praise and reveal His character.

(Dt. 10:14; Jb. 12:7-10, 41:11; Ps. 24:1, 36:6, 104:11-14, 21, 24-25, 27-30, 145:16, 21, 148:7, 10, 150:6; Mt. 6:26; Lk. 12:24; Rom. 1:20)

We believe all creation, including animals, will be set free from its slavery to corruption into the freedom of the glory of the children of God; that God will bring all things in heaven and on earth together under one head, Jesus the Christ; and through the Lord Jesus Christ will bring about a new heaven and a new earth that will reflect right relationships in all of creation, including between humans and animals.

[Is. 11:6-9, 65:17, 25; Hos. 2:18; Rom. 8:22; Eph1:9-10; Col. 1:15-23; Rev. 5:13, 21:1-5]

We Understand

We understand from Scripture that humans are uniquely created in the image and likeness of God and so have greater worth than every animal; but that God has given all animals the breath of life, that He sustains them, that they belong ultimately to Him, and that He has declared them "good," indicating they have value to Him independent of human use.

(Gn. 1:26-28; Ps. 8:5-8, 104:11-14; Jon. 4:11; Mt 6:26, 10:31; Lk. 12:7, 24)

We understand from Scripture that God has given us all animals into our hand and for food as part of our responsible rule; but as we live in a fallen world and are prone to sin, we also have the capacity and inclination to cause suffering instead of care for animals and to act cruelly towards them.

(Gn. 9:1-17; Ex. 26:14; Lv. 17:13; Prov. 12:10; Hos. 4:3; Hb. 2:17; Act. 10:13-15)

We understand from Scripture the responsible rule over and care of animals that God has given us on His behalf, and that this rule is to reflect His rule and character. This responsible rule and compassionate care of animals is expressed in God's instruction to

His people in His word, regarding the right treatment of animals, and that the principles behind these instructions, rooted in the unchanging character of God, still apply today.

(Ex. 23:4-5, 19, 34:26; Lv. 22:26-28, Lv. 25:7; Dt. 22:1-4, 6-7; 25:4)

We Resolve

We resolve to rule and treat all animals as living valued creatures, deserving of compassion, because they ultimately belong to God, because He has created them, declared them good, given them the breath of life, covenanted with them, and entrusted them to our responsible rule. So while animals have been given into our hand and for food this does not mean we can treat them as objects or act cruelly towards them.

We resolve to examine all our practices relating to how we treat the domesticated animals that live among us and provide us with companionship, food, and service as well how we treat animals that live in the wild apart from us; and hold them all up to Biblical principles for compassionate care and responsible rule, in light of God's view of them and His actions toward them.

We resolve to exercise our responsible rule in part by confronting any and all cruelty against animals, seeing it as a violation of our rule and an affront to the ultimate Ruler who created, values, and sustains these animals.

We resolve that because all kinds of animals are created by God and are sustained by Him, we need to work for the protection and preservation of all the kinds of animals God has created, while prioritizing human needs.[1]

An Evangelical Statement on Responsible Care for Animals: Explanatory Essay

WE OFFER THIS explanatory essay as a window into our interaction with the Bible's implications for animal stewardship. It is not a fully-rendered argument or a finished product. We offer it, however, with the prayer that it will provide additional insight and clarity about what we intend and don't intend by the various claims and conclusions we make in the Statement. Please feel free to interact with us regarding any aspect of this essay.

Preface

First paragraph

Jesus Christ is Lord, and "By Him all things were created, both in the heavens and on the earth, visible and invisible, whether thrones or dominions or rulers or authorities—all things have been created through Him and for Him." (Col. 1:16) As such we hold that our view of all living creatures, as our view of everything, must be thoroughly shaped, informed and tested against Scripture.

The first paragraph of the *Preface*, quoting Col. 1:16 explains why a statement like this is both necessary and appropriate. In drafting this statement, we have no wish or desire to place this issue on a pedestal or hold it up as of premier importance. We do, however, believe the apostle Paul when he writes *"All Scripture is God-breathed and profitable for teaching, for reproof, for correction, for training in righteousness; so that the man of God may be adequate, equipped for every good work."* (2 Tim. 3v16-17.[2]

We thus affirm that when we consider living creatures, and specifically animals in this document, that our thinking must come from Scripture, which trains us in righteousness, and reproves and corrects us when we err. This is surely just one area and component of the vast fullness of Christian discipleship, but nevertheless in this area, as in all areas, our minds must not be conformed to the pattern of this world, but instead must be transformed so that we might approve the good, pleasing and perfect will of God.

Second paragraph

The following then aspires to be a holistic Biblical approach to an understanding of how we treat an especially vulnerable subset of all God's creatures: animals. While we recognize that all living creatures deserve respect as part of God's creation, we want to help focus attention on animals, as these creatures can be most subject to irresponsible and cruel treatment by humans.

This second paragraph narrows our focus from all living creatures down to an especially vulnerable subset, animals. We do this because we think animals comprise the subset of living

2   Scripture taken from the New American Standard Bible® Copyright © 1960, 1962, 1963, 1968, 1971, 1972, 1973, 1975, 1995 by the Lockman Foundation. Used by permission.

creatures where most (but not all) of the more complex ethical considerations are manifest. In addition, because of their greater dependence on humans, animals are also more exposed to the possibility of irresponsible and cruel treatment by humans.

A Note on Structure

The accompanying Statement has been divided into three sections: Beliefs, Understandings and Resolutions. The Beliefs section seeks to identify, in contextually appropriate ways, the key passages that shape and inform our theological foundation for responsible care for animals. The Understandings section begins to interpret and apply these theological foundations and to draw out certain key principles from them. The final section, the Resolutions section, seeks to apply these theological foundations and key principles to our current situation.

Beliefs

First paragraph

> We believe that God created the heavens and the earth; that He created a multitude of living creatures, each after their own kind, including animals; that he gave them the breath of life; and that he declared all of this "good."
>
> (Gn. 1:1, 20-25, 30; 6:17; 7:15, 22; Ps. 104:29-30)

It is, of course, highly appropriate to begin this Statement at the beginning, in Genesis. In the creation account we see the awesome creative majesty of God at work. God's creative work regarding living creatures begins in verse 20. On the fifth day, God creates all the water creatures and birds, each after their own kind. Verse 21 ends with the affirmation that "God saw that it was good." Of interest also is that in verse 22, for the first time in the creation account, we see God giving a blessing and commanding the sea creatures to be fruitful and multiply and the birds to multiply.

The first paragraph of the Statement also refers to God's creation, on the sixth day, of living creatures from the earth, each after their own kind: the beasts of the earth, the cattle, the creeping things[3]. It is worth noting that there is no blessing or command to be fruitful here for these animals. However there is the divine affirmation in verse 25, "God saw that it was good." Lastly, before moving on to the culmination of the sixth day – man – it is necessary to address the description of animals as having "the breath of life." This term is typically associated with the creation of humanity (i.e., Genesis 2:7), however, the same Hebrew term is used to describe animals in Genesis 1:30.[4]

Second paragraph

> We believe God uniquely created humankind in his own image and likeness, in contrast to creatures, including animals, who are created after their own kind; that He appointed humankind to rule over all living creatures, including animals; that God blessed Adam and Eve and commanded them to be fruitful and multiply and to fill the earth; that God instructed them to subdue the earth; that He gave them every seed bearing plant for food; and that God declared all that He had made, "very good."
>
> (Gn. 1:26-31; Ps. 8:4-8; 1 Cor. 15:39; James 3:9)

The second paragraph rightly begins with the absolute belief that humanity is unique, completely distinct and alone is created in the image and likeness of God. The truth of humanity's uniqueness is clearly taught by Scripture, both in the creation account and in passages such as Psalm 8:4-8, 1 Cor. 15:39 and James 3:9.

---

3   *The terms are likely meant to be all-inclusive of animals that are not fish or fowl.*

4   *We are not claiming there is an equivalence between animals and humans. But we believe it is important for our better appreciation of animals to understand that this term is also used to refer to them.*

This complete and utter distinctiveness of humanity is not only ontological in nature. The second clause of the paragraph notes that God "appointed humankind to rule over all living creatures, including animals," Humans were given the sole appointment to rule over animals.

We think it is important to note that the word "rule"[5] used to describe human authority over animals, however, does not imply severe treatment. Moses tells the Israelites not to "rule over" (*radah*) indentured Israelites "harshly." So, it's possible to exercise *radah* in a way that respects the one being ruled.

The first half of verse 28 includes the second and last blessing in the creation account, where God blesses Adam and Eve and commands them to "Be fruitful and multiply, and fill the earth." We wish to fully affirm this divine command, still in force today.

We also wish to be as clear as possible about our affirmation that God gave Adam and Eve "every seed bearing plant for food." Our intent here is simply to be faithful to the whole creation account and note this part of Genesis 1:30. Our Statement goes on to say that this situation passed away after the flood[6] and that eating meat is affirmed in the New Testament.[7] Thus, while we include this clause for biblical faithfulness, we reject the belief and strongly disagree with any who would seek to use this verse (or consequently this Statement) to argue that the Bible mandates a vegetarian or vegan diet.

The last clause reminds us of the final affirmation that God gives in verse 31, that all of creation together is "very good." While this affirmation by the Creator of the exceeding goodness of all creation is well known to us, we must not let that familiarity dull the wonder and power of this truth and its implications for our view of all creation, including animals. The God of the heavens has declared all He made exceedingly good.

---

5   *Hebrew,* הדר *(radah)*

6   *Genesis 9:3*

7   *Luke 24:42 and Acts 10:13-15 for example*

Third paragraph

We believe that when sin entered the world through human rebellion it corrupted all relationships, firstly between humanity and God, but also relationships between people and between humankind and animals.

(Gn. 3:14, 4:8, 6:12-13, 49:6; Ex. 23:4-5; Prv. 12:10; Hos. 4:1-3; Hb. 2:17; Rom. 5:12, 8:20-21)

This third paragraph acknowledges the consequence of sin not only for humans but for the whole of creation, including animals. While we must never lose sight of the primary consequence of sin on humanity, that as the apostle Paul writes, "all have sinned and fall short of the glory of God,"[8] we are right, nevertheless, to recognize the systemic effects of sin upon all of creation.[9]

We see the initial impact of this consequence in the Fall itself and the curse meted out on the serpent. God told the serpent it is "cursed more than any livestock and more than any wild animal" (Genesis 3:14). But, the curse did not stop there. The use of the comparative "more than" tells us the curse on the serpent was more severe, but that the serpent wasn't the only recipient of the curse. All animals fell under the curse to some degree.

Furthermore, in the account of the flood in Genesis 6, we read "all flesh had corrupted their way upon the earth."[10] This asserts some sort of corruption of all living creatures, including animals.[11] In response, God decided to wipe out most of humanity, birds, and land-based animals. The birds and land-based

---

8   Romans 3:23

9   Romans 8:20-21

10   Genesis 6:12

11   *The exact phrase "all flesh", לֹב (kol) רְשָׂב (basar) appears eight times in Genesis chapters 6-8 [6:12, 13, 17, 19, 7:15, 16, 21, 8:17], with six of these occurrences referring specifically to the creatures taken on board the ark. It is for this reason we think the 6:12 reference suggest the wider understanding of corruption, though, clearly, this is primarily about human corruption.*

animals were not destroyed because of any moral failure on their part. Their corruption was due either to the effects of the curse at the Fall, or, as some commentators suggest, as a result of the failure of humans to appropriately fulfill their responsibility toward them. In support of this latter theory, we note that after the Flood, we continue to see a call to responsible treatment of animals.[12]

Fourth paragraph

We believe that after the flood God caused all animals to fear humankind and gave them into our hand and for food; that God included animals in the covenant he made after the flood and commands us to show the same respect and concern for the life and welfare of animals that He does.

(Gn. 3:21, 6:19, 8:1, 8:9, 9:1-17; Ex. 23:4-5, 12, 19, 34:26; Dt. 25:4; Jon. 4:11; Acts 10:13-15)

The fourth paragraph begins with the events of the flood. Here we see manifest God's concern for the preservation of all the different kinds of living creatures and the responsible rule and care for them required of humanity. God commanded Noah,

"And of every living thing of all flesh, you shall bring two of every kind into the ark, to keep them alive with you; they shall be male and female. Of the birds after their kind, and of the animals after their kind, of every creeping thing of the ground after its kind, two of every kind will come to you to keep them alive" (Genesis 6:19-20).

We continue to see God's concern manifest in Genesis 7:24 and 8:1 which states,

"the water prevailed upon the earth one hundred and fifty days. But God remembered Noah and all the beasts and all the cattle that were with him in the ark; and

---

12   *Genesis 49:6, Exodus 23:4-5 and Proverbs 12:10*

God caused a wind to pass over the earth, and the water subsided."

We wish to also note that Noah emulates God's concern for all creatures later in chapter 8 with his care for the dove:

"Then he sent out a dove from him, to see if the water was abated from the face of the land; but the dove found no resting place for the sole of her foot, so she returned to him into the ark, for the water was on the surface of all the earth. Then he put out his hand and took her, and brought her into the ark himself" (Genesis 8:8-9).

After the flood, we see God causing all animals to fear humans. He gives us authority over them and gives them to us for food.[13] Further, this paragraph reminds us that the covenant God made in Genesis 9 is not just with Noah, but with all living creatures on the ark. Four additional times God reiterated their inclusion in the covenant.[14] The fact that God considered it right to include animals in such a covenant is an important consideration for us as we think about our attitude toward animals.

The inclusion of animals in the Noahic covenant is just one instance of His obvious concern for animals. Scripture also contains numerous instances in which humanity is expected to show the same respect and care for animals that God does, most notably Exodus 23:4-5, 19 and 34:26; Deuteronomy 25:4; and Jonah 4:11.[15] While human behavior is of primary concern in these passages, we note that this is in relationship to animals. For example, Jonah 4:10-11 reads:

"Then the Lord said, "You had compassion on the plant for which you did not work and which you did not cause to grow, which came up overnight and perished overnight. Should I not have compassion on Nineveh, the great city in which there are more than 120,000 persons who do

---

13   *Genesis 9:2-3*

14   *After the initial reference in v. 10, the following four are verses 12, 15, 16 and 17.*

15   *Others include Leviticus 22:26-28, 25:7; and Deuteronomy 22:1-4, 6-7*

not know the difference between their right and left hand, as well as many animals?"

Fifth paragraph

We believe that all animals ultimately belong to God, are sustained by Him, and exist to bring Him praise and reveal His character.

(Dt. 10:14; Jb. 12:7-10, 41:11; Ps. 24:1, 36:6, 104:11-14,21, 24-25, 27-30, 145:16, 21, 148:7, 10, 150:6; Mt. 6:26; Lk. 12:24; Rom. 1:20)

A key foundation for the care and concern for animals mentioned in the previous paragraphs is the truth affirmed throughout Scripture that because God created animals, they, along with all of creation, belong to Him, are sustained by Him, and exist to bring Him praise and reveal His character.

The fifth paragraph affirms that God is the ultimate owner of not only the earth, but all its inhabitants. Psalm 24:1 is perhaps the most well-known passage expressing this truth: "The earth is the Lord's, and all it contains, the world, and those who dwell in it." Other passages that echo this theme include Deuteronomy 10:14, Job 41:11, and Psalm 104:24-25. All these passages affirm that while humans have rule over the animals, they ultimately belong, like all of creation, to God. Thus, by implication, we are responsible to Him for how we treat them.

Along with God's ultimate ownership of animals, Scripture speaks of God's ongoing provision for animals. Passages including Job 12:7-10 and Psalms 36:6, 104:10-14 and 145:16 all express the continued dependence of animals on God.

The third clause of this paragraph highlights the repeated refrain in Scripture that part of God's purpose for animals is that they would bring Him praise and reveal His character. We must rightly reject any attempt to idolize or divinize animals and be vigilant against this distortion[16] Nevertheless, we see the Old Testament, Jesus, and Paul pointing to the role of creation, including animals, in helping us to understand God.

---

16   *Romans 1:22-23*

For example, the same passage in which Paul rightly warns against idolizing creation, he also earlier notes, "For since the creation of the world His invisible attributes, His eternal power and divine nature, have been clearly seen, being understood through what has been made, so that they are without excuse." (Romans 1:20)

Psalms 145:21, 148:7-10 and 150:6 offer additional examples of this function of animals. Jesus helps us here, as well. He says, ***"Look at the birds of the air, that they do not sow, nor reap nor gather into barns, and yet your heavenly Father feeds them. Are you not worth much more than they?"*** (Matthew 6:36) Clearly, the consideration of the worth of animals is not Jesus' primary focus in this passage, but we note that our Lord said the way God cares for birds tells us something important about His commitment to us.

Sixth paragraph

> We believe all creation, including animals, will be set free from its slavery to corruption into the freedom of the glory of the children of God; that God will bring all things in heaven and on earth together under one head, Jesus the Christ; and through the Lord Jesus Christ will bring about a new heaven and a new earth that will reflect right relationships in all of creation, including animals.
>
> (Is. 11:6-9, 65:17, 25; Hos. 2:18; Rom. 8:22; Eph. 1:9-10; Col. 1:15-23; Rev. 5:13, 21:1-5)

Both the Old Testament and the New are clear that Christian eschatological hope encompasses all of creation. As John Stott observes regarding the Romans 8 passage:

> "Paul now writes from a cosmic perspective. The suffering and glory of the old creation (the material order) and of the new (the people of God) are integrally related to each other. Both creations are suffering and groaning now; both are going to be set free together. As nature shared in the curse, and now

shares in the pain, so it will also share in the glory."[17]

This new heaven and new earth will reflect *shalom*, the harmonious right relationships that the prophets speak about. Both Isaiah and Hosea include animals in their description of what this will look like.[18]

Understandings Section

First paragraph

We understand from Scripture that humans are uniquely created in the image and likeness of God and so have greater worth than every animal; but that God has given all animals the breath of life, that He sustains them, that they belong ultimately to Him and that He has declared them "good," indicating they have value to Him independent of human use.

(Gn. 1:26-28; Ps. 8:5-8, 104:11-14; Jon. 4:11; Mt 6:26, 10:31; Lk 12:7, 24)

This first paragraph categorically affirms the uniqueness and greater worth of humans compared to animals, witnessed to in both Old and New Testaments. Yet we also see an affirmation of the value of animals. God declared them "good" prior to the creation of humans. His ownership of them communicates an understanding of their value, as well. These facts suggest that animals have value to God independent of human use.[19] We also see, for example, in Jonah 4:11, that God expressed compassion not just for young children but also for the many animals in Nineveh.

God created animals, declared them good, and owns them. Consequently, while humanity rules over all animals, and they

---

17   Stott, J, *The Message of Romans, Bible Speaks Today Commentaries, p.*238

18   *Isaiah* 11:6-9, 65:25 *and Hosea* 2:18

19   *Wright, C, Old Testament Ethics and the People of God, IVP,* 2004

have been given to us for food, we cannot treat them as inanimate objects and in ways that debase their inherent God-given value.

Second paragraph

> We understand from Scripture that God has given us all animals into our hand and for food as part of our responsible rule; but as we live in a fallen world and are prone to sin, we also have the capacity and inclination to cause suffering instead of care for animals and to act cruelly towards them.

> (Gn. 9:1-17; Ex. 26:14; Lv. 17:13; Prov. 12:10; Hos. 4:3; Hb. 2:17; Acts 10:13-15)

God's giving of animals to us for food began with Noah and continues into the New Testament. Jesus himself ate meat and fish[20] and Paul affirms eating meat in both his letters to the Romans and the Corinthians.[21] In addition, Leviticus makes reference to hunting for food and Exodus to the use of animal skins in the building of the Tabernacle.[22]

However, this paragraph reminds us that because of our sinful nature we sometimes act in ways that either directly or indirectly cause cruelty and suffering to animals. Scripture is clear that such behavior is sinful.[23]

Indeed, cruelty and suffering is sinful because it is a distortion of the God ordained office we hold and a debasement of creatures that belong to Him. Cruelty towards animals is wrong, not only because of what they are, but also because of who God is and who He created us to be.[24]

---

20   *Luke 24:41-43; 22:7-8, and 13-15*

21   *Romans 14:2-3; 1 Corinthians 10:25*

22   *Exodus 36:19; Leviticus 17:13*

23   *Proverbs 12:10, Hosea 4:3, and Habakkuk 2:17*

24   *Leviticus 19:2*

Third paragraph

We understand from Scripture the responsible rule over and care of animals that God has given us on His behalf, and that this rule is to reflect His rule and character. This responsible rule and compassionate care of animals is expressed in God's instruction to His people in His word, regarding the right treatment of animals, and that the principles behind these instructions, rooted in the unchanging character of God, still apply today.

(Ex. 23:4-5, 19, 34:26; Lv. 22:26-28, Lv. 25:7; Dt. 22:1-4, 6-7; Dt. 25:4)

The third paragraph provides an overview of passages that discuss the treatment of animals and the normative principles at play. Of course, with any ethical norms derived from the Old Testament we must be clear how these principles apply today in light of the New Testament. We believe though that these ethical principles are rooted in the unchanging character of God and so with proper exegesis and application they still have relevance today.

Resolutions Section

This section seeks to correctly apply the previous acknowledgements rooted in biblical teaching to our contemporary actions and attitudes. We recognize that it is most likely here that differences among followers of Christ are likely to emerge.

First paragraph

We resolve to rule and treat all animals as living valued creatures, deserving of compassion, because they ultimately belong to God, because He has created them, declared them good, given them the breath of life, covenanted with them, and entrusted them to our responsible rule. So while animals have been given into our hand this does not mean we can treat them as objects or act cruelly towards them.

This first resolution seeks to attest to the imperative of humanity's responsible rule of all living creatures, here specifically, animals. Humans have no authority over animals that is not a delegated authority from God. Our rule over living creatures is not an absolute monarchy allowing us to do what we wish, but a vice-regency under and according to the rule of the King. As this rule has been granted to us by the ultimate Ruler, it must be on His terms, on His behalf, and for His glory.

The resolution also summarizes and elaborates on the inherent worth that God gives living creatures, including animals. It is derived by biblical passages that affirm God's ownership and sustenance of animals, along with the concept of "rule" revealed in Genesis 1:28.[25] Animals are not 'objects' but living creatures, valued by God. Our rule over them must reflect this reality.

We wish to be abundantly clear that by affirming animals as valued living creatures, we are not equating them with us or elevating them to our level. Just as Scripture is clear on the their status as living creatures valued by God, it is also clear on humanity's greater value, uniqueness, rule and sole status as God's image bearers.

Second paragraph

> **We resolve** to examine all our practices relating to how we treat the domesticated animals that live among us and provide us with companionship, food, and service as well how we treat animals that live in the wild apart from us; and hold them all up to Biblical principles for compassionate care and responsible rule, in light of God's view of them and His actions toward them.

This resolution seeks to expound on our mandate from the Creator to rule responsibly. It reminds us all to examine our

---

25   *Please see the comments in the explanation of the second paragraph of the Beliefs section.*

current treatment of animals to determine whether we are rightly fulfilling this mandate. As the paragraphs notes, this includes our treatment of different types of animals in every circumstance.

We must ask ourselves important questions about how we treat individual animals but also what sort of societal treatment we, explicitly or implicitly, encourage and support by our actions and attitudes.

Our answers to these questions must be shaped and thoroughly informed by Scripture. Clearly some of these issues are not clear-cut and require prudential wisdom to discern. Nevertheless, we affirm that this wisdom must find its source in our Creator God and that discussions among Evangelicals on these issues must always be rooted in His Holy Word which "is God-breathed and profitable for teaching, for reproof, for correction, for training in righteousness; so that the man of God may be adequate, equipped for every good work."[26]

Third paragraph

> **We resolve** to exercise our responsible rule in part by confronting any and all cruelty against animals, seeing it as a violation of our rule and an affront to the ultimate Ruler who created, values, and sustains these animals.

This resolution follows naturally from the preceding two. As animals are living creatures valued by God and humanity has been appointed to rule them, we are thus required to name and confront distortions of that rule. Indeed, as the second paragraph of the Understanding section notes, animal "cruelty and suffering is sinful because it is a distortion of the God ordained office we hold and a debasement of creatures that belong to Him."

By highlighting this responsibility, we by no means wish to elevate this sinfulness above others, but simply wish to recognize that *"there is not one righteous, not even one"* and that

---

26   2 Timothy 3:16-17

cruelty to animals is one of the many ways in which we sin and rebel against our rightful Ruler and Creator.

Fourth paragraph

We resolve that because all kinds of animals are created by God and are sustained by Him, we need to work for the protection and preservation of all the kinds of animals God has created, while prioritizing human needs.

This resolution draws primarily from the principles found in the early chapters of Genesis. It seeks to blend the truths that all animals have been created by God, that their diversity is part of His creative activity, and that He has taken action to preserve them. At the same time it recognizes that animals have been given into humanity's hand for food.

Concluding Words

We are keenly aware that this brief essay leaves many unanswered questions, but we are confident that we have established the exegetical basis for the Statement. We welcome further elaboration on these arguments as well as constructive criticism. It is our prayer that this Statement will help to unify Evangelicals around a basic, essential body of commitments that can help us develop a more biblical, consistent and responsible ethic toward our animal co-inhabitants of planet earth. May God bless this effort for His glory.

View the signatures of support for the statement at www.everylivingthing.com.

Assemblies of God

General Information

The Assemblies of God was founded in the United States in 1914 in the midst of an international Pentecostal revival. Today, it is a member of the world's largest Pentecostal association: the World Assemblies of God Fellowship. It characterizes itself as having a fourfold mission: "evangelism, discipleship, worship, and compassion."[27]

More information about the Assemblies of God, including the church's beliefs, structure, and history, can be found by going to http://ag.org/

Number of Members in the U.S.: 3.1 million[28]

Number of Members Worldwide: 61.9 million[29]

27   Assemblies of God. "Brief History of the Assemblies of God," accessed July 30, 2015. http://ag.org/top/About/History/index.cfm

28   Assemblies of God. "AG ACMR and Related U.S. Statistics, 2004-2014." accessed July 30, 2015. http://agchurches.org/Sitefiles/Default/RSS/AG.org%20TOP/AG%20Statistical%20Reports/2015%20(year%20 2014%20reports)/AcmrRpt2014.pdf

29   Assemblies of God, "AG Worldwide Churches and Adherents, 1987-2014,"accessed July 30, 2015. http://agchurches.org/Sitefiles/Default/RSS/AG.org%20TOP/AG%20Statistical%20Reports/2015%20(year%20 2014%20reports)/AdhWW%202014.pdf

Official Statements on Animals

God created all life, but human beings are "the cap-stone of God's creative activity"

The governing body of the Assemblies of God, known as the General Council, has issued a series of position papers representing the church's official stance on a number of controversial issues impacting contemporary society. In its Position Paper on the Doctrine of Creation, the General Council states that while "everything that exists" is created by God, human beings are the "capstone" and "zenith of God's creative activity."

- 'In the beginning God created the heavens and the earth' (Genesis 1:1).[30] The Bible begins with the story of creation, declares at the outset that God is the Creator, and reiterates this understanding of origins from Genesis to Revelation...In the Genesis narratives, and throughout the Old and New Testaments, the Bible emphasizes that God is Creator, not only of the earth and its inhabitants, but of everything that exists (Exodus 20:11; Nehemiah 9:6; Psalm 146:6; Acts 14:17; Revelation 4:11; 10:6).[31]

- [O]rder, progress, and climax are all woven into the biblical account of creation...Progress can be seen in...the increase of personal attention God gave to His creative work. Of the vegetation we read that God said, "'Let the land produce vegetation'...And it was so" (Genesis 1:11, 12). Of the animals we read that God said, "Let the land produce living creatures'... And it was so" (vv. 24-25). But of the human race God, using strikingly personal and plural language, said,

---

30   *Bible citations for all AG statements come from The Holy Bible, New International Version.*

31   *The General Council of the Assemblies of God, Position Paper: The Doctrine of Creation (Springfield: The General Council of the Assemblies of God, revised 2014), 1 http://ag.org/top/Beliefs/Position_Papers/pp_downloads/PP_The_Doctrine_of_Creation.pdf*

"'Let us make mankind'…So God created mankind… male and female he created them" (vv. 26-27). The human race is thus the capstone of God's creative activity…The creation story depicts human beings as the zenith of God's creative activity.[32]

Created in the image of God, human beings "may rule… over all the creatures"

Of all God's creatures, writes the AG's General Council, only human beings are created in the divine image. This bestows upon humanity the right to "rule…over all the creatures."

- Significantly, it was only humans of whom God said, 'Let us make mankind ['human being,' not exclusively 'male']³³ in our image, in our likeness.' (1:26), 'so that they may rule…over all the creatures' (1:26). Neither the previous inanimate or animate creation was so described. In those creative activities, God has simply said, "'Let there be'…And it was so" (as in Genesis 1:6-7).[34]

Human rule should treat all creatures "as gifts from God…to be appreciated and cherished"

In addition to Position Papers approved by its General Council, the AG also has created a series of documents "endorsed by the church's Commission on Doctrinal Purity and the Executive Presbytery." Among these is a document on Environmental Protection, which clarifies the intended nature of humanity's rule over creation. According to this document, humanity's rule should be exercised as a form of stewardship in which all creatures, including "animals, fish, and fowl," are recognized as gifts from God "to be appreciated and cherished."

- The Assemblies of God believes everyone needs to be a good steward of *all* God's creation–including the earth. As clearly indicated in Scripture, we believe the earth was created by God (Genesis 1:1-31; Isaiah

---

32 *Ibid,* 2-3.

33 *Textual clarification appears in the AG original.*

34 *General Council of the Assemblies of God,* 3-4.

37:16)…[W]e feel Christians must act responsibly in their use of God's earth as we rightly harvest its resources. As stated in Genesis 1:27-30, we believe God has given mankind alone complete dominion (authority) over the earth's resources. These resources include the land, the water, the vegetation, and the earth's minerals; as well as the animals, fish, and fowl. Like the earth, we acknowledge these to be gifts from God to mankind; and as gifts they are to be appreciated and cherished.[35]

Animals may be used to satisfy vital human needs but they should not be mistreated

According to the Commission on Doctrinal Purity, God permits humans to use animals to satisfy our needs as long as the animals "are not mistreated." "There is no justification in Scripture," says the Commission, "for needless abuse and mistreatment of animals."

- The Bible recognizes that animals are a source of food for humans. It also gives humans dominion over the animal world—and by implication over the plant world (Genesis 1:26, 28). There is also an instance in Scripture where selective breeding of animals took place (Genesis 30). Some recent research has sought to produce milk through genetic engineering that would be therapeutic and enriched for the benefit of those who drink it. Such research would seem to be acceptable as long as the animals used in the research are not mistreated. Animal life does not have the standing in God's sight that human life has, but there is no justification in Scripture for needless abuse and mistreatment of animals.[36]

35   Commission on Doctrinal Purity and the Executive Presbytery of the Assemblies of God, "Environmental Protection," accessed August 1, 2015. http://ag.org/top/Beliefs/contempissues_02_environment.cfm

36   Commission on Doctrinal Purity and the Executive Presbytery of the Assemblies of God. "Genetic Alteration and Cloning," accessed July 30, 2015. http://ag.org/top/Beliefs/contempissues_14_genetics.cfm

Historical References
on Animals

John McConnell, Jr.: "We love God [and therefore should have] an appreciation for his creation."

John McConnell, Jr., whose parents were founding members of the Assemblies of God and who, himself, was a longtime member of the church, credits his Pentecostal origins with inspiring him to establish the first Earth Day in 1970. According to McConnell, the love of human beings for God should give us an appreciation for God's creation. Genesis instructs us, says McConnell, to be "caretakers upon earth" and a "Christ-like view [would] be to recognize Earth as a precious gift that is our responsibility to protect and nurture."

- Many readers will be surprised to learn that the founder of the original Earth Day was a Pentecostal... [T]he life of John McConnell, Jr. demonstrates that one can love Jesus and care for His creation; these two attitudes are not mutually exclusive...He boldly declared, 'If there had been no Christian experience in my life there would be no Earth Day—or at least I would not have initiated it.'[37]

- John McConnell, Jr.'s interest in earth-care developed in part from his own lifelong study of Scripture. He explains his simple logic, stating, 'We love God... [and therefore should] have an appreciation for his creation.' To clarify and define this logical 'appreciation,' McConnell, Jr. cites Psalm 115:16, 'The earth has been given to the children of men.' He connects this promise to the command in Genesis

---

37   *Nicole Sparks and Darrin J. Rodgers, "John McConnell, Jr. and the Pentecostal Origins of Earth Day," Assemblies of God Heritage Vol. 30, (2010), 17, 23, accessed August 1, 2015. http://www.ifphc.org/pdf/Heritage/2010.pdf*

1:28, that humanity is to 'subdue' the earth. 'We're caretakers upon earth...'Subdue the earth'—I think that meant to take care of it'...McConnell's call is not for earth worship, but for responsible stewardship of the earth that all people share.[38]

- McConnell often found the Christian response to the call for earth-care and environmental responsibility, however, to be less than encouraging. Challenging the apathy and dismissal of environmental concerns, McConnell, Jr. wrote: 'Don't most evangelicals neglect responsibility and care of Earth because they are taught that Earth will soon pass away and is of relative unimportance in comparison with heaven and eternity? Wouldn't a more Christ-like view be to recognize Earth as a precious gift that is our responsibility to protect and nurture?'[39]

- John even views Christian participation in Earth Day as an opportunity to be a witness: 'While Earth Day is non-sectarian and non-political (people of all religions and no religion participate), it provides a great opportunity for Christians to show the power of prayer, the validity of their charity and their practical concern for Earth's life and people.' McConnell encourages Christians to lead the way in living out the kingdom of heaven on earth. As McConnell, Jr. observes, 'The cutting edge of freedom and order has often been people with a strong love for Jesus and what he taught.'[40]

---

38   *Ibid*, 23.
39   *Ibid*, 23-24.
40   *Ibid*, 24.

Contemporary Reflections
on Animals

God gives us "stewardship" over His earth and will
"hold us accountable for how we use" it

The Bible gives human beings dominion over the earth, say articles in the AG magazine *Pentecostal Evangel*. Dominion, however, is a commission to exercise stewardship over God's creation not a license to abuse it, says the magazine. Environmental stewardship "is one of the logical consequences of our belief that God is creator," reports one article. It requires that we "care for the creation and become responsible to do that," recognizing that God will "hold us accountable for how we use His provisions."

- 'The stewardship of God's creation is one of the logical consequences of our belief that God is Creator,' says Assemblies of God General Secretary James Bradford, who holds a Ph.D. in aerospace engineering. 'Even though the contemporary environmental movement has its unbiblical extremes, we as believers should understand our mandate to care for and protect what our Heavenly Father has created. According to the Genesis 1 mandate, we are co-administrators of His creation.'[41]

- Stewardship is taking responsibility for the things God has called us to do, one of which is to care for creation. With 'environmental stewardship,' we take the commission in Genesis to care for the creation and become responsible to do that. God has given

---

41   *Christina Quick, "AG News: Bible Believers Join Environmentalism Discussion," Pentecostal Evangel, August 29 (2013), accessed August 1, 2015. http://ag.org/top/News/index_articledetail.cfm?Process=DisplayArticle&targetBay=c97d4d5c-a325-4921-9a9e-e9fbddd9c-dce&ModID=2&RSS_RSSContentID=26420&RSS_OriginatingChannelID=1184&RSS_OriginatingRSSFeedID=3359&RSS_Source=search*

us dominion over the earth to use it, not to abuse it... God goes on to say He's going to hold us accountable for how we use His provisions.[42]

Engaging with animals and the natural world can provide children with physical and spiritual benefits

When we take proper care of God's creation, we receive both spiritual and physical benefits, says *Pentecostal Evangel* staff writer Christina Quick. For example, playing outdoors and interacting with animals can help children's "cognitive skills and ability to learn." It also can reduce childhood stress, "obesity, diabetes, attention deficit hyperactivity disorder (ADHD), and depression," while at the same time helping children learn "important life lessons like responsibility and compassion." In addition, reports Quick, interacting with the nonhuman world can provide parents with opportunities to talk with children about God.

- These days, a growing number of kids are simply staying indoors. Instead of observing ants in the grass or stirring puddles with sticks, they're watching television, scanning the Internet and playing video games...

  [According to best-selling author, Richard Louv], '[W]hile today's youngsters are better informed about environmental issues than previous generations, they have little firsthand knowledge of the natural world. They can expound on rain forest ecology, but they've barely explored their own backyards'...[I]t's no coincidence there are so many reports of obesity, diabetes, attention deficit hyperactivity disorder (ADHD) and depression among juveniles...'The natural world is an antidote to many of the things that are true threats to children. Time outdoors can affect cognitive skills and ability to learn. It can also reduce stress.

---

42   *Staff, "Conversation: Tri Robinson, Creation Stewardship," Pentecostal Evangel, September 9 (2007), accessed August 1, 2015. http://tpe. ag.org/Conversations2007/4870_Robinson.cfm*

'Being outdoors supplies the fresh air, sunshine and physical exercise children need for optimal health, [Assemblies of God minister, Christina] Powell says. 'Additionally, time outdoors helps children learn about the marvels of God's creation, instilling a sense of wonder for the natural world and providing opportunities for joy of discovery.'[43]

- From pets, children learn important life lessons like responsibility and compassion.[44]

- [E]ngaging in outdoor activities with...children opens up conversations about spiritual topics. On a recent camping trip...a frightening bear sighting led to a discussion about backing away from certain situations in life.

'There's nothing like roasting marshmallows around a campfire and looking at the stars to get everyone in a contemplative mood,' [says Royal Rangers national commander, Doug Marsh]...'In that setting, the moments come when your kids really reflect on things. We're often able to talk about God in ways that aren't possible even during...daily family devotions at home.'[45]

Engaging with animals can provide adults with physical and spiritual benefits

Caring for animals can provide adults with physical and spiritual benefits, reports the AG's Senior Adult Ministries magazine, *Primeline*. Having a pet "can help reduce elevated blood pressure and assist in driving away the blues" and some animals

---

43   Christina Quick, "Go Inside and Play: Today's Kids Favor Nintendo over Nature," Pentecostal Evangel (2007), accessed August 1, 2015. http://tpe.ag.org/Articles2007/48881_Newslead.cfm#author

44   Rose McCormick Brandon, "The Gift of a Loyal Pet," Pentecostal Evangel, July 13 (2008), accessed August 1, 2015. http://tpe.ag.org/Articles2008/4914_Loyal.cfm

45   Quick, "Go Inside and Play."

"can detect the onset of death and be alert to some early-stage cancers."

- We are told by experts that having a pet can help reduce elevated blood pressure and assist in driving away the blues. These reasons seem to suggest that nearly everyone needs a pet of some sort. People who live alone may find a pet to be good company...Pets love you unconditionally. Share your love and time with them and reap the benefits.[46]

- Since the day God gave Adam the joyful task of naming animals, people have bonded with them... Veterinarian Mike Hord...says, 'God has given us a directive to care for animals, but their value in our lives goes far beyond that. Studies are proving that relationships with animals are good for your health.' One study...showed decreased blood pressure readings in patients who adopted a pet...[According to Hord], animals can detect the onset of death and be alert to some early-stage cancers. 'But what's most important is that we, as Christians, respect them, care for them and enjoy them because they contribute a lot to the quality of our lives.'[47]

Creation can help build Christian faith and provide a nonthreatening way to talk to others about God

Creation reveals God's "invisible qualities," says *Pentecostal Evangel*. It provides us with assurance of God's existence and with reassurance that God can be trusted in all things. Appreciating the nonhuman world can lead people to a belief in God, says the

---

46   *Senior Adult Ministries, "Adopt a Pet," Primeline: Practical Living, accessed July 30, 2015. http://sam.ag.org/primeline/practical/ index.cfm?targetBay=e3b41bd7-a714-4fe5-ab4d-fea7432e36e1&Mo- dID=2&Process=DisplayArticle&RSS_RSSContentID=6492&RSS_Orig- inatingChannelID=1149&RSS_OriginatingRSSFeedID=3491&RSS_ Source=*

47   *Brandon.*

magazine, and provide a "nonthreatening way to begin talking to people about the Lord."

- Romans 1:20 says, 'For since the creation of the world God's invisible qualities—his eternal power and divine nature—have been clearly seen, being understood from what has been made, so that men are without excuse.' We have the assurance of God's existence because He has revealed himself through His creation. Therefore, every Christian should be concerned about the creation because it's a revelation of God, and it's a means to the unsaved world.[48]

- As soon as you say 'Amen' at the end of a prayer, what do you do? Weeks or months may pass without a visible answer from God. Do you patiently wait or at some point start wondering, questioning God?...

Let the animal kingdom build your faith while you wait for that answer. Pick any animal, bird or insect. It doesn't matter what creature you choose. Since the Garden of Eden, its kind has followed whatever instincts God placed inside it.

Certain birds and butterflies know when to migrate. Other animals know when to hibernate. Salmon know when to swim against the current, but not against the instincts God gave them. God clearly declared His control of the animal kingdom (see Job 38, 39). That told Job regardless of his situation God was still in control.

While waiting for God to answer that certain prayer, let every sign of the changing seasons, every star, every animal following its instincts, help you trust God. Let them remind you He keeps the universe together with orderliness. Let them assure you He's also working right now on the best answer to your prayer.[49]

---

48 *Staff.*

49 *William E. Richardson, "After You Say 'Amen,'" Pentecostal Evan-*

- I love observing and learning about all of God's creation…An appreciation for the wonders of nature can indeed lead people to a belief in God (see Romans 1), and it can be a nonthreatening way to begin talking to people about the Lord…When one enjoys God's creation, and shares it, it can open doors.[50]

Christians have a "moral duty" to treat animals "with the mercy of our Maker"

Although the Bible "affirms the greater value of humans," it also affirms that even the most humble sparrow has value in the eyes of God, says AG minister Christina Powell. Humanity, "created in the image of God," has a special responsibility and moral duty to reflect "the character of God" by treating animals with mercy, attending to their needs, and, says the AG's *For Every Woman* magazine, shaping laws that "respect the animal world as God's handiwork."

- While the Bible affirms the greater value of humans who are uniquely made in the image of God, the Bible also teaches that God values the sparrow…As Christians, we need to respect all life as God's creatures, treating them humanely. As Proverbs 12:10 states, 'The righteous care for the needs of their animals.'… We honor God, the Creator of both man and animals, when we properly care for His creation. Embracing the sanctity of human life need not devalue the worth of animals.[51]
- God…gave humanity dominion over the rest of the animals….Yet, those created in the image of God

gel, March 16 (2007), accessed August 1, 2015. http://tpe.ag.org/DailyBoostArchive/March_07/20070316.cfm

50   Ken Horn, "Vantage Point: Creation Evangelism," Pentecostal Evangel (2008), accessed August 1, 2015. http://tpe.ag.org/Articles2008/4909_Vantage.cfm

51   Christina M.H. Powell, "More Valuable Than Sparrows: Measuring Human Worth," Enrichment Journal: Enriching and Equipping Spirit-Filled Ministries (2012), accessed August 1, 2015. http://enrichmentjournal.ag.org/201202/201202_126_more_valuable.cfm

carry the responsibility of reflecting the character of God. God does not forget the needs of the sparrow (Luke 12:6). Similarly humans must not overlook the needs of creation. We must treat animals humanely.[52]

• Christians have a moral duty to respect the animal world as God's handiwork. This means finding out how animals are treated in research labs and on factory farms, and helping shape laws that determine their treatment. We must make sure we and others treat animals 'with the mercy of our Maker.'[53]

52   Christina M.H. Powell, "Biotechnology: Becoming Responsible Stewards of Knowledge," Enrichment Journal: Enriching and Equipping Spirit-Filled Ministries (2011), accessed August 1, 2015. http://enrichmentjournal.ag.org/201102/201102_112_biotechnology.htm.cfm

53   Chuck Colson, "Are Animals Persons?" reprinted in Assemblies of God, For Every Woman: Resources, Advice, and Guidance for Today's Woman (2004), accessed August 1, 2015. http://women.ag.org/informing_display.aspx?id=2160&langtype=1033

Church of God in Christ

General Information

The Church of God in Christ (COGIC) was founded in the Holiness tradition in 1897 and was chartered in 1907. Its membership is predominantly African-American, it is one of the oldest Pentecostal denominations in the world, and it is the largest Pentecostal denomination in the United States.[54]

More information about Church of God in Christ, including the church's beliefs, structure, and history, can be found by going to: http://cogic.org

Number of Members in the U.S.: 5 million[55]

Number of Members Worldwide: over 6 million[56]

---

54   See *Church of God in Christ, "The Founder & Church History,"* accessed July 30, 2015. http://www.cogic.org/our-foundation/the-founder-church-history/. See also *Church of God in Christ, "Our Foundation,"* accessed July 30, 2015. http://www.cogic.org/our-foundation/

55   *COGIC, "The Founder & Church History."*

56   *COGIC, "Our Foundation."*

Official Statements on Animals

In the beginning, God gave Man authority over animals and the rest of His creation

Since 2002, candidates for ordination into the Church of God in Christ have been given a training catechism designed to instruct them "in the fundamental truths of the Bible" and to expand "on the Articles of Religion listed in the official manual of the Church of God in Christ" (Preface). According to this book, entitled *Understanding Bible Doctrine As Taught In The Church of God In Christ*, God created the first human beings for "the Lord's pleasure" and "to exercise authority over God's creation." The original humans were sinless, wise, and immortal. It was humanity's original intelligence that allowed man "to name the entire animal creation."

- Why was man created? For the Lord's pleasure…[and t]o exercise authority over God's creation…Where did man come from? Man was created from the dust of the earth…Adam and Eve were the first human beings…The whole human race descended from this single pair…What was the original nature of man? Spiritually, man possessed the nature of God…Thus, he was perfect, holy, or sinless. Mentally, man was so intelligent that he was able to name the entire animal creation…He knew wrong from right…and was given a free will to choose between the two. Physically, man was immortal…[57]

When Adam and Eve sinned, they forfeited humanity's right to rule creation

According to COGIC's training catechism, Satan tempted Adam and Eve to eat from the forbidden fruit. When they did so, they committed treason against God and lost their right to rule creation. That right now belongs to Satan.

---

57   *Bishop P. A. Brooks and Charles Hawthorne, Understanding Bible Doctrine As Taught In The Church Of God In Christ, Centennial Edition (Detroit: Church of God in Christ, 2002), 23.*

- What happened to change man's nature? Satan, in the form of a serpent, tempted Eve to take of the forbidden fruit...Eve 'took of the fruit thereof, and did eat, and give also unto her husband with her, and he did eat' (Gen. 3:6)[58]...In so doing, Adam sinned against God...In so doing, Adam committed high treason. He turned his God-given authority to legally rule the earth over to Satan. At that point, Satan became the god of this world.[59]

Sanctification allows us to perform "good works" within creation

Although creation currently is ruled by Satan, humanity is not free to denigrate life. "Saints" (all those who are saved) are called by the church to renew their "whole nature in the image of God": living exemplary lifestyles and performing good works.

- Sanctification is the gracious and continuous operation of the Holy Ghost, by which He delivers the justified sinner from the pollution of sin, renews his whole nature in the image of God and enables him to perform good works.[60]
- What impact should this doctrinal truth have on saints today? Saints should make proper preparation so as to be ready for the Lord...Saints should live in earnest expectation of Christ's return...Saints should have an exemplary lifestyle.[61]

---

58   Bible citations for all COGIC statements come from The Holy Bible, King James Version

59   Brooks and Hawthorne, 23.

60   Church of God in Christ, "What We Believe," accessed July 30, 15. http://www.cogic.org/our-foundation/what-we-believe/

61   Brooks and Hawthorne, 37-38.

Contemporary Reflections on Animals

COGIC calls upon its leaders to commit themselves to reversing social trends that threaten creation

In a 2007 Apostolic Missive, COGIC's Presiding Bishop, The Most Reverend Charles E. Blake, Sr., called upon the church to provide leadership in reversing current "ill-conceived" social trends, including trends that threaten the environment.

- Let me add that while we have such a rich heritage, the global challenges of the future must be embraced as our 'call' to train, develop, and commission a new generation of leaders. A band of leaders who are equally committed to reversing the ill-conceived trends of urban centers, family disintegration, violence in our communities, global famine and disease, environmental threats, political upheaval, moral leadership deficiency, poverty, and the loss of our youth to subcultures that rob our precious human commodity of their Divinely-inspired destiny. Our future, if we are to remain a constructive influence in society, must be guided by godly principles that penetrate the culture and bring glory to our God. We must take the high road of integrity and authentic leadership around the world. Church of God in Christ, we must lead! And lead we will![62]

The protection of creation is essential for the achievement of basic human rights

COGIC's leaders have demonstrated their commitment to "reversing...ill-conceived trends" by becoming signatories on three interfaith documents that identify environmental sustainability and health—including the sustainability and health of

---

62   *The Most Reverend Charles E. Blake, Sr., Presiding Bishop, Church of God in Christ, "The Centennial Proclamation: An Apostolic Missive, September 2007."*

vulnerable animals—as essential for the achievement of basic human rights. By focusing on such diverse topics as climate change, reduced biodiversity, and environmental toxins, these documents remind Christians that "any damage that we do to God's world is an offense against God Himself."

- Human-Induced Climate Change is Real and increasing international instability, which could lead to more security threats to our nation...

  The Earth's natural systems are resilient but not infinitely so, and human civilizations are remarkably dependent on ecological stability and well-being. It is easy to forget this until that stability and well-being are threatened...

  Low-lying regions, indeed entire islands, could find themselves under water. (This is not to mention the various negative impacts climate change could have on God's other creatures)[63]...Millions of people could die in this century because of climate change, most of them our poorest global neighbors...

  Christians must care...because we love God the Creator and Jesus our Lord, through whom and for whom the creation was made. This is God's world, and any damage that we do to God's world is an offense against God Himself (Gen. 1; Ps. 24; Col. 1:16).

  Christians must care...because we are called to love our neighbors, to do unto others as we would have them do unto us, and to protect and care for the least of these as though each was Jesus Christ himself (Mt. 22:34-40; Mt. 7:12, Mt. 25:31-46).

  Christians...are reminded that when God made humanity he commissioned us to exercise stewardship over the earth and its creatures. Climate change is the latest evidence of our failure to exercise proper

---

63   *Parenthetical statement in original text.*

stewardship, and constitutes a critical opportunity for us to do better (Gen. 1:26-28).[64]

- The world's faiths and traditions share an understanding of the need for balancing the health of society and the environment. There are significant links between ill health—including reproductive ill health—and environmental degradation. Environmental toxins such as industrial chemicals, air pollution and pesticides are linked to numerous health problems, including infertility, reproductive cancers and birth defects. Policy makers and members of civil society should promote greater understanding of the linkages between the environment and reproductive health, and encourage integrated actions to address both these areas.[65]

- The Universal Declaration of Human Rights demands meeting basic human needs. The abject and dehumanizing conditions of extreme poverty to which more than a billion people are currently subjected, must be decisively altered. The human destruction of the environment has to be stopped. The process of achievement of the Millennium Development Goals...represents a key indicator of

---

64   Evangelical Environmental Network, "Evangelical Climate Initiative," (2006), Claims 1 & 2, accessed July 30, 2015. Signatories include Presiding Bishop Charles E. Blake, Sr., Church of God in Christ. http://creationcare.org/climate-realists-energy-optimists/evangelical-climate-initiative/

65   United Nations International Interfaith Network for Development and Reproductive Health, A Faith-Filled Commitment to Development Includes a Commitment to Women's Rights and Reproductive Health: Religious Reflections on the Millennium Development Goals, (Washington, DC: International Interfaith Network for Development and Reproductive Health, 2005). Signatories include Rev. Osagyefo Uhuru Sekou, Church of God in Christ. http://www.un-ngls.org/orf/un-summit-interfaith.pdf

the commitment of States to realise human rights for all.[66]

- Millennium Development Goal 7: Ensure Environmental Sustainability. Target 1: Integrate the principles of sustainable development into country policies and programmes and reverse the loss of environmental resources. Target 2: Reduce biodiversity loss, achieving…a significant reduction in the rate of loss. (a) Marine areas and land conservation need greater attention. (b) Deforestation slows and more forests are designated for biodiversity conservation. (c) The number of species threatened with extinction is rising rapidly. (d) Fish stocks require improved fisheries management to reduce depletion.[67]

---

66   World Council of Churches, "2008 Faith in Human Rights Statement," (2008), Preamble, section II, paragraph 9, page 5. Reproduced on COGIC website. Signatories include Presiding Bishop Charles E. Blake, Sr. Church of God in Christ, accessed July 30, 2015. http://www.cogic.org/wp-content/uploads/2012/09/FINAL-DRAFT-OF-RESPONSE-TO-CRITICISM-OF-FAITH-IN-HUMAN-RIGHTS-DECLARATION.pdf

67   United Nations, The Millennium Development Goals Report (New York: United Nations, 2008), 36-39. http://www.un.org/millennium-goals/2008highlevel/pdf/newsroom/mdg%20reports/MDG_Report_2008_ENGLISH.pdf. Support for Millennium Development Goals affirmed in World Council of Churches, "2008 Faith in Human Rights Statement."

The Church of Jesus Christ of Latter-day Saints

General Information

The Church of Jesus Christ of Latter-day Saints (LDS) is the official name of the religion commonly called the Mormon Church. It claims to be the original church established by Jesus Christ while He was mortal and was restored, under His direction, by Joseph Smith, Jr. in 1830. According to Smith, an angel appeared to him and revealed an account of God's dealings with ancient inhabitants of North America. Mormon, one of the last prophets of these people, collected and edited the accounts of the history of these people and their encounter with the risen Christ, who was said to have appeared to them shortly after his resurrection in the Holy Land. The angel led Smith to this ancient record and provided him with the tools necessary to translate it. This text has come to be known as the *Book of Mormon*.[68]

More information about the LDS, including the church's beliefs, structure, and history, can be found by going to: http://lds.org.

Number of Members in the U.S.: 6.4 million

Number of Members Worldwide: 15.3 million[69]

---

68   *General Information for the LDS was provided via email by the Correlation Intellectual Property department of The Church of Jesus Christ of Latter-day Saints, July 15, 2015.*

69   *US and International membership numbers were provided via email by the Correlation Intellectual Property department of The Church of Jesus Christ of Latter-day Saints, July 15, 2015.*

Official Statements on Animals

Humans may use animals, but they are to be used "sparingly" and "with thanksgiving"

The sacred canon of the LDS consists of four texts: the Bible, the *Book of Mormon*, the *Book of Doctrine and Covenants*, and the *Pearl of Great Price*. According to the Book of Doctrine and Covenants (D&C), animals are provided by God for human use, but God has ordained that they should be used "sparingly" and "with thanksgiving". The D&C also states that God is pleased when we refrain from using animals entirely, except "in times of winter, or of cold, or famine."

- Yea, flesh also of beasts and of the fowls of the air, I, the Lord, have ordained for the use of man with thanksgiving; nevertheless they are to be used sparingly; And it is pleasing unto me that they should not be used, only in times of winter, or of cold, or famine.[70]

- For, behold, the beasts of the field and the fowls of the air, and that which cometh of the earth, is ordained for the use of man for food and for raiment, and that he might have in abundance. But...wo be unto man that sheddeth blood or that wasteth flesh and hath no need.[71]

Humans are accountable to God for the ways in which we use His creatures

Although God has "ordained" all creation "for the use of man," He also commands us to exercise our power responsibly,

---

70   The Church of Jesus Christ of Latter-day Saints, ed. *The Doctrine & Covenants of The Church of Jesus Christ of Latter-day Saints Containing Revelations Given to Joseph Smith, the Prophet with Some Additions by His Successors in the Presidency of the Church*, (Salt Lake City: The Church of Jesus Christ of Latter-day Saints, 2013), 89:12-13, accessed August 1, 2015. https://www.lds.org/scriptures/dc-testament/dc/89?lang=eng

71   *Ibid*, 49:19-21, https://www.lds.org/scriptures/dc-testament/dc/49?lang=eng

says the D&C, warning that we will be held "accountable" for our stewardship choices.

- …a commandment I give unto you…That every man may give an account unto me of the stewardship which is appointed unto him. For it is expedient that I, the Lord, should make every man accountable, as a steward over earthly blessings, which I have made and prepared for my creatures.[72]

Animals have souls and are destined for "eternal felicity" with humans

In "The Book of Moses," a separate book within the canonical *Pearl of Great Price*, we are told that every living thing was created "spiritually" by God before being given physical form on earth. All creatures—plant, animal, and human—possess their own unique soul, and, according to *The Doctrine and Covenants*, are destined for "eternal felicity" on a transformed earth where all "enmity" between humans and animals will cease.

- …I, the Lord God, made the heaven and the earth, And every plant of the field before it was in the earth, and every herb of the field before it grew. For I, the Lord God, created all things, of which I have spoken, spiritually, before they were naturally upon the face of the earth…And I, the Lord God, formed man from the dust of the ground, and breathed into his nostrils the breath of life; and man became a living soul…nevertheless, all things were before created; but spiritually were they created…And out of the ground made I, the Lord God, to grow every tree, naturally… And it became also a living soul. For it was spiritual in the day that I created it…And out of the ground I, the Lord God, formed every beast of the field, and every fowl of the air; and commanded that they

---

72   *Ibid,* 104:13, *https://www.lds.org/scriptures/dc-testament/ dc/104.13?lang=eng#12*

should come unto Adam, to see what he would call them; and they were also living souls…[73]

- Q. What are we to understand by the four bests, spoken of in [Revelations 4:6]?

  A. They are figurative expressions, used by the Revelator, John, in describing heaven, the paradise of God, the happiness of man, and of beasts, and of creeping things, and of the fowls of the air; that which is spiritual being in the likeness of that which is temporal; and that which is temporal in the likeness of that which is spiritual; the spirit of man in the likeness of his person, as also the spirit of the beast, and every other creature which God has created.

  Q. Are the four beasts limited to individual beasts, or do they represent classes or orders?

  A. They are limited to four individual beasts, which were shown to John, to represent the glory of the classes of beings in their destined order or sphere of creation, in the enjoyment of their eternal felicity.[74]

- And the end shall come, and the heaven and the earth shall be consumed and pass away, and there shall be a new heaven and a new earth. For all old things shall pass away, and all things shall become new, even the heaven and the earth, and all the fullness thereof, both men and beasts, the fowls of the air, and the fishes of the sea; And not one hair, neither mote, shall be lost, for it is the workmanship of mine hand.[75]

73   *The Church of Jesus-Christ of Latter-day Saints, ed. The Pearl of Great Price: A Selection from the Revelations, Translations, and Narrations of Joseph Smith First Prophet, Seer, and Revelator to The Church of Jesus Christ of Latter-day Saints,* (Salt Lake: The Church of Jesus Christ of Latter-day Saints, 2015), *Moses 3:4-19, accessed August 1, 2015. https://www. lds.org/search?q=moses+3%3A4-20&domains=scriptures&lang=eng*

74   *The Doctrine & Covenants, 77:2-3. https://www.lds.org/scriptures/dc-testament/dc/77?lang=eng*

75   *Ibid, 29:23-25. https://www.lds.org/scriptures/dc-testament/*

- And prepare for the revelation which is to come, when the veil of the covering of my temple, in my tabernacle, which hideth the earth, shall be taken off, and all flesh shall see me together. And every corruptible thing, both of man, or of the beasts of the field, or of the fowls of the heavens, or of the fish of the sea, that dwells upon all the face of the earth, shall be consumed; And also that of element shall melt with fervent heat; and all things shall become new, that my knowledge and glory may dwell upon all the earth. And in that day the enmity of man, and the enmity of beasts, yea, the enmity of all flesh, shall cease from before my face.[76]

Historical References on Animals

Joseph Smith: Men must "lose their vicious dispositions and cease to destroy the animal race"

The LDS suffered from persecution in its early days and its members frequently were compelled to resettle their church. In 1834, while leading his followers through the prairies of Illinois, Joseph Smith saw his brethren attempt to kill three rattlesnakes that had entered their campsite. Smith told the men to stop, exhorting them to "become harmless before the brute creation" and to "lose their vicious dispositions and cease to destroy the animal race."

- In pitching my tent we found three massasaugas or prairie rattlesnakes, which the brethren were about to kill, but I said, 'Let them alone—don't hurt them! How will the serpent ever lose his venom, while the servants of God possess the same disposition, and

dc/29.23-25?lang=eng#22

76   Ibid, 101:23-26. https://www.lds.org/scriptures/dc-testament/dc/101?lang=eng

continue to make war upon it? Men must become harmless, before the brute creation; and when men lose their vicious dispositions and cease to destroy the animal race, the lion and the lamb can dwell together, and the sucking child can play with the serpent in safety.' The brethren took the serpents carefully on sticks and carried them across the creek. I exhorted the brethren not to kill a serpent, bird, or an animal of any kind during our journey unless it became necessary in order to preserve ourselves from hunger.[77]

Joseph Smith: God will redeem all that He has made, "whether beasts, fowls, fishes, or men"

Smith was granted frequent revelations concerning the correct interpretation of biblical passages. According to Smith, the final book of the Bible reveals that animals exist in heaven, that all animals will be saved by God, and that some animals are "perfect...like angels in their sphere."

- John saw the actual beast in heaven, showing to John that beasts did actually exist there, and not just to represent figures of things on the earth...he saw every creature that was in heaven,—all the beasts, fowls and fish in heaven,—actually there, giving glory to God...John learned that God glorified Himself by saving all that His hands had made, whether beasts, fowls, fishes, or men.[78]

- Says one, 'I cannot believe in the salvation of beasts.' Any man who would tell you this could not be, would tell you that the revelations are not true. John heard the words of the beast giving glory to God, and

77   Joseph Smith, History of the Church of Jesus Christ of Latter-day Saints: Period 1, History of Joseph Smith, the Prophet, Vol. II, B.H. Roberts ed. (Salt Lake City: Deseret News, 1904), 71-72.

78   Joseph Smith, History of the Church of Jesus Christ of Latter-day Saints: Period I. History of Joseph Smith, the Prophet, Vol. V (Salt Lake City: Deseret News, 1909), 343.

understood them. God who made the beasts could understand every language spoken by them.[79]

Brigham Young: Animals will receive salvation

After Joseph Smith was killed in 1844, Brigham Young took his place as president and prophet of the LDS. Young praised animals for being more obedient than men to God's laws and promised that animals, like humans, will receive salvation.

- Are these great weaknesses to be found in the birds of the air, in the fishes of the sea, or in the beasts of the field? No. The animal, vegetable, and mineral kingdoms abide the law of their Creator; the whole earth and all things pertaining to it, except man, abide the law of their creation.[80]

- ...always keep in view that the animal, vegetable, and mineral kingdoms—the earth and its fulness—will all, except the children of men, abide their creation—the law by which they were made, and will receive their exaltation.[81]

Brigham Young: Only true need, not convenience or sport, justify killing animals

In preparation for a grasshopper blight that was predicted to destroy the crops of a nascent LDS settlement, Brigham Young reminded his followers that even insects are "creatures of God" who serve a purpose in God's creation. Their inconvenience to humanity, said Young, does not justify their extermination, unless human survival is at stake. Likewise, after viewing "immense herds of buffalo" that blackened the prairies, Young told his followers that the vast numbers did not justify hunting more animals than were needed. Only true need, not

---

79   Ibid, 343-344.

80   Brigham Young, Journal of Discourses: Delivered by President Brigham Young, His Two Counsellors, the Twelve Apostles, and Others, Vol. 9, G.D. Watt and J.V. Long, ed., (Liverpool: George Q. Cannon Publ., 1862), 246.

81   Brigham Young, Journal of Discourses: Delivered by President Brigham Young, His Two Counsellors, the Twelve Apostles, and Others, Vol. 8, G.D. Watt and J.V. Long, ed., (Liverpool: George Q. Cannon Publ., 1861), 191.

convenience or sport, said Young, could justify killing one of God's creatures.

- According to present appearances, next year [1868] we may expect grasshoppers to eat up nearly all our crops. But if we have provisions enough to last us another year, we can say to the grasshoppers—these creatures of God—you are welcome. I have never had a feeling to drive them from one plant in my garden; but I look upon them as the armies of the Lord...[82]

- Thursday, May 6 (1847)—Traveled nineteen miles. The prairie appeared black being covered with immense herds of buffalo. Friday, May 7—I preached in camp and advised the brethren not to kill any more buffalo or other game until the meat was needed.[83]

Brigham Young: "The more kind we are to animals, the more peace will increase"

According to Young, there is a direct connection between the way we treat animals and the amount of strife that exists on the earth. "[T]he more kind we are to animals," said Young, "the more will peace increase."

- Let the people be holy, and the earth under their feet will be holy. Let the people be holy, and filled with the spirit of God, and every animal and creeping thing will be filled with peace; the soil of the earth will bring forth in its strength, and the fruits thereof will be meat for man. The more purity that exists, the less is the strife; the more kind we are to animals, the

---

82   Brigham Young, Journal of Discourses: Delivered by President Brigham Young, His Two Counsellors, and the Twelve Apostles, Vol. 12, G.D. Watt and J.V. Long, ed. (Liverpool: Albert Carrington, 1869), 121.

83   Brigham Young, "May 6, 1847," Journals, April 4-July 31, 1847, excerpted by Heritage Gateways (2015), accessed July 31, 2015. http://heritage.uen.org/journals/Wc586467fc2327.shtml and Ibid, "May 7, 1847," accessed July 31, 2015. http://heritage.uen.org/journals/Wc589b91b453ce.shtml

more will peace increase, and the savage nature of the brute creation will vanish away.[84]

Contemporary Reflections on Animals

David O. McKay (1951-1970): A "true" Latter-day Saint is kind to animals

In the 20th century, several LDS presidents have extolled the virtue of kindness toward animals. President David O. McKay, for instance, equated a "true" Latter-day Saint with someone who is kind to all God's creatures.

- A true Latter-day Saint is kind to animals, is kind to every created thing, for God created all.[85]

Joseph Fielding Smith (1970-72): animal cruelty is a sin that will be punished by God

President Joseph Fielding Smith said cruelty to animals leads to cruelty to humans, is a sign of the absence of true religion, and will be punished by God.

- ...doing wrong to animals is but a stepping stone to the doing of wrong to our fellow men.[86]

- Kindness to animals and to all living things is one good way of expressing true religion. Cruelty to the dumb creation always shows an absence of the true religious spirit; and in most cases, is simply barbarous.[87]

---

84   Brigham Young, Journal of Discourses, Vol I (Liverpool: F.D. and S.W. Richards, 1851), 203.

85   David O. McKay as reprinted in Gerald E. Jones, "The Gospel and Animals," Ensign, August (1972), accessed August 1, 2015. https://www.lds.org/ensign/1972/08/the-gospel-and-animals?lang=eng

86   Joseph F. Smith, compiled by Richard D. Stratton, Kindness to Animals and Caring for the Earth: Selections from the Sermons and Writings of Latter-day Saint Church Leaders (Portland: Inkwater Press, 2004), 66.

87   Ibid, 67.

- I believe that cruelty to a caged bird is a sin in the sight of God; and if those who do it, or permit it, are not somewhere held accountable, there is no such thing as justice.[88]

Joseph Fielding Smith: Jesus died so that all creatures might have immortal life

President Joseph Fielding Smith affirmed the long-held LDS position that Jesus died for the salvation of all God's creatures, including animals.

- We have the assurance that through the sacrifice made on the cross all mankind and every other creature, even the earth itself, are redeemed from death and shall receive the resurrection and be restored to immortal life.[89]

- So we see that the Lord intends to save, not only the earth and the heavens, not only man who dwells upon the earth, but all things which he has created. The animals, the fishes of the sea, the fowls of the air, as well as man, are to be recreated, or renewed, through the resurrection, for they too are living souls.[90]

Joseph Fielding Smith: Hunting for sport is wicked

President Joseph Fielding Smith was appalled by men's "blood-thirsty desire to kill and destroy animal life." For Smith, hunting is wicked unless it is required for food.

- I never could see why a man should be imbued with a blood-thirsty desire to kill and destroy animal life. I have known men—and they still exist among us— who enjoy what is, to them, the 'sport' of hunting birds and slaying them by the hundreds, and who will come in after a day's sport, boasting of how many harmless birds they have had the skill to slaughter, and day after day, during the season when it is lawful

---

88   *Ibid , 63.*

89   *Ibid, back cover.*

90   *Joseph Fielding Smith, as reprinted in Jones.*

for men to hunt and kill (the birds having had a season of protection and not apprehending danger) go out by scores or hundreds, and you may hear their guns early in the morning on the day of the opening, as if great armies had met in battle; and the terrible work of slaughtering the innocent birds goes on.[91]

- I do not believe any man should kill animals or birds unless he needs them for food, and then he should not kill innocent little birds that are not intended for food for man. I think it is wicked for men to thirst in their souls to kill almost everything which possesses animal life. It is wrong, and I have been surprised at prominent men whom I have seen whose very souls seemed to be athirst for the shedding of animal blood.[92]

Spencer W. Kimball (1973-85): It is wicked to take the life of animals unnecessarily

President Spencer W. Kimball, Joseph Fielding Smith's successor as LDS president, spoke approvingly of Smith's opposition to hunting. Kimball affirmed that it is "wicked...[and] a shame" to shed the blood of animals unnecessarily.

- Now, I also would like to add some of my feelings concerning the unnecessary shedding of blood and destruction of life. I think that every soul should be impressed by the sentiments that have been expressed here by the prophets. And not less with reference to the killing of innocent birds is the wildlife of our country that live upon the vermin that are indeed enemies to the farmer and to mankind. It is not only wicked to destroy them, it is a shame, in my opinion. I

---

91   *Joseph Fielding Smith, Gospel Doctrine: Selections from the Sermons and Writings of Joseph F. Smith (Salt Lake City: The Deseret News, 1919), 334.*

92   *Ibid.*

think that this principle should extend not only to the bird life but to the life of all animals.[93]

93   Spencer W. Kimball, "Fundamental Principles to Ponder and Live," *Ensign*, November (1978), 43, *accessed August 1, 2015. https://www.lds. org/ensign/1978/11/fundamental-principles-to-ponder-and-live?lang=eng*

The Episcopal Church

General Information

The Episcopal Church arrived in the American colonies in 1607. Originally an extension of the Church of England, it became an autonomous institution after the American Revolution. Today, The Episcopal Church is a member of the Anglican Communion—a worldwide fellowship of churches that acknowledge the Archbishop of Canterbury as their spiritual head but have independent ecclesial authority.[94]

More information about The Episcopal Church, including the church's beliefs, structure, and history, can be found by going to: http://www.episcopalchurch.org

Number of Members in the U.S.: 1.89 million

Number of Members Worldwide: 2.06 million[95]

---

94   The Episcopal Church, "The History of the American Church" (1999), accessed August 1, 2015. http://www.episcopalchurch.org/page/history-american-church

95   Michael Gryboski, "Episcopal Church Continues Downward Trend According to Report," The Christian Post, November, 1 (2013), accessed August 1, 2015. http://www.christianpost.com/news/episcopal-church-continues-downward-trend-according-to-report-107906/

Official Statements on Animals

God creates, sustains, and redeems all creation, having "ecstatic joy in and love for" all creatures

The Episcopal Church has included statements about animals in several of its official documents, including its *Book of Common Prayer*, *Catechism of Creation*, legislative resolutions, and liturgical resources. These documents affirm that God is the creator, sustainer, and redeemer of all creation. God's continuing relationship with and care for creation reveal God's "ecstatic joy in and love for all creatures wild and tame."

- Genesis 1 teaches that the one true God calls the universe into existence, and all of creation responds to God's call...It is dependent upon its Creator for its continuing existence and for all of the powers and capacities it possesses.[96]

- Genesis 2…emphasizes God's immanence or intimate relationship with creation. In the story of the making of the garden … God is present to every creature in creating it and giving it sustenance.[97]

- Psalm 104…describes God continually giving all living things life, food, and shelter, and through the Holy Spirit renewing the face of the earth. God is always creating, sustaining, renewing, and blessing.[98]

- [T]he book of Job, chapters 38-41, reveals God's… ecstatic joy in and love for all creatures wild and tame.[99]

- In metaphorical and mystical language, St. Paul writes that the resurrection of Christ marks the

96   *The Domestic and Foreign Missionary Society of the Protestant Episcopal Church, Catechism of Creation: An Episcopal Understanding, First Edition, Revised* (2005), 5. *http://episcopalscience.org/wp-content/uploads/2011/06/CreationCatechism.pdf*

97   *Ibid.*

98   *Ibid.*

99   *Ibid.*

beginning of a process that will bring not only humanity but the whole of creation into a new state of being and relationship with God… Likewise, the image of 'a new heaven and a new earth' (Rev. 21:1-4) symbolically conveys not the destruction of the old but its transformation into the new…[I]n some inexpressible way, the whole of creation will be taken up into the life of God (1 Cor. 15). What this new creation may be remains a mystery, yet it constitutes the ground of Christian hope.[100]

Humans are created in God's image to love and care for all creatures as God loves and cares for them

The Bible states that human beings are created in the divine image and that we have dominion over the earth. This statement, says The Episcopal Church, must be understood not as a license to dominate and destroy creation but as an invitation "to represent the caring, compassionate Creator who looks upon Creation with love."

- Genesis 1:26-28 teaches that God brought forth man and woman in the divine image and likeness, enabling them to enter into an intimate relationship with God and one another. And God gave humankind the responsibility to tend and serve the garden (Gen. 2:6), i.e., to care for 'this fragile earth, our island home' (Eucharistic Prayer C)… God invites humanity into a covenantal relationship of love for God, for all humankind and for the whole creation.[101]

- The Holy Bible declares our obligation to care for God's creation. What specifically does the Bible say about this obligation? Genesis 1:26-28 states that human beings are created in God's 'image and likeness' and given dominion over all other creatures. 'Dominion' does not mean 'domination,' but refers to the need for humans to exercise responsibility for

---

100   *Ibid,* 7.

101   *Ibid.*

the earth as God's representatives. In Genesis 2, the human beings are given the garden to tend and serve, symbolizing our obligation to care for creation.[102]

- The idea of humans made in the 'image of God' was not God's invitation to act like a dictator or lord over Creation, but rather to represent the caring, compassionate Creator who looks upon Creation with love.[103]

- The God who is Love unconditionally loves all of the creation and not merely us who are able to enter into a conscious relationship with God. We may express the divine image and likeness by loving the creation as God loves it, and by exercising stewardship and earth-keeping as an act of love.[104]

Our stewardship of God's creation is a moral issue; Christ will require an accounting of our actions

God's love for all creatures and our own commission to mirror God's love make stewardship a moral issue. Too often, says the Episcopal Church, we have failed in our stewardship of creation and have fallen into sin. We must now repent our past actions and prepare to "give an accounting to Christ for our stewardship," knowing that "judgment awaits 'those who destroy the earth.'"

- First, why is environmental stewardship a religious issue? Why is it a concern for the Church to address? We have a responsibility to care for God's Creation and for one another. The Earth is rapidly losing its sustenance, upon which we can 'multiply' and 'subdue' and develop. The problem is not only

---

102   *Ibid, 16.*

103   *The Executive Council and The Environmental Stewardship Team of The Episcopal Church, "Environmental Stewardship," (1994), 243. http://episcopalarchives.org/e-archives/blue_book/reports/1994/ bb_1994-Ro12.pdf*

104   *Committee on Science, Technology and Faith, 17.*

scientific or political or industrial. It is a moral and spiritual problem throughout.[105]

- There are those who do not believe that confronting environmental concerns should have national focus or the backing of the Church. But we believe this is properly the Church's concern, as 'the earth is the Lord's and the fullness thereof' (Psalm 24:1). As reverence for God's Creation and our role in Creation requires spiritual and moral leadership, government leaders and scientists throughout the world have begun to respect this sacred stance.[106]

- We humans have fallen into sin…and expressions of greed, lust for power, neglect, and a willingness to turn a blind eye work against the mandate to be good stewards and keepers of God's good earth.[107]

- Most holy and merciful Father:
  We confess to you and to one another,
  And to the whole communion of saints
  In heaven and on earth,
  That we have sinned by our own fault
  In thought, word, and deed;
  By what we have done, and by what we have left undone…
  Accept our repentance, Lord.
  For our waste and pollution of your creation, and our lack of
  Concern for those who come after us,
  Accept our repentance, Lord
  Restore us, good Lord, and let your anger depart from us;

---

105   *Environmental Stewardship Team, Environmental Stewardship,*
243.

106   *Ibid,* 244.

107   *Committee on Science, Technology and Faith,* 17.

Favorably hear us, for your mercy is great[108]

- The New Testament teaches that Christ came to redeem the whole of creation and not merely human beings (Rom. 8:19-22; Eph. 1:10; Col. 1:20, 2 Cor. 5:19), and makes the sobering declaration that judgment awaits 'those who destroy the earth' (Rev. 11:18). Therefore, we should be just as concerned about the physical state of the earth as we are with the spiritual state of God's human sons and daughters.[109]
- [W]e...must give an accounting to Christ for our stewardship...We want him to say to us, 'Well done, good and faithful stewards' (cf. Matt. 25:22).[110]

Stewardship obligates us to "support the humane and merciful treatment" of animals

Animals are part of God's creation and fall within our stewardship obligations, says The Episcopal Church. We must, therefore, exercise "responsible care of animals" and "support the humane and merciful treatment of all of God's Creatures."

- *Resolved*, that the 74th General Convention recognize that responsible care of animals falls within the stewardship of creation.[111]

---

108   *The Episcopal Church, ed., The Book of Common Prayer: and Administration of the Sacraments and Other Rites and Ceremonies of the Church Together with The Psalms of David According to the Use of The Episcopal Church (New York: Church Publishing Incorporated, 1979), 267-268.*

109   *Committee on Science, Technology and Faith, 19.*

110   *Ibid.*

111   *The Episcopal Church General Convention, "Resolution #2003-D016: Support Ethical Care of Animals," Journal of the General Convention of...The Episcopal Church, Minneapolis, 2003 (New York: General Convention, 2004), 253. http://www.episcopalarchives.org/cgi-bin/acts/acts_resolution.pl?resolution=2003-D016*

- *Resolved*, that this 76th General Convention reaffirm that all animals are a part of All Creation, for which we are called to be stewards of God's gifts.[112]
- *Resolved*, that the 76th General Convention support the humane and merciful treatment of all of God's Creatures.[113]

Economic activities that endanger or cause suffering to animals are immoral and should be prohibited

Responsible care of God's animals means that activities that adversely impact endangered species or that cause animal suffering (for example, puppy mills and factory-farms) should be prohibited. The Episcopal Church reminds its members that "all economic policy has a moral dimension" and calls upon its members to "identify and advocate for legislation" that adheres "to ethical standards in the care and treatment of animals."

- *Resolved*, that all economic policy has moral dimensions and consequences for all human beings; and that global economies should be facilitated in consideration of the interconnectedness of all God's Creation.[114]

---

112   *The Episcopal Church General Convention, "Resolution #2009-C078: Direct the Development of Liturgies for the Loss of a Companion Animal," Journal of the General Convention of...The Episcopal Church, Anaheim, 2009 (New York: General Convention, 2009), 791. http://www.episcopalarchives.org/cgi-bin/acts/acts_generate_pdf.pl?resolution=2009-C078*

113   *The Episcopal Church General Convention, "Resolution #2009-D015: Urge Dioceses to Educate on Environmental Decisions Affecting Animal Species," Journal of the General Convention of...The Episcopal Church, Anaheim, 2009 (New York: General Convention, 2009), 629. http://episcopalarchives.org/cgi-bin/acts/acts_generate_pdf.pl?resolution=2009-D015*

114   *The Episcopal Church General Convention, "Resolution #2012-A012: Urge Governments to Follow Principles in Adopting Trade Policies," Journal of the General Convention of...The Episcopal Church, Indianapolis, 2012 (New York: General Convention, 2012), 211-212. http://www.episcopalarchives.org/cgi-bin/acts/acts_generate_pdf.pl?resolution=2012-A012*

- *Resolved*, that The Episcopal Church encourage its members to ensure that husbandry methods for captive and domestic animals would prohibit suffering in such conditions as puppy mills, and factory farms; and be it further

  Resolved, that The Episcopal Church's Peace and Justice Office identify existing guidelines to educate its members to adhere to ethical standards in the care and treatment of animals; and be it further

  Resolved, that The Episcopal Church, through its Office of Government Relations, identify and advocate for legislation protecting animals and effective enforcement measures.[115]

- *Resolved*, that the General Convention urge Diocesan Environmental Commissions of Committees to provide information to educate our congregations about decisions that would affect the lives and health of endangered species, farmed food animals and domesticated animals; and be it further

  Resolved, that each congregation be encouraged to refer this resolution to their outreach committee or other such venue in order to ensure the education and dissemination of information to their members about endangered species, farmed food animals and domesticated animals.[116]

Liturgical rites and prayers "provide pastorally for people caring for animals"

The Episcopal Church recognizes that our commission to love all God's creatures means that we need ways to bless the entry of animals into our lives, celebrate their relationship with us, and mourn their departure. In order to satisfy this need, The

---

115   *Episcopal General Convention, "Support Ethical Care of Animals,"* 253.

116   *Episcopal General Convention, "Decisions Affecting Animal Species,"* 629.

Episcopal Church has developed liturgical materials for use during the Feast of St. Francis (the patron saint of animals) or during other occasions when pastoral care is needed.

- *Resolved*, that the 77th General Convention make available the following liturgical materials, for use in a variety of settings to provide pastorally for people caring for animals:
  'Service at the loss of a beloved animal...At the adoption of an animal...For a lost or missing animal... For a sick animal...For one whose beloved animal has died...At the euthanizing of an animal...For the suffering of animals during warfare...For the loss of a farm animal...At the death of a wild animal.'[117]

- *At the adoption of an animal:* 'God, whose nature and whose name is Love: We thank you for this new relationship between N. [and N.] and this animal A. Let their home be filled with kindness and care; let them be the delight of one another's hearts; and watch over and keep them from this day forward in safety and peace; for your Name's sake. Amen.'[118]

- *General Blessing:* 'Most high, omnipotent good Lord, grant your people grace to renounce gladly the vanities of the world; that, following the way of blessed Francis, we may for love of you delight in your whole creation with perfectness of joy...We thank you for giving us these pets who bring us joy. As you take care of us, so also we ask your help that we might take care of those who trust us to look after them. By

---

117   *The Episcopal General Convention*, "Resolution #2012-A054: *Authorize Rites for Care of Animals," Journal of the General Convention of...* *The Episcopal Church, Indianapolis*, 2012 (*New York: General Convention,* 2012), 1. *http://www.episcopalarchives.org/cgi-bin/acts/acts_generate_pdf. pl?resolution=2012-A054*

118   *Ibid*, 4.

doing this, we share in your own love for all creation. We ask this in Jesus' name. Amen.'[119]

- *At the death of a wild animal:* 'Almighty God, who make the beasts of the wild move in beauty and show forth the glory of your Name: We grieve the death of this creature, whose existence was a reminder to us of your creative presence in the world. We give you thanks for that which was never ours to claim, but only to behold with wonder; through Jesus Christ our Redeemer, who lives and reigns with you and the Holy Spirit, one God, for ever and ever. Amen'[120]

Historical References on Animals

God "careth for all things." It is our duty to "prevent from all abuse the creatures he has made"

The Episcopal Church (or the Protestant Episcopal Church in the United States of America, as it was known at the time) was the first Christian denomination in the United States to issue an official condemnation of animal cruelty. This statement, released in 1817 by the House of Bishops, called upon members to avoid "amusements" that involve "cruelty to the brute creation." Although the 1817 statement spoke only of the damage to human souls caused by cruel behavior, additional statements released in 1874 and 1922 refocused the spotlight directly on animals, proclaiming them to be loved by God and deserving to be protected by us.

- The House of Bishops, solicitous for the preservation of the purity of the Church, and the piety of its members, are induced to impress upon the Clergy

---

119   *The Episcopal Church, "The Blessing of the Animals," St. Francis Day Resources, accessed July 30, 2015, 1. http://www.episcopalchurch.org/ files/st_francis_day_resources.pdf*

120   *Episcopal General Convention, "Rites for Care of Animals,"* 3.

the important duty, with a discreet but earnest zeal, of warning the people of their respective cures, of the danger of an indulgence in those worldly pleasures, which may tend to withdraw the affections from spiritual things. And especially on the subject of gambling, of amusements involving cruelty to the brute creation, and of theatrical representations, to which some peculiar circumstances have called their attention. They do not hesitate to express their unanimous opinion that these amusements, as well from their licentious tendency as from the strong temptation to vice which they afford, ought not to be frequented.[121]

- The Christian soul is sensitive to the love of God, and loves all things in Him, and for His sake. It loves even the dumb creatures He has made, because He condescends to be the God of the sparrow, and considered the very cattle that were in Nineveh. Gentleness to the animals which serve us, protection to the dependent flock which typifies the chosen people of God, pity for the callow brood in the fragile nest, are lessons which men of love are not ashamed to impress upon themselves and upon their children.[122]

- Whereas, we are taught by our Lord that not even a sparrow falls to the ground without our heavenly father's knowledge, and in other ways he careth for all things; we proclaim in consequence that it is our

121   Protestant Episcopal Church in the United States of America. "House of Bishops, May 27, 1817," Journal of the Proceedings of the Bishops, Clergy, and Laity, of the Protestant Episcopal Church in the United States of America, Assembled in a General Convention, Held in St. John's Chapel, in the City of New York, From October 6th to October 28th, Inclusive, in the Year of Our Lord 1847. (New York: Daniel Dana, Jr., 1847), 229.

122   Protestant Episcopal Church in the United States of America. Debates of the House of Deputies in the General Convention of the Protestant Church in the United States of America, Held in New York City, October, A.D. 1874 (Hartford: M.H. Mallory and Company, Printers, 1874), 426.

duty to be kind and considerate and to prevent from all abuse all the creatures he has made. Therefore be it resolved, the house of Bishops concurring, that this Convention acknowledges man's responsibilities for the humane care and treatment of his faithful friends and servants, the domestic animals …Resolved, that this Convention express its sympathetic interest with the work of all societies whose aim is the protection of the friendless and the wronged; and while wishing all such societies God's blessing, also pledges itself to interest and assistance in their work.[123]

Anyone who "will not be merciful to his beast, is a beast himself" and "the Devil in human form"

Prominent clergy within the Anglican Convention have followed, and sometimes anticipated, official church statements on animals: recognizing the damage caused to the human soul by cruelty to animals, affirming the intrinsic value of animals, and denouncing humanity's role in animal suffering. Anyone who is unmerciful to animals, say these clergy, "is a beast himself" and would be depicted as "the Devil in human form" if animals "were able to formulate a religion."

- [H]e that will not be merciful to his beast, is a beast himself.[124]

- It is also an unproved assumption that the domination of the planet by our own species is a desirable thing, which must give satisfaction to its Creator. We have devastated the loveliness of the world; we have exterminated several species more beautiful and less vicious than ourselves; we have enslaved the rest of the

---

123   *Protestant Episcopal Church in the United States of America. Journal of the General Convention of the Protestant Episcopal Church in the United States of America, Held in the City of Portland from September Sixth to September Twenty-Third, inclusive, in the Year of Our Lord 1922 (New York: The Abbott Press, 1923), 116-117.*

124   *Rev. Thomas Fuller, The Holy State and the Profane State (London: William Pickering, 1840), 18.*

animal creation, and have treated our distant cousins in fur and feathers so badly that beyond doubt, if they were able to formulate a religion, they would depict the Devil in human form.[125]

Contemporary Reflections on Animals

We have a "Christian commitment" to make choices that provide "greater life for other creatures"

The Presiding Bishop of The Episcopal Church, Katharine Jefferts Schori, encourages Episcopalians to put church teachings into action by living in a manner that respects "the dignity of our fellow creatures." From the garbage we create to the methods of travel we use to the food we eat, says Schori, our day-to-day decisions impact the well-being of our human and nonhuman neighbors. Our Christian commitment should be to live in a manner that brings "greater life for other creatures" and a "more abundant life...for the whole world."

- [C]onsider how your daily living can be an act of greater life for other creatures...We are beginning to be aware of the ways in which our lack of concern for the rest of creation results in death and destruction for our neighbors. We cannot love our neighbors unless we care for the creation that supports all our earthly lives. We are not respecting the dignity of our fellow creatures if our sewage or garbage fouls their living space. When atmospheric warming, due in part to the methane output of the millions of cows we raise each year to produce hamburger, begins to slowly drown the island homes of our neighbors in the South Pacific, are we truly sharing good news? The food we eat, the energy we use, the goods and foods we buy,

---

125   *Rev. William Ralph Inge, "The Idea of Progress," The Romanes Lecture 1920 (Oxford: At the Clarendon Press, 1920). 13-14.*

the ways in which we travel, are all opportunities—
choices and decisions—to be for others, both human
and other. Our Christian commitment is for this—
that we might live that more abundant life, and that
we might do it in a way that is for the whole world.[126]

Choices that protect endangered species and their habitats are an important part of stewardship

The Episcopal Church's commitment to all God's creatures
has inspired church members to take action against creation's
most pressing problems, including species extinction. "The
human population explosion...accompanied by exploitation of
fossil fuels" has contributed to the "wholesale death" of species,
says Presiding Bishop Schori. In order to protect vulnerable species from extinction, we must change our ways and practice a
stewardship of "life" not "death." One Diocese that is attempting to put this call into action is the Episcopalian Diocese of
Western Massachusetts, which is addressing extinction "pressure
due to the current pace of climate change" by shifting part of
its "investments from fossil fuels to renewable energy." Another
example of faith put into action can be found in a letter written
by the House of Bishops of The Episcopal Church to the United
States Senate opposing the opening of the Arctic Wildlife Refuge
to oil and gas exploration.

- We profess that God has planted us in a garden to care
  for it and for all its inhabitants, yet we have failed to
  love what God has given us...The human population
  explosion of recent millennia, accompanied by
  exploitation of fossil fuels in recent centuries, have
  moved this planetary system out of dynamic
  equilibrium...We are making war on the integrity of
  this planet. The result is wholesale death as species
  become extinct at unprecedented rates, and human

---

126   *The Most Rev. Dr. Katharine Jefferts Schori, Presiding Bishop, The
Episcopal Church, "Presiding Bishop's Message for Easter 2008," March 11
(2008), accessed August 1, 2015. http://www.episcopalchurch.org/library/
article/presiding-bishops-message-easter-2008*

beings die from disease, starvation, and the violence of war unleashed by environmental chaos and greed. A crisis is a decision point, a time of judgment. We can choose to change our destructive and overly consumptive ways, or we can ignore the consequences of our actions and slowly steam like proverbial frogs in a soup pot. We still have some opportunity to choose, but that Kairos moment will not last long. We have before us this day life and death. Which will we choose?[127]

- [I]ncreased extinction pressure on plant and animal species due to the current pace of climate change… combined with other sources of habitat loss, degradation and over-exploitation…[have inspired] the Diocese of Western Massachusetts…to shift about 20 percent of its $60 million of investments from fossil fuels to renewable energy. 'We took a vote after a long, hard debate. It reflects the bishop's commitment.'[128]

- *Resolved*, the House of Bishops of the Episcopal Church, USA…sends to the United States Senate the following message:

As the Bishops of the Episcopal Church, USA, we want to express our commitment to the vision of reconciliation of all peoples and share a common scriptural and theological belief that we have a responsibility to care for God's creation. We support protecting the Arctic National Wildlife Refuge fully. To risk the destruction of an untouched wilderness

127   *The Most Rev. Katharine Jefferts Schori, Presiding Bishop and Primate, The Episcopal Church, "Keynote Address," The Climate Change Crisis (2015), accessed August 1, 2015. http://www.episcopalchurch.org/ posts/publicaffairs/climate-change-crisis-forum-now-available-viewing*

128   *Episcopal News Service, World's largest climate action march: Episcopalians protest for change, September 23 (New York: The Episcopal Church, 2014). http://www.episcopalchurch.org/library/article/ world's-largest-climate-action-march-episcopalians-protest-change*

and an ancient culture violates our theological mandate to be caretakers of creation...

[T]he Arctic is an important habitat and home for many species, including the Arctic peregrine falcon, gyrfalcon, golden eagle, snowshoe hare, ptarmigan, polar bear, grizzly bear, musk ox, threatened spectacled eider, wolves, smaller mammals and water fowl. The psalmist proclaims, 'O Lord, how manifold are thy works! In wisdom hast thou made them all; the earth is full of your creatures' (Psalm 104)...

For these reasons and others, we ask you to oppose opening the Arctic National Wildlife Refuge to oil and gas exploration and development."[129]

Small, daily actions, such as our eating and purchasing choices, are an important part of stewardship

Compassionate stewardship reveals itself in the small, as well as the large, choices we make in our daily lives. Paying attention to what we eat and what we buy can be practical and effective ways to demonstrate compassion for animals, says Presiding Bishop Schori.

- There is much we can do, in small and large ways. We can pay attention to what we eat. Learn what fisheries are sustainable and which are not, and change your buying habits appropriately. Eat lower on the food chain...and demand a higher standard of environmentally accountable production...All of the Pauline language about the body of Christ applies equally to the body of God's creation. We are all part of one larger body, none of us lives for ourselves alone, and indeed our very meaning is dependent on our relationships with God and each other.[130]

---

129   *The Episcopal Church House of Bishops, House of Bishops calls on U.S. Senate to protect Arctic National Wildlife Refuge, March 14* (2005), *accessed August 1,* 2015. *http://www.episcopalchurch.org/library/article/house-bishops-calls-us-senate-protect-arctic-national-wildlife-refuge*

130   *The Most Rev. Dr. Katharine Jefferts Schori, Presiding Bishop, The*

Evangelical Lutheran Church in America

General Information

The Evangelical Lutheran Church in America (ELCA) traces its origins to the 16th century Protestant Reformation and the mid-17th century immigration of Lutherans to the Americas. It achieved its current form in 1988 when three previously independent churches merged together to form the largest Lutheran denomination in the United States.[131]

More information about the ELCA, including the church's beliefs, structure, and history, can be found by going to http://www.elca.org/

Number of Members in the U.S.: 3.86 million[132]

Episcopal Church, Healing Our Planet Earth: Stewardship of the Earth, April 12 (2008), *accessed August 1, 2015. http://www.episcopalchurch.org/posts/jeffertsschori/healing-our-planet-earth-stewardship-earth*

131   *Evangelical Lutheran Church in America, "History," accessed July 31, 2015. http://elca.org/About/History*

132   *Evangelical Lutheran Church in America, "ELCA Facts," accessed July 30, 2015. http://www.elca.org/News-and-Events/ELCA-Facts?_ga=1. 26557501.1430856676.1438307167*

Official Statements on Animals

"All creation, not just humankind, is viewed as 'very good' in God's eyes"

The Evangelical Lutheran Church in America has developed a series of Social Statements that "are meant to...set policy for the ELCA and guide its advocacy and work as a publically engaged church."[133] The Statements are adopted only after they receive approval by two-thirds of the ELCA Churchwide Assembly and, once adopted, are considered official declarations of church teaching and policy. Several of these statements have touched, directly or indirectly, on animals, their place in creation, and their relationship with God and with humanity. According to the ELCA's Social Statements on Genetics and on Creation, respectively, God loves all creatures "from the amoeba to the person." This love, says the ELCA, means that all creatures have "a God-given integrity and value," irrespective of any value they may or may not have for humanity.

- God blesses the world and sees it as 'good,' even before humankind comes on the scene. All creation, not just humankind, is viewed as 'very good' in God's eyes (Genesis 1:31)... God showers care upon sparrows and lilies (Matthew 6:26-30), and brings 'rain on a land where no one lives, on the desert, which is empty of human life' (Job 38:26).[134]

- Because each participant of creation depends ultimately upon God and is tasked by God, they are

---

133   *Evangelical Lutheran Church in America, "Social Statements,"* accessed July 30, 2015. *https://www.elca.org/faith/faith-and-society/social-statements?_ga=1.214666775.1223707317.1433702321*

134   *Bible citation from The Holy Bible, New Revised Standard Version. Evangelical Lutheran Church in America, "A Social Statement on Caring for Creation: Vision, Hope, Justice,"* (1993), 2. *http://download.elca.org/ELCA%20Resource%20Repository/EnvironmentSS.pdf?_ga=1.20453339 2.1223707317.1433702321*

not simply resources for human well-being or parts of a greater good; they are good in themselves.[135]

- God's creative action brings forth a dynamic, varied, evolving, interdependent community of abundance and life. In this creation, each participant has a relationship to God and has a God-given integrity and value.[136]

- Respect is a directive grounded in the dignity and integrity of created life (Exodus 20:11-17). For Lutheran Christians, respect follows from God's regard for all life as precious, from the amoeba to the person. Human beings cannot love as God loves, but the minimal response of innovative stewards to other members of the community of life is to recognize their givenness and to perceive their inherent or intrinsic value.[137]

We are kin to all creatures and must include them in our "sphere of moral consideration"

Both biology and the Bible tell us that we are related to and interdependent with all creatures, says the ELCA. Our kinship and interdependence, as well as God's word and example, teach us that "the sphere of moral consideration must encompass all of nature, not simply the immediate circle of human beings."

- All living beings exist because of common biological structures and processes, and all share fundamental dependencies and interdependencies. All life forms are related one to another.[138]

- Humanity is intimately related to the rest of creation. We, like other creatures, are formed from the earth

135   Evangelical Lutheran Church in America, "A Social Statement on Genetics, Faith and Responsibility," (2011), 10. http://download.elca.org/ELCA%20Resource%20Repository/GeneticsSS.pdf?_ga=1.247702279.12 23707317.1433702321

136   Ibid, 9.

137   Ibid, 16.

138   Ibid, 15.

(Genesis 2:7, 9, 19). Scripture speaks of humanity's kinship with other creatures (Psalm 104, Job 38-39). God cares faithfully for us, and together we join in singing the 'hymn of all creation' (*Lutheran Book of Worship*, page 61; Psalm 148). We look forward to a redemption that includes all creation (Ephesians 1:10).[139]

- Solidarity recognizes a kinship within all of nature that issues from God's creative activity (Psalms 104 and 148). It recognizes the fundamental human continuity and interdependence with all living things and natural resources on the earth. It expresses the contention that the interests of the entire community of life should be legitimate concerns when decisions are made and actions evaluated.[140]

- Today, the meaning of 'common good' or 'good of all' must include the community of all living creatures. The meaning also should extend beyond the present to include consideration for the future of the web of life. The sphere of moral consideration is no longer limited to human beings alone.[141]

- The sphere of moral consideration must encompass all of nature, not simply the immediate circle of human beings.[142]

Human "dominion" is a "special responsibility…to serve and keep God's garden"

Although the Bible states that humans have "dominion" over animals and the earth, this commission is not "a license to dominate and exploit," says the ELCA. Instead, dominion is correctly understood as an invitation to imitate the "shepherd king who takes the form of a servant." When we serve "all members of the community of life"—living "within the covenant God makes

139   ELCA, "Creation," 2.
140   ELCA, "Genetics," 23.
141   Ibid, 15.
142   Ibid, Prologue, 3.

with every living thing"—then we have grasped what Genesis means when it says we are created in the image of God, says the church.

- Humans, in service to God, have special roles on behalf of the whole of creation. Made in the image of God, we are called to care for the earth as God cares for the earth. God's command to have dominion and subdue the earth is not a license to dominate and exploit. Human dominion (Genesis 1:28; Psalm 8), a special responsibility, should reflect God's way of ruling as a shepherd king who takes the form of a servant (Philippians 2:7), wearing a crown of thorns.[143]

- God creates human beings as interdependent with the whole creation and as responsible to provide oversight as stewards who care for that creation. It is a vocation, a calling to continue what God is already doing for the earth—a calling to respect and promote the creation's flourishing. In this sense, Genesis understands the human species as being created 'in the image of God' (Genesis 1:26-28).[144]

- According to Genesis 2:15, our role within creation is to serve and to keep God's garden, the earth. 'To serve,' often translated 'to till,' invites us again to envision ourselves as servants, while 'to keep' invites us to take care of the earth as God keeps and cares for us (Numbers 6:24-26).[145]

- [T]he ELCA articulates an ethic of universal human obligation to serve the flourishing of the created order.[146]

---

143   ELCA, "Creation," 2-3.

144   ELCA, "Genetics," 10.

145   ELCA, "Creation," 3.

146   ELCA, "Genetics," 15.

- [W]e are to live within the covenant God makes with every living thing (Genesis 9:12-17; Hosea 2:18)…We are to love the earth as God loves us.[147]

"When the interests of life forms conflict, Christians must discern…ways that respect all"

Although all creatures are loved by God and have value in and of themselves, not all creatures have identical needs or require identical treatment. Differences between and within species, however, do not justify decisions "based solely on human interests." Instead, says the ELCA, humanity is obligated to "care for the basic needs of…all other life forms" and must look to resolve conflicting interests in "ways that respect all." "The good of the community of life," summarizes the ELCA, "should now serve as the overarching value to guide moral reflection and action."

- As reciprocity between humans does not always mean strict mutuality or equal treatment, so, too, reciprocity between humans and the community of life requires careful discrimination and judgment. Reciprocity must always mean that the community of life, its members and individuals, has moral standing that needs to be taken into account in discernment and deliberation for action.[148]

- [H]umans should not claim for themselves authority to make decisions based solely on human interests. They should consider both the integrity of the other participants in the community of life and their tasks before God. The human vocation as innovative stewards must be guided by the goal to respect and promote the earth's abundance for the sake of the community of life.[149]

---

147   ELCA, "Creation," 3.

148   ELCA, "Genetics," 14-15.

149   Ibid, 10.

- When the interests of life forms conflict, Christians must discern morally relevant differences and seek to resolve these dilemmas in ways that respect all.[150]
- The principle of sufficiency obligates human beings to care for the basic needs of others and all other life forms. It is grounded in the belief that God provides abundance that is sufficient for all.[151]
- [T]he ELCA articulates an ethic of universal human obligation to serve the flourishing of the created order.[152]
- The good of the community of life should now serve as the overarching value to guide moral reflection and action.[153]

Economic activity should serve the wellbeing of all God's creatures, now and into the future

Economic activity that focuses on "providing for people's wants" is unsustainable both ecologically and socially, says the ELCA. In order to be sustainable over time, economic activity needs to focus on the "wellbeing of both nature and human communities…now and in the future."

- 'Sustainability' is the capacity of natural and social systems to survive and thrive together over the long term. What is sufficient in providing for people's wants often is in tension with what can be sustained over time. Sustainability has implications for how we evaluate economic activity in terms of its ongoing effects on the wellbeing of both nature and human communities. Economic life should help sustain humans and the rest of creation—now and in the future.[154]

150   *Ibid, 17.*

151   *Ibid, 21.*

152   *Ibid, 13.*

153   *Ibid, 15.*

154   *Evangelical Lutheran Church in America, "A Social Statement on Sufficient, Sustainable Livelihood for All" (1999), 14. http://download.elca.*

Preference should be given to public policies that protect vulnerable species and habitat

In an attempt to put its Social Statements into action, the ELCA has declared that it will favor public policies that protect the environment, including policies that protect "species and their habitats."

- This church will favor proposals and actions that... seek: to protect species and their habitats; to protect and assure proper use of marine species; and to protect portions of the planet that are held in common, including the oceans and the atmosphere.[155]

Science must respect all life as precious and avoid "frivolous or abusive" research on animals

ELCA Social Statements support care and compassion for all God's creatures, even those within laboratory settings. Although this position does not necessitate the cessation of all animal testing, it does require the cessation of "frivolous or abusive treatment" of "experimental subjects."

- [N]ot every possible [scientific] enhancement or innovation should be pursued. Promotion must not violate the fundamental directive of respect. Efforts toward enhancement or innovation must be evaluated also through the norms of justice and wisdom.[156]
- Christian faith views all life as precious and given, such that respect and gratitude must govern even the sacrifice of life in which humans are inevitably involved, such as...aspects of scientific research... [R]esearch on animals, such as mice, may require the death of individual experimental subjects. The directive of respect, however, rules out frivolous or abusive treatment.[157]

---

org/ELCA%20Resource%20Repository/Economic_LifeSS.pdf?_ga=1.4313
9621.1223707317.1433702321
155   ELCA, "Creation," 11.
156   ELCA, "Genetics," 20.
157   Ibid, 17.

Historical References on Animals

Martin Luther: "God's entire divine nature is wholly and entirely in all creatures"

The ELCA traces its origins to the protestant reformer Martin Luther, whose "Small Catechism," "Large Catechism," and "Smalcald Articles" continue to be regarded as official statements of the faith. While Luther's other writings do not hold doctrinal status within the church, they do form part of the church's history and demonstrate that animals have been part of Lutheran theological reflection from the church's earliest days.

According to Luther, human sin has rendered us "crazy and foolish": no longer able to clearly discern God's will, even with the help of Scriptures. Animals, said Luther, are wiser than we are. If we were to pay close attention to them, we would see "God's almighty power and wonderful works clearly shine" for "God's entire divine nature is wholly and entirely" present within all creatures, even the smallest and least significant.

- But man has become crazy and foolish, since he fell away from God's word and command, so that henceforth there is no creature living that is not wiser than he; and a little finch, that can neither speak nor read, is his teacher and master in the Scriptures, although he has the whole Bible and his reason to help him.[158]

- In all things, in the least creatures, and in their members, God's almighty power and wonderful works clearly shine.[159]

---

158   Martin Luther, *Commentary on the Sermon on the Mount*, trans. Charles A. Hay (Philadelphia: Lutheran Publication Society, 1892), 342.
159   Martin Luther, *The Table Talk of Martin Luther*, trans. William Hazlitt (New York: HG Bohn, 1857), 28.

- God's entire divine nature is wholly and entirely in all creatures, more deeply, more inwardly, more present than the creature is to itself.[160]

Luther: God holds animals in "high esteem" and cares about their wellbeing

According to Luther, God loves animals and "holds them in such high esteem that he daily feeds them" and takes personal pleasure in caring for them.

- Thus Christ now speaks:...you daily see how your heavenly Father feeds the little birds in the field, without their having any care...[H]e holds them in such high esteem that he daily feeds them, as if he had only these to care for; and he takes pleasure in it, that they quite without care fly about and sing, as if they should say: I sing and am cheerful...[161]

Luther: On Judgment Day, animals will cry out against those who have abused them

All creatures "have speech intelligible to God and the Holy Spirit," said Luther. God hears their cries and will listen "on the last day" when "all creatures will utter an accusing cry against the ungodly who have shown them abuse here on earth."

- Just as we Christians endure many kinds of injustice and consequently sigh for and implore help and deliverance in the Lord's prayer, so do the creatures sigh. Although they have not human utterance, yet they have speech intelligible to God and the Holy Spirit, who mark the creatures' sighs over their unjust abuse by the ungodly.[162]
- Rightly was it said from the pulpit in former times that on the last day all creatures will utter an accusing

160   Martin Luther, Luther's Works, Vol. 37, ed. Helmut T. Lehmann (Philadelphia: Muhlenberg Press, 1959), 60.

161   Luther, Commentary on the Sermon on the Mount, 341.

162   Martin Luther, Luther's Epistle Sermons: Trinity Sunday to Advent Vol. III, trans. John Nicholas Lenker (Minneapolis: The Luther Press, 1909), Fourth Sunday after Trinity, paragraph 17.

cry against the ungodly who have shown them abuse here on earth, and will call them tyrants to whom they were unjustly subjected.[163]

Contemporary Reflections on Animals

"We cannot love God or our human neighbor without caring for creation"

The ELCA's commitment to creation-care has provided rich soil for the blossoming of contemporary moral reflections on animals. For Mark S. Hanson, the ELCA's Presiding Bishop from 2001-2013, God's care for creation and the intimate interconnection of "people, animals, and plants" means that "[w]e cannot love God or our human neighbor without caring for creation."

- We cannot escape the interconnectedness of the earth's fabric of life. Creation is the matrix of all our activities, both as human beings and as Christ's church. God gives us and all creatures life through the water, air, food, and all the other gifts that come to us from the earth. Everything we do both depends on these gifts, and has some kind of impact upon them. If these gifts are treated with contempt and abused, people, animals, and plants suffer together. If they are graciously received and cherished, people will flourish with the rest of creation. We cannot love God or our human neighbor without caring for creation.[164]

The current mass extinction of species at human hands is a sin and an offense to God

---

163   *Ibid, paragraph 18.*

164   *Mark S. Hanson, "A Commentary," Awakening to God's Call to Earthkeeping (2006), 11, accessed August 1, 2015. http://download.elca. org/ELCA%20Resource%20Repository/Awakening_To_Gods_Call_To_Earthkeeping.pdf?_ga=1.247772743.1358748120.1433638443*

For Lutheran theologian Larry L. Rasmussen, science may tell us that we are in the midst of a "great wave of extinction," but it is our moral and religious convictions that allow us to recognize this "genocide of creatures" as a "sin" that is a "rancid offense to the nostrils of the Triune God."

- We have become imperial unCreators in the Community of Life, terminators who deal death to birth itself. The sixth great wave of extinction, and the first at human hands, happens as we speak…

  To put the matter theologically: if the genocide of creatures, witting or unwitting, isn't sin, what on earth qualifies? If this isn't rancid offense to the nostrils of the Triune God, what is?…Killing nativity itself must count somewhere as worthy of repentance.

  'The earth belongs to all'…But it is true with equal force that 'all belongs to the earth.' This is our singular home, judging from all recent science. Perhaps when our moral emotions and religious convictions grasp both sides of this core belonging—the earth belongs to all and we all belong to earth—we will rightly name extinction 'sin' and begin to take our Eucharistic vow seriously.[165]

"Love of our…neighbors…demands a drastic change in U.S. animal farming" and meat consumption

Some ELCA members have interpreted the church's call to love God, neighbor, and creation as necessitating changes in our dietary habits and animal husbandry practices. Current Concentrated Animal Feeding Operations, known as CAFOs or Factory Farms, create unsustainable levels of atmospheric and aquatic pollution and treat animals with brutality. Eating just 20% less meat and advocating for changes in animal farming practices, says an ELCA blog, would improve the health and "environmental circumstances of everyone."

---

165   Larry L. Rasmussen, "Extinction and Sin," Journal of Lutheran Ethics, Volume 3, Issue 9 (2003), accessed August 1, 2015. http://www.elca.org/jle/articles/825?_ga=1.43757093.1223707317.1433702321

- 'Livestock production generates almost 20 percent of the world's greenhouse gases—more than the entire transportation sector. If Americans reduced meat consumption by just 20 percent, it would be as though we all switched from a sedan to a hybrid. (*New York Times*)'… 'Animal factory farms pollute U.S. waterways more than all other industrial sources combined. And you'd save more water by refraining from eating a pound of beef than you would by not showering for an entire year (*E-The Environmental Magazine*)'

   Asking Americans to reconsider their meat consumption does not seem to me to be an unreasonable request, especially considering most of us could do with more vegetables in our diet, anyway. It also seems so very straightforward. How many of your meals each week include meat? What is 20 percent of that figure? Switch at least that many of your meals each week to vegetarian selections. That's it! You'll improve the health of the planet and quite likely yourself at the same time. In the process, you'll also improve the environmental circumstances of everyone…[166]

- Love of our non-human neighbors surely demands a drastic change in U.S. animal farming. 'To visit a modern CAFO (Confined Animal Feeding Operation) is to enter a world that, for all its technological sophistication, is still designed according to Cartesian principles: animals are machines incapable of feeling pain. Since no thinking person can possibly believe this any more, industrial animal agriculture depends on a suspension of disbelief on the part of the people who operate it and a willingness to avert

166   Nancy Michaelis, "Eat Less Meat," ELCA Blogs, accessed July 11, 2015. http://elca.org/News-and-Events/blogs/elcaworldhunger/431?_ga=1 .18583097.1223707317.1433702321

your eyes on the part of everyone else.'[167] If all of us meat-eaters knew how brutally, how unnaturally our food animals are raised and slaughtered, I think there'd be a fully deserved outcry of anguish. It is incumbent on a biblical people to help make known this phenomenon in our food production, a relatively recent development, and to advocate intensely for change.[168]

Pantries, pet blessings, and prayers help churches incorporate animals into their moral circle

At both the national and local level, the ELCA is striving to weave its message of compassion for all God's creatures into its sermons, educational programs, and community outreach. Examples of these efforts include food pantries for pets and church services that incorporate animal blessing ceremonies and prayers.

- It all started when Diane Donahue, a member of St. Peter's Lutheran Church, an ELCA congregation in Port Jervis, NY, noticed that a dog in her neighborhood looked rather hungry....When looking back on this night, Diane says, 'God planted a seed in me.' She immediately presented her plan to her pastor, Patt Kaufman, to form a pet food pantry that would provide food for pets throughout the community.[169]

- For the past eight years, St. James [Lutheran Church in Grosse Pointe, MI] has celebrated St. Francis Day

---

167   *Quote from Margaret Talbot, New York Times Magazine, 15 December 2002, p. 133.*

168   *Charles Lutz, "Loving My Neighbor in the Whole of God's Creation," Journal of Lutheran Ethics, Volume 3, Issue 3 (2003), accessed August 1, 2015. http://www.elca.org/JLE/Articles/876?_ga=1.248701831. 1223707317.1433702321*

169   *Brandi Maczik, "Caring for the Animals," Living Lutheran: Lively Engagement in Faith & Life (2013), accessed August 1, 2015. http://www. elca.org/en/Living-Lutheran/Blogs/2013/07/~/link.aspx?_id=280CF-CBDD36C4DB5816F79B99AB58FA7&_z=z&_ga=1.46171943.122370 7317.1433702321*

with a blessing of the animals…The service is short so as not to 'test the patience of the animals,' as [Pastor Gerald Spice] puts it. Each year it features singing St. Francis' 'All Creatures of Our God and King,' a reading of the creation story from Genesis, a brief homily, and a litany of blessing for the pets present… 'Once we started doing the blessing, folks loved it,' Gerald says. 'Especially some of the older members who live alone, their pets are real companions to them,' he continues. 'They're also really important to young families. Children love their pets and become very attached.'[170]

- [Pastor] Michael Mueller…and St. Andrew [Lutheran Church in Racine, WI]…have embraced the Season of Creation, an optional four-week season in the church year usually celebrated during the month of September…[The season concludes] with an outdoor service where everyone gathers with their pets, and each animal—humans included—is blessed with health and well-being…[171]

- In the Book of Sirach we read, 'The compassion of human beings is for their neighbors, but the compassion of the Lord is for every living thing'. Remembering that that is the God whose blessings we ask, let us pray: 'Gracious God, we ask that you would give us will and wisdom to be good stewards as we tend these your creatures before us whom you have given into our care. Make us always aware of

170   Staff, "Blessing of the Animals," Living Lutheran: Lively Engagement in Faith & Life(2013), accessed August 1, 2015. http://www.elca.org/en/Living-Lutheran/Stories/2013/05/~/link.aspx?_id=CBEFC-5D3A5844D399E8E96E77C0B510B&_z=z&_ga=1.248614407.1223707317.1433702321
171   Aaron Cooper and David Rhoads, "The Season of Creation,"Living Lutheran: Lively Engagement in Faith & Life, (2012), accessed August 1, 2015. http://www.elca.org/en/Living-Lutheran/Stories/2013/05/~/~/link.aspx?_id=8A5893E771D24297ADD633D93EABBABA&_z=z

their needs as well as our own, so that your whole creation may proclaim your praise. We ask this in the name of your son Jesus Christ our Good Shepherd. Amen.'[172]

- Let us pray: 'Almighty God, we ask your blessing upon these [name animals], that they may have good health, adequate feed, plentiful pastures, and companionship of the flock/herd. Give them good stewards who will be faithful in their care, feeding them, and protecting them from danger. Bless their relationships with humankind and other living things so that, together in the web of life which you have brought into being, all creatures may fulfill your purpose. Amen.'[173]

172   *Pastor George L. Murphy, The Blessing of Farm Animals: An Occasional Liturgical Resource, (The Lutheran Alliance for Faith, Science, and Technology). Reprinted by Evangelical Lutheran Church of American, "Resource Repository," accessed July 11, 2015. http://download.elca.org/ ELCA%20Resource%20Repository/Blessing_Farm_Animals.pdf?_ga=1.20 9748629.1223707317.1433702321*
173   *Ibid.*

The Lutheran Church– Missouri Synod

General Information

The Lutheran Church–Missouri Synod (LCMS) was established in 1847 by German immigrants seeking religious freedom to practice their confessional faith. The church is characterized by belief in the Bible as the literal and inerrant Word of God and acceptance of *The Book of Concord: The Confessions of the Lutheran Church* as the normative statement of the faith.[174]

More information about The Lutheran Church–Missouri Synod, including the church's beliefs, structure, and history, can be found by going to: http://www.lcms.org

Number of Members in the U.S.: 2.28 million[175]

174   *The Lutheran Church – Missouri Synod, "History of the LCMS," accessed July 31, 15. http://www.lcms.org/aboutus/history*

175   *The Lutheran Church – Missouri Synod, "Synod Stats: Membership drops, giving increases," September 28 (2011), accessed August 1, 2015. http://blogs.lcms.org/2011/synod-stats-membership-drops-giving-increases*

Official Statements on Animals

God "created all things," but man is "the principal creature of God"

The Lutheran Church–Missouri Synod (LCMS) considers the Bible and *The Book of Concord* to be the only definitive statements of its faith, doctrine, and principles. In order to help its members better understand these texts and their application to contemporary issues, the LCMS has created a "Belief and Practice" section on its website. In this section, the church confesses faith in God as the Creator of "all things." Yet while everything is created by God, says the church, "man" is His "principal creature...specially created in the image of God."

- We believe, teach, and confess that God, by the almighty power of His Word, created all things. We also believe that man, as the principal creature of God, was specially created in the image of God, that is, in a state of righteousness, innocence, and blessedness.[176]

Man came "into being through the direct creative action of God" not "through a process of evolution"

The biblical assertion that the universe was created in six days, says the LCMS, is to be understood literally, not figuratively. Because the universe came into being over the course of a single week, human beings could not have evolved from animals or other "lower forms of life." Instead, says the church, humans are created "through the direct creative action of God."

- We teach that God has created heaven and earth, and that in the manner and in the space of time recorded in the Holy Scriptures, especially Gen. 1 and 2, namely, by his almighty creative word, and in six days.[177]

---

176   The Lutheran Church–Missouri Synod, "A Statement of Scriptural and Confessional Principles, Principle V: Original Sin," Belief and Practice (1973), accessed August 1, 2015. http://www.lcms.org/doctrine/scriptural-principles#V

177   Lutheran Church–Missouri Synod, "A Brief Statement of the

- We therefore reject the…notion that man did not come into being through the direct creative action of God, but through a process of evolution from lower forms of life, which in turn developed from matter that is either eternal, autonomous or self-generating.[178]

Animals "do not have immortal souls," but it is possible they will be with us in our "eternal home"

In response to a question concerning the presence of animals in heaven, the LCMS states that "animals do not have immortal souls," but it is possible—although not certain—that they will be present in "our eternal home [which] is a new earth."

- Since animals do not have immortal souls, we might think the answer [to the question of animals in heaven] is no. Several facts, however, make one hesitant to be satisfied with a simple 'no.' Our eternal home is a new earth (Is. 65:17ff; 2 Peter 3:13; Rev. 21:1). Is. 65:25 speaks of it as a place in which the wolf and the lamb live together peacefully.

  This may be figurative language, but one other passage suggests animals might be in our eternal home. Rom. 8:21 says that 'the creation itself will be liberated from its bondage.' In this present, sin-cursed world, we inflict suffering on animals, and they inflict suffering on us. At Christ's coming, when this world is freed from the effects of sin, animals, too, will be freed from suffering.

  The text also says the creation will be 'brought into the glorious freedom of the children of God.' That might mean there may be plants and animals in the new earth as there were in the first earth. If there are animals on the new earth, they will be good creatures of God as the animals of the first earth were.

Doctrinal Position of the Missouri Synod: On Creation," Belief and Practice (1932), accessed August 1, 2015.http://www.lcms.org/doctrine/doctrinal-position#creation

178   LCMS, "Original Sin."

In short, the answer is a cautious 'maybe.'[179]

Historical References on Animals

Martin Luther: God holds animals in "high esteem" and cares about their well-being

The LCMS considers *The Book of Concord* to be the definitive expression of its faith. Within this book are three sections consisting of works by Martin Luther: "The Smalcald Articles," "The Small Catechism," and "The Large Catechism." While these are the only writings by Luther that are regarded as official statements of the Lutheran faith, Luther's others writings form part of the church's history and demonstrate that animals have been part of Lutheran theological reflection from the church's earliest days.

According to Luther, God loves animals and "holds them in such high esteem that he daily feeds them" and takes personal pleasure in caring for them.

- Thus Christ now speaks:…you daily see how your heavenly Father feeds the little birds in the field, without their having any care…[H]e holds them in such high esteem that he daily feeds them, as if he had only these to care for; and he takes pleasure in it, that they quite without care fly about and sing, as if they should say: I sing and am cheerful…[180]

Luther: Animals can help us recognize God's presence within creation

Prior to the fall of Adam and Eve, humanity had perfect knowledge of "God's word and command," says Luther. Since

179   The Lutheran Church–Missouri Synod, "Frequently Asked Questions/LCMS Views, The Bible FAQS: Animals in Heaven?" Belief and Practice, accessed July 30, 2015. http://www.lcms.org/faqs/lcmsviews#animals

180   Martin Luther, Commentary on the Sermon on the Mount, trans. Charles A Hay (Philadelphia: Lutheran Publication Society, 1892), 341.

the fall, our knowledge has become imperfect. Creation can help us recover some of our lost wisdom if we allow God's creatures to teach us about God's power and divine nature.

- But man has become crazy and foolish, since he fell away from God's word and command, so that henceforth there is no creature living that is not wiser than he; and a little finch, that can neither speak nor read, is his teacher and master in the Scriptures, although he has the whole Bible and his reason to help him.[181]

- In all things, in the least creatures, and their members, God's almighty power and wonderful works clearly shine.[182]

Luther: On Judgment Day, animals will cry out against those who have abused them

All creatures "have speech intelligible to God and the Holy Spirit," said Luther. God hears their cries and will listen "on the last day" when "all creatures will utter an accusing cry against the ungodly who have shown them abuse here on earth."

- Just as we…endure many kinds of injustice and consequently sigh for and implore help and deliverance in the Lord's prayer, so do the creatures sigh. Although they have not human utterance, yet they have speech intelligible to God and the Holy Spirit, who mark the creatures' sighs over their unjust abuse by the ungodly.[183]

- Rightly was it said from the pulpit in former times that on the last day all creatures will utter an accusing cry against the ungodly who have shown them abuse

---

181   *Ibid*, 342.

182   *Martin Luther, The Table Talk of Martin Luther, trans. William Hazlitt (New York: HG Bohn, 1857), 28.*

183   *Martin Luther, Luther's Epistle Sermons: Trinity Sunday to Advent, Vol. III trans. John Nicholas Lenker (Minneapolis: The Luther Press, 1909), Fourth Sunday after Trinity, Romans 8:18-22, paragraph 17.*

here on earth, and will call them tyrants to whom they were unjustly subjected.[184]

Contemporary Reflections on Animals

God has "infinite compassion." His "governance extends over all creatures"

In 1970, the LCMS' Commission on Theology and Church Relations issued a study document entitled "Creation in Biblical Perspective." This document initially was intended to be an examination of the creation account in the book of Genesis but quickly expanded to include creation narratives in other biblical texts. When looked at in the context of the entire Bible, concluded the Commission, the doctrine of creation can be seen to touch upon every aspect of Christian theology, including questions of evil, redemption and restoration, and humanity's role in the created world. In 2010, the Commission revisited the question of humanity's role in creation in a report entitled "Together with All Creatures: Caring for God's Living Earth." According to these reports, God is the creator, sustainer, and redeemer of all creatures and has compassion over both "man and beast." God is concerned for the welfare of all creatures, extending His benevolence "even to the animal world."

- ...God continues to look after His creation. He persists in creating man and beast. He continues to provide sustenance for His creatures. He rules the universe, the nations, individuals. We are reminded that He looks out for the welfare of oxen and even of sparrows (Matt. 10:29).[185]

---

184   *Ibid, paragraph 18.*

185   *The Lutheran Church–Missouri Synod Commission on Theology and Church Relations, Creation in Biblical Perspective: Report of the Commission on Theology and Church Relations (1970), 8, accessed August 1, 2015. http://www.lcms.org/Document.fdoc?src=lcm&id=427*

- God's governance extends over all creatures. Those who fear Him experience it as infinite compassion (Ps. 78:38ff). His benevolence extends even to the animal world (Jonah 4:11; Deut. 25:4; Luke 12:6; Matt. 10:29).[186]

God has given humanity "special responsibilities for His creation"

Humanity has a special calling within creation, say the LCMS reports. Although we share much in common with God's other creatures, only human beings have been entrusted with the care of "the garden home that God created for all of His creatures."

- God has given His human creatures both special privileges and special responsibilities for His creation. God formed His human creatures to take care of His earth. He did not give this responsibility to other creatures—not even to the angels. Herein lies our distinctive calling as humans. While we share much in common with other creatures, we do not share with them a common responsibility for taking care of—or for ruining—the garden home that God created for all of His creatures. That responsibility is ours alone as human creatures.[187]

Our care of God's creatures should be one of "servant-hood that focuses on the well-being of the other"

The earth belongs to God, says the Commission, and we are under His "jurisdiction…and…accountable to Him in all things." We have sinned against God and failed in our care of creation by treating "other creatures less as 'fellow creatures' and more as objects and commodities." We must repent our past "tyranny" and exercise care of creation through "servanthood that focuses

---

186   Ibid, 7.

187   The Lutheran Church-Missouri Synod Commission on Theology and Church Relations, Together with All Creatures: Caring for God's Living Earth, A Report of the Commission on Theology and Church Relations (St. Louis: The Lutheran Church – Missouri Synod, 1970), 39. http://www. lcms.org/Document.fdoc?src=lcm&id=341

on the well-being of the other." According to the LCMS, "…the question raised here is not one of human life versus animal life. It is a question of how we shall…live with God, with one another, and with creation for the sake of the flourishing of life."

- First, God called us to care for *His* earth. Although God entrusted us with the earth and placed it into our hands, this does not mean that God gave it to us in such a way that He absented Himself from His creation or relinquished His ownership of it. The earth still belongs to Him. It remains His earth (Deut. 10:14; Ps. 24:1; Ps. 95:4-5, 7).[188]

- The Biblical teaching that God is the Creator and man is His creature places man under the jurisdiction of God and makes him accountable to Him in all things. Autonomous man is man in rebellion against his Creator.[189]

- The dominion that God gave His human creatures is often abused, carried out to the detriment of creation. First the fall into sin resulted in a rejection of God's gifts of creation. Rather than seeing creation as a gift received, human beings came to see it as something that belonged to them as a right. Greed and pride replaced gratitude and humility. Second, when we no longer see other animals and birds as fellow creatures, tyranny follows. A view of life in which 'It's all about me' will displace a view of servanthood that focuses on the well-being of the other. Even when we seek the preservation of nature and the creatures who live within it, more often than not it will be only for our pleasures and purposes (e.g., that we might have nice scenery)…Third, as a result of sin, we see and treat other creatures less as 'fellow creatures' and more as objects and commodities. In the pursuit of our own needs and desires, it has become easier to objectify

---

188   LCMS, *Together with All Creatures*, 47.

189   LCMS, *Creation in Biblical Perspective*, 11.

other creatures by seeing them as little more than raw resources that serve our thirst for the acquisition of possessions.[190]

- The heart of original sin ultimately lies in the refusal to accept our creaturely limits. As it did with Adam and Eve, this refusal brings disastrous consequences in our relationships to God, others, and the wider creation. As Christians who embrace the gift of our creatureliness we need to learn to live as creatures... This means we accept that we are part of a whole interconnected web of life within which each creature is a gift to the other. We see our lives as human creatures defined not by the freedom to exceed limits in the pursuit of personal fulfillment but by the freedom to limit ourselves for the sake of the other. ...Thus the question raised here is not one of human life versus animal life. It is a question of how we shall...live with God, with one another, and with creation for the sake of the flourishing of life.[191]

Christians should speak out "on practices that we know are inhumane and cruel"

Too often, says the LCMS, Christians have remained silent on the issue of animal cruelty, despite having "good reason for urging compassion on their fellow nonhuman creatures." The church suggests that Christians oppose "practices that we know are inhumane and cruel" or, by default, opposition will be left in secular hands that may not hold Christian values.

- [W]here are the Christian voices objecting to the abuse of animals? Matthew Scully, a speech writer in the George W. Bush administration suggests that it is 'by default...others with no religious faith are left to champion the causes of animals' because Christians have so little to say on practices that we know are inhumane and cruel. In fact, he suggests that if it

---

190   LCMS, *Together with All Creatures,* 50-51.

191   *Ibid,* 84, 90.

were not to oppose the radicalism of animal rights groups, many Christian thinkers would say nothing at all about the compassionate treatment of animals. This is a shame because Christians have good reasons for urging compassion for their fellow nonhuman creatures without demeaning the value of humans.[192]

Unregulated puppy mills raise troubling questions about the way we treat our pets

Since most of us have direct contact with animals only through our pets, says the Commission on Theology and Church Relations, practicing compassion toward animals logically begins with issues surrounding these animals. Regulating puppy mills provides a good place to start.

- Today, most of us do not have direct contact with animals other than our pets…How do we care for our pets and other animals? In most states, dog fighting and cock fighting have been outlawed but puppy mills often remain unregulated.[193]

Food animals should be "allowed to live as God intended prior to giving their lives for us"

Eating animals was not part of God's original intention for creation," says the LCMS Commission, it was "a concession to a fallen world." In recognition of this point, we should show compassion toward food animals by ensuring that they are "allowed to live as God intended prior to giving their lives for us." To do this, says the Commission, we should make an effort to purchase cage-free eggs and free range beef, pork, and poultry whenever possible.

- Eating animals was not part of God's original intention for creation. It was a concession to a fallen world. When we eat meat, we eat what [Thomas] Berry calls 'the broken body of creation.' In recognition of these two points, we can ask, 'How were the animals that we eat allowed to live out their brief lives?' This is

---

192   *Ibid, 97-98.*
193   *Ibid, 99.*

not only to ask whether they were healthy with the help of antibiotics and vaccines. It is to ask a larger question. Were cows and hogs allowed to see the sun and feel the ground beneath them or to graze in the fields? Were turkeys and chickens allowed to spread their wings? We can choose to eat those animals that were allowed to live as God intended prior to giving their lives for us.[194]

- Buy certified, organically raised dairy products, eggs, cereals, fruit, and vegetables. Purchase range-fed beef, pork, and poultry. How we eat determines the way in which our food is raised. This can be expensive, but we can begin by choosing one food that we will eat this way, for example eggs from cage-free chickens or range-fed beef from a local farmer.[195]

Laboratory and wild animals should be treated kindly and never killed "only for the sake of killing"

Our mandate to care for all God's creatures extends even to the animals that we hunt and keep in laboratories, says the LCMS. Although God permits us to use animals for legitimate purposes, He does not permit us to "kill only for the sake of killing."

- How are laboratory animals, used in experimentation for cures and cosmetics, treated? How do we treat the animals that we hunt? Are they simply economic commodities? God allowed us to kill the beasts of field and forest for food, but not to kill only for the sake of killing.[196]

Endangered species should be protected. Their extinction "diminishes the song of creation"

"Of all the ecological problems we face," says the LCMS, "the one truly irreversible action to which we contribute" is the extinction of species. According to the Commission reports, we

194   *Ibid.*
195   *Ibid,* 102.
196   *Ibid,* 99.

must begin to ask ourselves if "we have a right to render any species extinct" and to remember that with each extinction "the song of creation becomes much diminished. The witness to God's work for unbelievers becomes muted."

- Of all the ecological issues we face, the extinction of species is the only truly irreversible action to which we contribute. The very word extinction may send chills down one's spine. It is 'not just the death of an individual—but of all the individuals—past, present, and potential—that collectively make up a species.' Consider the loss of the passenger pigeon, ivory-billed woodpecker, Carolina pigeon, and more recently, Yangtzee fresh water dolphin. Scientists estimate that over 170 amphibian species have gone extinct in recent years and another 30 to 50 percent are threatened with extinction. A number of interrelated reasons account for this. Conservation biologists summarize those factors with the acronym HIPPO. It stands for Habitat destruction, Invasive species, Pollution, Population, and Over harvesting or Over hunting…The question must be asked, do we have a right to render any species extinct?[197]

- 'Human beings are unique among creation not only because we have the choice about whether we will make our lives a reflection of God, but also because we can in our activity severely impair the ability of other members of creation to reflect God's grace.' When we do so, as in the case of species extinction, replacing the beauty of creation with…ugliness…we stifle their voices if not remove them from the choir. The song of creation becomes much diminished. The witness to God's work for unbelievers becomes muted.[198]

---

197   *Ibid*, 71-72.
198   *Ibid*, 111.

Presbyterian Church (U.S.A.)

General Information

The Presbyterian Church (U.S.A.), also known as the PC(USA), traces its history to the 16th century Protestant reformer John Calvin, whose biblical commentaries, sermons, and theological works are highly regarded within the church to this day. Presbyterianism came to the Americas in 1706 and achieved its current form in 1983 when the United Presbyterian Church in the USA and the Presbyterian Church in the U.S. merged to form the Presbyterian Church (U.S.A.), thereby healing a schism that had developed during the American Civil War.[199]

More information about the Presbyterian Church (U.S.A.), including the church's beliefs, structure, and history, can be found by going to: http://www.pcsusa.org/ministries/101

Number of Members in the U.S.: 1.8 million[200]

---

199   Presbyterian Church (U.S.A.), "Presbyterian 101: Presbyterian Distinctives, accessed July 31, 2015. http://www.presbyterianmission.org/ministries/101/distinctives/

200   Presbyterian Church (U.S.A.), "PC(USA) Congregations and Membership, 2001-2012, Table 1," accessed August 1, 2015. http://www.pcusa.org/site_media/media/uploads/research/pdfs/2012-cs-table1.pdf

Official Statements on Animals

All of creation "cries out in this time of ecological crisis"

In 1990, the PC(USA) issued an official report entitled *Restoring Creation for Ecology and Justice* that continues to be the authoritative statement of the church's environment policy. In this document, the PC(USA) states that rampant human population growth combined with unsustainable and unjust economic practices threaten "the entire realm of animals and plants." It is time we put aside our anthropocentric "understanding of justice," says the church, and recognize that "the neighbors that claim respect and concern include our nonhuman companions." "The cry of the nonhuman creation," warns the church, "joins the cry of the human victims of indifference and oppression."

- Creation cries out in this time of ecological crises...In the face of [growing] human [population] numbers... the question is not only whether the planet can carry those numbers, but what other creatures it can carry as well. The expansion of the human species threatens the entire realm of animals and plants, the total biotic community interacting with nonliving forces.[201]

- The impact made by modern civilization upon nature in this one century has wrought more damage than was done by human agency in all preceding centuries combined...The capacity of basic biological systems to regenerate themselves was severely impaired. Finite minerals were pumped and mined as if inexhaustible. The wastes and poisons from a global population that tripled and a global economy that multiplied many times exceeded the capacity of earth, air, and

---

201   202nd *General Assembly* (1990), *Presbyterian Church (U.S.A.), Restoring Creation for Ecology and Justice* (Louisville: Office of the General Assembly, Presbyterian Church [U.S.A.], 1990), 8, 17. https://www.presbyterianmission.org/site_media/media/uploads/environment/pdf/restoring-creation-for-ecology&justice.pdf

water to absorb them safely…Warnings abound that present trends are unsustainable and unjust. The cry of the nonhuman creation joins the cry of the human victims of indifference and oppression.[202]

- [T]he crisis of our time compels us to transcend the traditional, strictly anthropocentric understanding of justice. The neighbors that claim respect and concern include our nonhuman companions. The human community depends upon the biotic. Nature's systems are vulnerable. Earth is oppressed along with people.[203]

"Disrespect for living beings" has resulted in inhumane treatment of both domestic and wild animals

The PC(USA) recognizes "that all the creatures with whom we share the planet have value in their own right," independent of any value they may or may not have for human beings. Troubling questions arise about our "cruelty…to wildlife" and our "inhumane treatment of domestic animals" when we ask ourselves "how much animal suffering and what kind of genetic alterations of animals are justifiable for human benefit?" In light of the inherent value of animals, says the church, we should reexamine such practices as sports hunting, factory farming, animal research and testing, genetic alteration of animals, and the disruption of habitats of endangered species.

- There is increasing recognition that all the creatures with whom we share the planet have value in their own right. What then is an appropriate human relation to other animals, particularly animals raised for food or utilized in experiments? The key issues are how much animal suffering and what kind of genetic alterations of animals are justifiable for human benefit? These questions are especially urgent in relation to animals with advanced nervous systems.[204]

---

202   *Ibid,* 20.
203   *Ibid,* 31.
204   *Ibid,* 68.

- [Q]uestions arise concerning much that goes on: cruelty done to wildlife for the sake of profit or sport; inhumane treatment of domestic animals, including the 'factory farming' of livestock; often unwarranted use of animals in research and testing; development of biotechnology (the genetic alteration of plants and animals) which has unassessed potential, not only for food production, but for new inequities and new forms of disrespect for living beings; resistance to strong measures to curb 'acid rain,' despite mounting evidence of damage to trees, lakes, and fish; and massive destruction of the world's forests, accompanied by the extinction of enormous numbers of plant and animal species.[205]

God calls us to "respond to the cry of creation" by reflecting "God's love for all creatures"

According to the PC(USA), human beings have been "created in God's image" and been given a unique mission to act as stewards of our fellow creatures: a mission that should be pursued with joy, thanksgiving, and humility. All creatures, says the church's *Constitution*, are created, sustained and redeemed by a loving God. Our call to stewardship should "respond to the cry of creation" in ways that "reflect God's love for all creatures."

- Created in God's image, we humans are called by God to relate consciously, lovingly, caringly not only to the Creator but to all human and nonhuman companions.[206]
- In worship Christians rejoice and give thanks to God, who gives and sustains the created universe, the earth, all life, and all goods. They acknowledge God's command to be stewards. They confess their own failures in caring for creation and life. They rejoice in the promise of the redemption and renewal of the creation in Jesus Christ, proclaimed in the Word and

205   *Ibid,* 17.
206   *Ibid,* 25.

sealed in the Sacraments. They commit themselves to live as God's stewards until the day when God will make all things new.[207]

- Therefore, God calls the Presbyterian Church (U.S.A.) to respond to the cry of creation, human and nonhuman...Restoring creation is God's own work in our time, in which God comes both to judge and to restore. The Creator-Redeemer calls faithful people to become engaged with God in keeping and healing the creation, human and nonhuman.[208]

- [T]he 202nd General Assembly (1990) recognizes and accepts restoring creation as a central concern of the church, to be incorporated into its life and mission at every level.[209]

- As stewards of God's creation who hold the earth in trust, the people of God are called to: (a) use the earth's resources responsibly without plundering, polluting, or destroying, (b) develop technological methods and processes that work together with the earth's environment to preserve and enhance life, (c) produce and consume in ways that make available to all people what is sufficient for life, (d) work for responsible attitudes and practices in procreation and reproduction, (e) use and shape earth's goods to create beauty, order, health, and peace in ways that reflect God's love for all creatures.[210]

The destruction of a species is a "monstrous arrogance" that usurps "the prerogative of God"

"No one," says the PC(USA), "'owns' a species" and "anyone who would destroy species...takes...the prerogative of God." In

207   Presbyterian Church (U.S.A.), The Constitution of the Presbyterian Church (U.S.A.) Part II: Book of Order 2015-2017 (Louisville: The Office of the General Assembly, 2015), W-7.5002.

208   202nd General Assembly (1990), 8.

209   Ibid, 9.

210   Presbyterian Church (U.S.A.), W-7.5003.

the contiguous United States, points out the church, only 2 percent of our wilderness remains. If we are to protect endangered animals, concludes the church, we must "protect and expand remaining public wildlands…prohibit trade in endangered wild animals and…stop indiscriminate killing of wild animals."

- At the level of species all concepts of ownership ought to lapse; no one 'owns' a species. Anyone who would destroy species in the name of development takes, a monstrous arrogance, the prerogative of God.[211]

- The divinely given natural world is vanishing, while the 'built environment' of human culture has been increasing dramatically. About 96 percent of the contiguous United States is developed, farmed, grazed, timbered, or designated for multiple use. Only about 2 percent has been designated as wilderness, and another 2 percent, as yet little developed, might be suitable for wilderness…Maximum effort must be made through national, state, and local policy to protect the minimum of genuine wildlands that remain.[212]

- In addition to preserving a place for natural sectors and even some wildness within the built environment, responsible environmental policy provides for wild domains, to which human beings come only as visitors who do not remain.[213]

- Keep wildlife wild and free. Avoid irreversible change. Protect and expand remaining public wildlands… Respect life, the more sentient the more respect. Think of nature as a community, more than a commodity… Preserve wildlands in all the diverse kinds of American ecosystems, including wildlands near urban areas; and restore degraded wildlands, reintroducing all the original native fauna and flora where possible. Stop

211   202nd General Assembly (1990), 57.

212   Ibid, 56.

213   Ibid, 56-57.

cutting remaining pristine forests on public lands…
Prohibit trade in endangered wild animals and
endangered plants, or products derived from them.
Stop indiscriminate killing of wild animals.[214]

The integrity life is "to be valued above rights of property and its development"

According to the PC(USA), economic activities that presume "only human interests really count" jeopardize the well-being and survival of both vulnerable humans and animals. It is time, says the church, to adopt a "new humility" that values "people and all other living things…above rights of property and its development." If we are to live "in harmonious balance with creation and other creatures," says the church, we must place limits on "economic growth and material consumption."

- People and all other living things are to be valued above rights of property and its development.[215]
- The eco-justice crisis displays the anthropocentric attitude that only human interests really count. As economic development proceeds and cities expand, developers give little attention to the consequences for nonhuman creatures whose habitats are lost or threatened—birds, bears, elephants, the marine life in wetlands, and the many endangered species.[216]
- The grace of God's judgment brings a new humility, partly because it does expose the 'greedy for unjust gain.'[217]
- [T]he church should insist that economic values cannot justify the further reduction of the pristine natural environment. In the U.S., human needs can be met from the 96 percent of land that has already been domesticated.[218]

214   *Ibid*, 57-59.
215   *Ibid*, 23-24.
216   *Ibid*, 17.
217   *Ibid*, 23.
218   *Ibid*, 57.

- Stewardship, understood as caretaking or earthkeeping reflective of God's 'equivocal love for this world,' requires 'respect for the integrity of natural systems and for the limits that nature places on economic growth and material consumption,' and anticipates nonhierarchical social relations in harmonious balance with creation and other creatures.[219]

Historical References on Animals

John Calvin: Animals are "equally the children of God." We must treat them with justice

The Presbyterian Church (U.S.A.) has its roots in the writings of John Calvin (1509-1564). Although these writings are not binding on the church, they are part of its history.

According to Calvin, animals deserve to be treated with care and justice. Calvin listed the need to provide care for animals and children as one of the few acceptable reasons to be absent from church on Sundays.

- Now...God himself...prohibits the muzzling of the mouth of the ox that treadeth out the corn...[T] here is...force in this quotation, in which the Lord requires cattle to be taken care of...It is an unjust thing that the husbandman should lay out his pains to no purpose in plowing and thrashing, but that the end of his labor is the hope of receiving the fruits. As it is so, we may infer that this belongs to oxen also.[220]

---

219   *Ibid*, 47.

220   *John Calvin, Commentary on the Epistles of Paul the Apostle to the Corinthians, Vol 1, John Pringle, trans. (Edinburgh: The Calvin Translation Society, 1848), 295.*

- Everyone in each house is to come [to church] on Sundays, unless it be necessary to leave someone behind to take care of children or animals…[221]

John Calvin: God will require us to give an account of the way we have treated His creatures

God has placed the creatures of the earth in trust to humanity and one day will require us to give an account of the ways in which we have used or abused that trust, said Calvin. We should treat creation as though we constantly hear God whispering, "Give an account of your stewardship."

- [Scripture] declares that [earthly blessings] have all been given us by the kindness of God, and appointed for our use under the condition of being regarded as trusts, of which we must one day give account. We must, therefore, administer them as if we constantly heard the words sounding in our ears, 'Give an account of your stewardship.'[222]

John Calvin: Animals reflect God's wisdom. We should strive to understand and love them

For Calvin, animals provide a mirror that reflects the wisdom and goodness of God. Knowledge of God can be gained through knowledge of God's creatures, so we should "dwell long upon them" and fix them "deeply in [our] heart."

- God therefore presents before us in his creatures a bright mirror of his admirable wisdom, so that every one that looks upon the world, and the other works of God, must of necessity break forth in admiration of him, if he has a single spark of sound judgment.[223]
- It were, indeed, a strange defence for man to pretend that he has no ears to hear the truth, while dumb

---

221   John Calvin, The Library of Christian Classics, Volume XXII, Calvin: Theological Treatises, J.K.S. Reid, trans. (Philadelphia: The Westminster Press, 1954), 77.

222   John Calvin, Institutes of the Christian Religion, Vol II, Henry Beveridge, trans. (Edinburgh: T&T Clark, 1863), 35.

223   Calvin, Commentary on the Epistles of Paul, 84.

creatures have voices loud enough to declare it; to allege that he is unable to see that which creatures without eyes demonstrate, to excuse himself on the ground of weakness of mind, while all creatures without reason are able to teach. Wherefore, when we wander and go astray, we are justly shut out from every species of excuse, because all things point to the right path.[224]

- Undoubtedly, were one to attempt to speak in due terms of the inestimable wisdom, power, justice, and goodness of God, in the formation of the world, no grace or splendour of diction could equal the greatness of the subject. Still there can be no doubt that the Lord would have us constantly occupied with such holy meditation, in order that, while we contemplate the immense treasures of wisdom and goodness exhibited in the creatures as in so many mirrors, we may not only run our eye over them with a hasty, and as it were, evanescent glance, but dwell long upon them, seriously and faithfully turn them in our minds, and every now and then bring them to recollection.[225]

- Therefore, in order to be compendious, let the reader understand that he has a genuine apprehension of the character of God as the Creator of the world; first, if he attends to the general rule, never thoughtlessly or obliviously to overlook the glorious perfections which God displays in his creatures; and, secondly, if he makes a self application of what he sees, so as to fix it deeply on his heart.[226]

---

224   *John Calvin, Institutes of the Christian Religion, Vol I, Henry Beveridge, trans. (Edinburgh: T&T Clark, 1863), 62.*

225   *Ibid, 211.*

226   *Ibid, 157.*

Contemporary Reflections
on Animals

Human dominion should be understood as service, not as exploitation and domination

The PC(USA)'s General Assembly, which sets priorities for the church and is responsible for protecting it from errors in faith and practice,[227]asserts that human "dominion" over creation, granted in the book of Genesis, "is to be understood in the sense of 'service'…as care of and as commitment…to the well-being of nature." This assertion is echoed by the Presbyterian Hunger Program, a ministry of the PC(USA), which explains that Genesis can only be fully understood when it is read in conjunction with the other biblical creation narratives found in Psalms 8, 65, and 104, and Job 38-40. When these stories are looked at together, they reveal that "humans are simply one species in the vast choir of creation" and that all species have "value independent of how they might benefit human beings."

- It is to be noted…that the terms 'dominion' and 'subdue' in the Genesis account are not to be taken as giving humankind the right of 'exploitation.' Dominion is to be understood in the sense of 'service.' It is to be expressed as stewardship, as care of and as commitment, to the well-being of nature.[228]
- Genesis 1 is not the only account of God as creator in the Bible. Psalm 104, Psalm 65, Job 38-40, and Psalm 8 are other examples. While human beings are given a prominent role in Genesis 1 and Psalm 8, in

227   Presbyterian Church (USA) Office of the General Assembly, "General Assembly of the PC(U.S.A.), accessed 7/31/15. https://oga.pcusa.org/section/ga/ga/

228   Presbyterian Church in the United States General Assembly, "GA Minutes: The Dialogue between Theology and Science," (1982), 3, accessed August 1, 2015. http://www.pcusa.org/media/uploads/theologyandworship/pdfs/dialogue.pdf

[Psalm 104], as in the latter chapters of Job, humans are simply one species in the vast choir of creation. Psalm 104 describes an intricate system where all creatures are dependent on God for food. Here, the interplay between water, the landscape, and the rhythm of seasons sounds like an ecology textbook, and the human race receives no more attention than lions or wild goats. In the eyes of this hymn writer, the appropriate response to creation is not dominion but humility and praise.[229]

- Psalm 104:27-30 reminds us that we are not the only creatures God feeds. All creation is dependent on the breath of God and food from God's hands. Nor does nature exist to serve humanity: indeed most of the creatures mentioned have no economic value. Wild donkeys, wild goats, storks, and lions are all described as part of God's good creation with value independent of how they might benefit human beings. Even Leviathan, a fearsome sea monster, is not a predator or pest; it is God's plaything, formed to 'sport' in the water.[230]

Eating lower on the food chain is an act of justice that protects the earth, human health, and animals

The PC(USA) has committed itself to the development of resources dedicated to the restoration of creation. Among these resources is a curriculum designed by the Presbyterian Hunger Program (PHP) that reveals the connections between faith, food, and justice. The program materials suggest that church members "live our beliefs about justice" by reducing or eliminating the consumption of meat. The intensive factory farming of animals, says the PHP, has led to massive water pollution,

---

229   *Presbyterian Hunger Program, Just Eating? Practicing Our Faith at the Table: Readings for Reflection and Actions, 27, accessed August 1, 2015. http://www.pcusa.org/media/uploads/hunger/pdf/justeatpart.pdf. Additional information can be found at http://pcusa.org/justeating*

230   *Ibid, 27.*

adverse impacts on human health, an unjust distribution of vital resources, and the inhumane treatment of animals.

- Eating…can be an opportunity to thoughtfully live our beliefs about justice—a vehicle for practicing our faith… Good nutrition is stewardship of a gift God gave us—our bodies…Choose healthier sources of proteins…Animal proteins such as beef or whole milk dairy products come with a heavy helping of saturated fats. Vegetable proteins come with plenty of fiber and vitamins.[231]

- Seventy percent of all the grain in the United States goes to feeding herds of livestock. It takes up to sixteen pounds of grain to produce a pound of beef. In fact, the world's cattle alone consume a quantity of food equal to the caloric needs of 8.7 billion people— more than the entire human population on earth.[232]

- Human waste is an environmental problem in some places, but in the U.S. farm animals produce 130 times as much manure as we do.[233]

- In 2005, the American Cancer Society reported the results of an extensive study which confirmed that high consumption of red and processed meat increases your risk of colon cancer, the third most common cancer that annually kills 56,000 men and women in the U.S. High consumption was defined as only 3 or more ounces per day for men and 2 or more for women.[234]

- The meat industry does not always handle animals humanely.[235]

231   *Ibid, 1, 12.*
232   *Ibid, 22.*
233   *Ibid, 25.*
234   *Ibid, 16.*
235   *Ibid, 56.*

***Liturgical materials entreat God to "kindle in our
hearts a flame of love" for all creatures***

Other resources developed by the PC(USA) in support of
God's creation include liturgical materials such as the *Litany
of Creation's Agony and Hope*. In this prayer, God the Creator is
praised and human sins against creation confessed. "We destroy
habitat for the other creatures we are charged to care for," says
the litany, "herd them into tortuous confinement, and sacrifice
whole species...Kindle in our hearts a flame of love for you and
all our neighbors: from the lowliest creature that lives, to the
name that is the greatest of all."

- *Litany of Creation's Agony and Hope:*

  Leader: Gracious Creator, we praise you, for you
  brought forth the cosmos out of chaos, and created
  this shining jewel of heavens—this fragile earth, our
  island home.

  People: 'And God saw everything that God had made,
  and behold, it was very good.' (Genesis 1:31)[236]

  Leader: In the midst of this web of life, you brought
  forth the human race, and gave us the stewardship
  of all creation. You made a covenant with Noah,
  charging all living creatures together to be fruitful
  and multiply, and promising not to curse the ground
  for human sin.

  People: 'While the earth remains, seedtime and harvest,
  cold and heat, summer and winter, day and night,
  shall not cease.' (Gen. 8:22)

  Leader: But we have turned against you and betrayed
  your trust, and our human enterprise threatens the
  cycles of seedtime and harvest, cold and heat. We
  poison the waters, foul the sparkling air, and strip the
  living land of trees and topsoil. We destroy habitat for
  the other creatures we are charged to care for, herd
  them into tortuous confinement, and sacrifice whole
  species. We have turned against your creation, and

---

236   *Bible citations from English Standard Version.*

we have turned against each other, exploiting and oppressing our human and nonhuman neighbors. We have been prideful in our dominion, and trusted too much in our own wisdom. Even when we can see our wrong, we have been paralyzed by feelings of helplessness and isolation.

All: Gracious God, grant us the courage to turn around and participate in the world's future with new insight and humility. Give us wisdom and energy to meet the challenge of the eco-justice crisis with hope and purpose. Kindle in our hearts a flame of love for you and all our neighbors: from the lowliest creature that lives, to the Name that is the greatest of all. Amen.[237]

---

237   *Presbyterian Church (U.S.A.), Committee on Social Witness Policy in cooperation with Stewardship Communication Development Ministry Unit and Social Justice and Peacemaking Ministry Unit, Restoring Creation for Ecology and Justice: Responding to the Cry of Creation for Healing and Justice, Leader's Guide, 5-6, accessed August 1, 2015. http://www.pcusa.org/site_media/media/uploads/environment/pdf/restoring-leaderguide.pdf*

The Roman Catholic Church

General Information

The Roman Catholic Church is the world's largest Christian denomination, representing more than half of all Christians and more than one-sixth of the world's population. Final authority for the Church rests in the Magisterium: the College of Bishops headed by the pope (currently Pope Francis).[238]

More information about The Roman Catholic Church, including the Church's beliefs, structure, and history, can be found by going to: http://w2.vatican.va

Number of Members in the U.S.: 79.7 million
Number of Members Worldwide: 1.2 billion

---

238   Center for Applied Research in the Apostolate, "Frequently Requested Church Statistics: United States Data Over Time," accessed August 1, 2015. http://cara.georgetown.edu/caraservices/requestedchurchstats.html

Official Statements on Animals

Humans may use animals "within reasonable limits"

According to the *Catechism of the Catholic Church*, animals may be used to serve human purposes, but these uses must be kept "within reasonable limits" since "it is contrary to human dignity to cause animals to suffer and die needlessly."

- [I]t is legitimate to use animals for food and clothing. They may be domesticated to help man in his work and leisure. Medical and scientific experimentation on animals is a morally acceptable practice if it remains within reasonable limits and contributes to caring for or saving human lives. It is contrary to human dignity to cause animals to suffer and die needlessly.[239]

God entrusted animals to our "stewardship;" we must "reject the notion [of] absolute domination"

Although the Catholic Catechism states that humans may use animals for our own purposes, it also states that we are to act as God's stewards on earth. Pope Francis laments that Christians "at times" have misinterpreted God's gift of stewardship as a license to exercise "absolute domination" over other creatures. "[N]owadays," says the pope, "we must forcefully reject" this misinterpretation of Scripture and recognize that "indiscriminate exploitation" has left a "swath of destruction and death" in its path.

- God entrusted animals to the stewardship of those whom he created in his own image.[240]

- Although it is true that we Christians have at times incorrectly interpreted the Scriptures, nowadays we must forcefully reject the notion that our being created

---

239   The Holy See, *Catechism of the Catholic Church* (*Vatican City: Libreria Editrice Vaticana, 1993*), 2417-2418. *http://www.vatican.va/archive/ENG0015/__P8B.HTM*

240   *Ibid.*

in God's image and given dominion over the earth justifies absolute domination over other creatures.[241]

- There are other weak and defenceless beings who are frequently at the mercy of economic interests or indiscriminate exploitation. I am speaking of creation as a whole. We human beings are not only the beneficiaries but also the stewards of other creatures…Let us not leave in our wake a swath of destruction and death…[242]

Humans were created to be in relationship with God and all creatures. Rupture of this is sin

According to the Roman Catholic Church, the Bible teaches that God created human beings to live in harmony with God, with each other, and with all creation. The more we enter into these relationships, says Pope Francis, the more we mature and are "sanctified." However, says the pope, because of human actions, these "vital relationships have been broken, both outwardly and within us. This rupture is sin."

- The first man was not only created good, but was also established in friendship with his Creator and in harmony with himself and with the creation around him…[243]
- The human person grows more, matures more and is sanctified more to the extent that he or she enters into relationships, going out from themselves to live

241   Pope Francis, Encyclical Letter Laudato Si' of the Holy Father Francis On Care for Our Common Home (Vatican City: Libreria Editrice Vaticana, 2015), 67.http://w2.vatican.va/content/francesco/en/encyclicals/documents/papa-francesco_20150524_enciclica-laudato-si.html

242   Pope Francis, Apostolic Exhortation, Evangelii Gaudium, of the Holy Father Francis to the Bishops, Clergy, Consecrated Persons and the Lay Faithful on the Proclamation of the Gospel in Today's World (Vatican City: Libreria Editrice Vaticana, 2013), 215. http://w2.vatican.va/content/francesco/en/apost_exhortations/documents/papa-francesco_esortazione-ap_20131124_evangelii-gaudium.html

243   The Holy See, 374.

in communion with God, with others and with all creatures…[244]

- The laws found in the Bible dwell on relationships, not only among individuals but also with other living beings. 'You shall not see your brother's donkey or his ox fallen down by the way and withhold your help… If you chance to come upon a bird's nest in any tree or on the ground, with young ones or eggs and the mother sitting upon the young or upon the eggs; you shall not take the mother with the young' (Dt. 22:4, 6). Along these same lines, rest on the seventh day is meant not only for human beings, but also so 'that your ox and your donkey may have rest' (Ex. 23:12). Clearly, the Bible has no place for a tyrannical anthropocentrism unconcerned for other creatures.[245]

- The creation accounts in the book of Genesis…suggest that human life is grounded in three fundamental and closely intertwined relationships: with God, with our neighbour and with the earth itself. According to the Bible, these three vital relationships have been broken, both outwardly and within us. This rupture is sin.[246]

Animals are God's creatures. Each "must be cherished with love and respect"

"Animals are the creatures of God," says the Catholic Catechism, and each, says Pope Francis, "must be cherished with love and respect." Saint Francis of Assisi is the ideal model of "what it is to be human," says the pope, "for to him each and every creature was a sister united to him by bonds of affection. That is why he felt called to care for all that exists."

- Animals are God's creatures. He surrounds them with his providential care. By their mere existence they

---

244   *Francis, Laudato Si'*, 240.
245   *Ibid*, 68.
246   *Ibid*, 66.

bless him and give him glory. Thus men owe them kindness.[247]

- Because all creatures are connected, each must be cherished with love and respect, for all of us as living creatures are dependent on one another.[248]

- [Saint] Francis [of Assisi] helps us to see that an integral ecology calls for openness to categories which transcend the language of mathematics and biology, and take us to the heart of what it is to be human. Just as happens when we fall in love with someone, whenever he would gaze at the sun, the moon or the smallest of animals, he burst into song, drawing all other creatures into his praise. He communed with all creation...for to him each and every creature was a sister united to him by bonds of affection. That is why he felt called to care for all that exists.[249]

"Every creature has its own value and significance" with its own God-given place in the world

God loves every creature that He has made and enfolds "even the fleeting life of the least of beings...with his affection," says Pope Francis. According to the pope, we are called upon to mirror God's love by recognizing "that other living beings have a value of their own" and that each has been given a place in the world through "the Father's tenderness."

- [W]e are called to recognize that other living beings have a value of their own in God's eyes: 'by their mere existence they bless him and give him glory', and indeed, 'the Lord rejoices in all his works' (Ps. 104:31).[250]

- In the Judaeo-Christian tradition, the word 'creation' has a broader meaning than 'nature', for it has to do

---

247   *The Holy See*, 2416.

248   *Francis, Laudato Si*, 42.

249   *Ibid*, 11.

250   *Ibid*, 69.

with God's loving plan in which every creature has its own value and significance.[251]

- God's love is the fundamental moving force in all created things: 'For you love all things that exist, and detest none of the things that you have made; for you would not have made anything if you had hated it' (Wis. 11:24). Every creature is thus the object of the Father's tenderness, who gives it its place in the world. Even the fleeting life of the least of beings is the object of his love, and in its few seconds of existence, God enfolds it with his affection.[252]

"Through the greatness and the beauty of creatures one comes to know by analogy their maker"

Each creature, says the Church, "reflects in its own way a ray of God's infinite wisdom and goodness." Although no single creature possesses the fullness of God, says Pope Francis, each provides "a continuing revelation of the divine" and "a teaching which God wishes to hand on to us." Quoting from the Book of Wisdom, the pope concludes, that "[t]hrough the greatness and the beauty of creatures one comes to know by analogy their maker."[253]

- Each creature possesses its own particular goodness and perfection…Each of the various creatures, willed in its own being, reflects in its own way a ray of God's infinite wisdom and goodness.[254]
- The beauty of creation reflects the infinite beauty of the Creator and ought to inspire the respect and submission of man's intellect and will.[255]
- The Canadian bishops rightly pointed out that no creature is excluded from this manifestation of God:

251   Ibid, 76.

252   Ibid, 77.

253   *The Book of Wisdom is contained within the Catholic Bible but not within Protestant Bible editions.*

254   *The Holy See*, 339.

255   Ibid, 341.

'From Panoramic vistas to the tiniest living form, nature is a constant source of wonder and awe. It is also a continuing revelation of the divine'. The bishops of Japan, for their part, made a thought-provoking observation: 'To sense each creature singing the hymn of its existence is to live joyfully in God's love and hope.' This contemplation of creation allows us to discover in each thing a teaching which God wishes to hand on to us, since 'for the believer, to contemplate creation is to hear a message, to listen to a paradoxical and silent voice.'[256]

• The Spirit of life dwells in every living creature and calls us to enter into relationship with him.[257]

• [Saint] Francis, faithful to Scripture, invites us to see nature as a magnificent book in which God speaks to us and grants us a glimpse of his infinite beauty and goodness. 'Through the greatness and beauty of creatures one comes to know by analogy their maker' (Wis. 13:5).[258]

"We have only one heart." Cruelty towards animals leads to cruelty towards other human beings

"We have only one heart," says Pope Francis, "and the same wretchedness which leads us to mistreat an animal will not be long in showing itself in our relationships with other people." All creatures exist in a "universal communion" in which "indifference or cruelty towards fellow creatures" eventually "affects the treatment we mete out to other human beings."

• [W]hen our hearts are authentically open to universal communion, this sense of fraternity excludes nothing and no one. It follows that our indifference or cruelty towards fellow creatures of this world sooner or later affects the treatment we mete out to other human beings. We have only one heart, and the same

256   *Francis, Laudato Si', 85.*
257   *Ibid, 88.*
258   *Ibid, 12.*

wretchedness which leads us to mistreat an animal will not be long in showing itself in our relationships with other people. Every act of cruelty towards any creature is 'contrary to human dignity'. We can hardly consider ourselves to be fully loving if we disregard any aspect of reality...[259]

"Living our vocation to be protectors of God's handiwork is essential to a life of virtue"

According to the Church, protection of "God's handiwork... is not an optional or a secondary aspect of our Christian experience" but, rather, is "an essential part" of our faith. We must always remember, says Pope Francis, "that, where other creatures are concerned, 'we can speak of the priority of being over that of being useful.'"

- Living our vocation to be protectors of God's handiwork is essential to a life of virtue; it is not an optional or a secondary aspect of our Christian experience.[260]

- Christians...'realize that their responsibility within creation, and their duty towards nature and the Creator, are an essential part of their faith.'[261]

- In our time, the Church does not simply state that other creatures are completely subordinated to the good of human beings, as if they have no worth in themselves and can be treated as we wish. The German bishops have taught that, where other creatures are concerned, 'we can speak of the priority of being over that of being useful.'[262]

"Eternal life will be a shared experience...in which each creature...will take its rightful place"

Jesus is "present throughout creation," says Pope Francis, and is moving "all creatures...towards a common point of arrival,

259   *Ibid, 92.*
260   *Ibid, 217.*
261   *Ibid, 64.*
262   *Ibid, 69.*

which is God." This, says the pope, imbues each creature with God's "radiant presence" and reveals that eternal life "will be a shared experience of awe, in which each creature, resplendently transfigured, will take its rightful place."

- [A]ll creatures are moving forward with us and through us towards a common point of arrival, which is God, in that transcendent fullness where the risen Christ embraces and illumines all things.[263]

- The New Testament does not only tell us of the earthly Jesus and his tangible and loving relationship with the world. It also shows him risen and glorious, present throughout creation by his universal Lordship...This leads us to direct our gaze to the end of time, when the Son will deliver all things to the Father, so that 'God may be everything to every one' (1 Cor. 15:28). Thus, the creatures of this world no longer appear to us under merely natural guise because the risen One is mysteriously holding them to himself and directing them towards fullness as their end. The very flowers of the field and the birds which his human eyes contemplated and admired are now imbued with his radiant presence.[264]

- At the end, we will find ourselves face to face with the infinite beauty of God (cf. 1 Cor. 13:12), and be able to read with admiration and happiness the mystery of the universe, which with us will share in unending plenitude. Even now we are journeying towards the Sabbath of eternity, the new Jerusalem, towards our common home in heaven. Jesus says: 'I make all things new' (Rev. 21:5). Eternal life will be a shared experience of awe, in which each creature, resplendently transfigured, will take its rightful place and have something to give those poor men and

---

263   *Ibid*, 83.

264   *Ibid*, 100.

women who will have been liberated once and for all.[265]

Let us offer prayers "for inspiration to take up the commitment" to all God's creatures

At the end of *Laudato si'*, the Roman Catholic Church's official encyclical on the environment, Pope Francis proposes two prayers for creation: one that can be shared "with all who believe in a God who is the all-powerful Creator, while in the other we Christians ask for inspiration to take up the commitment to creation set before us by the Gospel of Jesus." Both prayers are reminders of the major themes put forward in the encyclical, including: God's presence in and love for all creatures, humanity's obligation to "protect the world" and "discover the worth of each thing…with awe and contemplation," and the unity of all creatures now and in the coming Kingdom.

- *A Prayer for Our Earth*

  All-powerful God, you are present in the whole universe
  and in the smallest of your creatures.
  You embrace with your tenderness all that exists.
  Pour out upon us the power of your love,
  that we may protect life and beauty.
  Fill us with peace, that we may love
  as brothers and sisters, harming no one.
  O God of the poor,
  help us to rescue the abandoned and forgotten of this earth,
  so precious in your eyes.
  Bring healing to our lives,
  that we may protect the world and not prey on it,
  that we may sow beauty, not pollution and destruction.
  Touch the hearts
  of those who look only for gain

---

265   *Ibid*, 243.

at the expense of the poor and the earth.
Teach us to discover the worth of each thing,
to be filled with awe and contemplation,
to recognize that we are profoundly united
with every creature
as we journey towards your infinite light.
We thank you for being with us each day.
Encourage us, we pray, in our struggle
for justice, love and peace.

- *A Christian Prayer in Union with Creation*
Father, we praise you with all your creatures.
They came forth from your all-powerful hand;
they are yours, filled with your presence and your
tender love.
Praise be to you!

Son of God, Jesus,
through you all things were made.
You were formed in the womb of Mary our Mother,
you became part of this earth,
and you gazed upon this world with human eyes.
Today you are alive in every creature
in your risen glory.
Praise be to you!

Holy Spirit, by your light
you guide this world towards the Father's love
and accompany creation as it groans in travail.
You also dwell in our hearts
and you inspire us to do what is good.
Praise be to you!

Triune Lord, wondrous community of infinite love,
teach us to contemplate you
in the beauty of the universe,
for all things speak of you.
Awaken our praise and thankfulness
for every being that you have made.
Give us the grace to feel profoundly joined
to everything that is.

God of love, show us our place in this world
as channels of your love
for all the creatures of this earth,
for not one of them is forgotten in your sight.
Enlighten those who possess power and money
that they may avoid the sin of indifference,
that they may love the common good, advance the
weak,
and care for this world in which we live.
The poor and the earth are crying out.
O Lord, seize us with your power and light,
help us to protect all life,
to prepare for a better future,
for the coming of your Kingdom
of justice, peace, love and beauty.
Praise be to you!
Amen.[266]

---

266   *Ibid, 246.*

Historical References
on Animals

St. Thomas Aquinas: God's goodness is present in all creatures and is "represented by them"

St. Thomas Aquinas (1225-1274 CE) noted that all creatures "come from the intention of…God…in order that His goodness might be…represented by them." Since no one creature can adequately represent His goodness, God created "many and diverse creatures that what was wanting to one…might be supplied by another."

- Hence we must say that the distinction and multitude of things come from the intention of the first agent, who is God. For He produced things into being in order that His goodness might be communicated to creatures, and be represented by them; and because His goodness could not be adequately represented by one creature alone, He produced many and diverse creatures, that what was wanting to one in the representation of the Divine goodness might be supplied by another. For goodness, which in God is simple and uniform, in creatures is manifold and divided; and hence the whole universe together participates in the Divine goodness more perfectly, and represents it better than any single creature whatever.[267]

St. Francis of Assisi preached to animals, extolled their virtues, and tended to their needs

In preparation for the canonization of St. Francis of Assisi (c. 1181-1226 CE), Pope Gregory IX commissioned an official biography to be written. This book, authored by one of the saint's earliest followers, described multiple occasions when Francis

---

267   *Thomas Aquinas, The 'Summa Theologica' of St. Thomas Aquinas, Part I. Fathers of the English Dominican Province, trans. (London: R&T Washbourne, Ltd, 1912), 255.*

preached to animals, rescued them from danger, provided them with food and comfort, and praised their nobility.

- During the time when (as has been said) many joined themselves to the brethren the most blessed father Francis was journeying through the valley of Spoleto, and came to a spot near Bevagna where a very great number of birds of different sorts were gathered together...When he saw them...Francis the most blessed servant of God left his companions in the way and ran eagerly towards the birds. When he was come close to them and saw that they were awaiting him, he gave them his accustomed greeting. But, not a little surprised that the birds did not fly away (as they are wont to do) he was filled with exceeding joy and humbly begged them to hear the word of God: and, after saying many things to them he added: 'My brother birds, much ought ye to praise your Creator, and ever to love Him who has given you feathers for clothing, wings for flight, and all that ye had need of. God has made you noble among His creatures, for He has given you a habitation in the purity of the air, and, whereas ye neither sow nor reap, He himself doth still protect and govern you without any care of your own.'

...[O]nce when he was staying at the fortress of Greccio, one of the brethren brought him a live leveret that had been caught in a snare; and when the blessed man saw it he was moved with compassion... [T]he holy father, caressing him with maternal affection, let him go, so that he might freely return to the woodland...He was also moved by the same feeling of pity towards fish, for if they had been caught, and he had the opportunity, he would throw them back alive into the water, bidding them beware of being caught a second time.

Another time...he met a man carrying two lambs, bound and hanging over his shoulders, which he was taking to market to sell. When blessed Francis heard them bleating he was moved with compassion, and came near and touched them, showing pity for them like a mother towards her crying child. And he said to the man...'take the cloak I am wearing for their price, and give the lambs to me.'...When he had received the lambs he...gave them back to the man, charging him never to sell them or do them hurt, but to keep them, feed them, and take good care of them.

He picked up worms from the way that they might not be trodden on, and ordered honey and the best wine to be provided for bees that they might not perish from want in the cold of winter. He called by the name of brother all animals, though in all their kinds the gentle were his favourites. Who is sufficient to tell all these things? For that Original Goodness, which shall be all in all, shone forth already to this Saint as all in all.[268]

Contemporary Reflections on Animals

Pope John Paul II: Only humans have immortal souls but animals may have mortal souls

During a general audience in January of 1990, Pope John Paul II stated that both "man" and "animal" are created from the "spirit or breath of God" and "under this aspect man... appears in solidarity with all living beings." This statement was interpreted by some as a papal declaration that animals have souls. In 2002, Pope John Paul II partially clarified his position on this issue by stating that only human souls are immortal—a

---

268   *Thomas of Celano, The Lives of Saint Francis of Assisi, A. G. Ferrers Howell, trans. (London: Methuen & Co, 1908), 58-60, 77, 297.*

statement that leaves open the possibility that animals have mortal souls.

- We read that, after having formed man from the dust of the ground, the Lord God 'breathed into his nostrils the breath of life; and man became a living being' (Gen. 2:7)… In man there is a breath or spirit similar to the breath or spirit of God. When the Book of Genesis speaks in chapter two of the creation of the animals (v. 19), it does not hint at such a close relationship with the breath of God…Other texts, however, admit that the animals also have a vital breath or wind and that they received it from God. Under this aspect man, coming forth from the hands of God, appears in solidarity with all living beings.[269]
- At the centre of the whole creation, He placed us, human beings, with our inalienable human dignity. Although we share many features with the rest of the living beings, Almighty God went further with us and gave us an immortal soul, the source of self-awareness and freedom, endowments that make us in His image and likeness (cf. Gen. 1:26-31; 2:7).[270]

Pope John Paul II and the ITC: In "the fullness of time," God will "unite all things to him"

In 1990, 25 years before Pope Francis released his encyclical on the environment, Pope John Paul II wrote that in "the fullness of time" God will make "new heavens and a new earth"

---

269   *Pope John Paul II, "The Creative Action of the Divine Spirit, General Audience, January 7, 1990" (Vatican City: Libreria Editrice Vaticana, 1990), accessed February 2, 2009. http://www.humanesociety.org/assets/pdfs/faith/pope-john-paul-ii-general.pdf*

270   *Pope John Paul II, "Common Declaration on Environmental Ethics: Common Declaration of John Paul II and the Ecumenical Patriarch His Holiness Bartholomew I, Monday 10 June 2002" (Vatican City: Libreria Editrice Vaticana, 2002), accessed August 1, 2015. http://w2.vatican.va/content/john-paul-ii/en/speeches/2002/june/documents/hf_jp-ii_spe_20020610_venice-declaration.html*

in which Christ will "reconcile to himself all things." A similar statement was made in 2002 by the International Theological Commission (ITC), a group of 30 international Catholic theologians who are appointed by the Pope as advisors to the Magisterium. According to the ITC, animals "by their very existence...bless God and give him glory" and will be restored with "the whole of creation in an eschatological and definitive moment of harmony."

- Christians believe that the Death and Resurrection of Christ accomplished the work of reconciling humanity to the Father, who 'was pleased...through (Christ) to reconcile to himself *all things*, whether on earth or in heaven, making peace by the blood of his cross' (Col. 1:19-20). Creation was thus made new (cf. Rev. 21:5). Once subjected to the bondage of sin and decay (cf. Rom. 8:21), it has now received new life while 'we wait for new heavens and a new earth in which righteousness dwells' (2 Pt. 3:13). Thus, the Father 'has made known to us in all wisdom and insight the mystery...which he set forth in Christ as a plan for the fullness of time, to unite *all things* in him, all things in heaven and things on earth' (Eph. 1:9-10).[271]

- Animals are the creatures of God, and, according to the Scriptures, he surrounds them with his providential care (Mt. 6:26). Human beings should accept them with gratitude and, even adopting a eucharistic attitude with regard to every element of creation, to give thanks to God for them. By their very existence the animals bless God and give him

271   Pope John Paul II, "Message of His Holiness Pope John Paul II for the Celebration of the World Day of Peace: 1 January 1990: Peace with God the Creator, Peace with all of Creation" (Vatican City: Libreria Editrice Vaticana, 2002), 4, accessed August 1, 2015. http://w2.vatican.va/content/ john-paul-ii/en/messages/peace/documents/hf_jp-ii_mes_19891208_xxiii- world-day-for-peace.html

glory: "Bless the Lord, all you birds of the air. All you beasts, wild and tame, bless the Lord" (Dn. 3:80-81). In addition, the harmony which man must establish, or restore, in the whole of creation includes his relationship to the animals. When Christ comes in his "glory, he will 'recapitulate' the whole of creation in an eschatological and definitive moment of harmony."[272]

Cardinal Ratzinger: The "industrial use" of animals violates biblical "relationship(s) of mutuality"

Before becoming Pope, Benedict XVI (known at the time as Cardinal Joseph Ratzinger) was asked if humans are allowed to eat animals. He replied that we are "not forbidden" to use animals for food, but that any use of animals must conform to the biblical directive to treat animals with respect. "Industrial use of creatures"—the large-scale, confined rearing of animals—contradicts this directive, said Ratzinger.

- …we can see that [animals] are given into our care, that we cannot just do whatever we want with them. Animals, too, are God's creatures and even if they do not have the same direct relation to God that man has, they are creatures of his will, creatures we must respect as companions in creation…[Man] should always maintain his respect for these creatures, but he knows at the same time that he is not forbidden to take food from them. Certainly, a sort of industrial use of creatures, so that geese are fed in such a way as to produce as large a liver as possible, or hens live so packed together that they become just caricatures of birds, this degrading of living creatures to a commodity seems to me in fact to contradict the

---

272   International Theological Commission, "Communion and Stewardship: Human Persons Created in the Image of God" (Vatican City: Libreria Editrice Vaticana, 2002), 79, accessed August 1, 2015. http://www.vatican.va/roman_curia/congregations/cfaith/cti_documents/rc_con_cfaith_doc_20040723_communion-stewardship_en.html

relationship of mutuality that comes across in the Bible.[273]

U.S. Conference of Catholic Bishops: Agricultural practices should protect wildlife

The United States Conference of Catholic Bishops has a long history of involvement with agricultural policy issues. At their 2003 General Meeting, the full body of bishops reviewed the church's agricultural policies and approved a document that supports the protection of human life, soil quality, and wildlife. In this document, entitled "For I Was Hungry and You Gave Me Food: Catholic Reflections on Food, Farmers, and Farmworkers," the bishops state that "all creation is a gift" and that "caring for animals [is a] form of stewardship" that should be practiced with "reverence and respect."

- Care for God's creation is a central calling for believers. Agricultural and food policies should reward practices that protect human life, encourage soil conservation, improve water quality, protect wildlife, and maintain the diversity of the ecosystem.[274]

- All creation is a gift. Scripture tells us that 'the earth is the Lord's, and all it holds' (Ps. 24:1). All of us, especially those closest to the land, are called to special reverence and respect for God's creation. Nurturing and tilling the soil, harnessing the power of water to grow food, and caring for animals are forms of this stewardship.[275]

273   Joseph Cardinal Ratzinger, God and the World: A Conversation with Peter Seewald, (San Francisco: Ignatius Press, 2002), 78-79.

274   United States Conference of Catholic Bishops, Committee on Domestic Policy, For I Was Hungry and You Gave Me Food: Catholic Reflections of Food, Farmers, and Farmworkers, (Washington, DC: United States Conference of Catholic Bishops, 2003), Pastoral Reflection – Part 5, Criteria for Agricultural Policy and Advocacy: Protecting God's Creation, accessed August 1, 2015. http://www.usccb.org/issues-and-action/human-life-and-dignity/agriculture-nutrition-rural-issues/for-i-was-hungry-pastoral-reflection-part-5.cfm

275   Ibid, Catholic Social Teaching & Agriculture, Section VI, Respect

U.S. Conference of Catholic Bishops: Factory farms should be regulated and monitored

According to the U.S. Conference of Catholic Bishops, Catholic teachings call into "question certain farming practices," including the factory farming of animals. These practices, say the bishops, should be regulated and monitored in order to ensure that animals are treated as God's creatures.

- Catholic teaching about stewardship of creation leads us to question certain farming practices, such as the operation of massive confined animal feeding operations. We believe that these operations should be carefully regulated and monitored so that environmental risks are minimized and animals are treated as creatures of God.[276]

U.S. Conference of Catholic Bishops: Let us pray that God will "make us all true friends of animals"

The U.S. Conference of Catholic Bishops has made available prayers and liturgies celebrating creation and emphasizing our responsibility to protect God's creatures. In "Other Prayers for Animals," the bishops remind us that God intends us to be friends to animals and to treat them with "a gentle heart of compassion."

---

for Creation. http://www.usccb.org/issues-and-action/human-life-and-dignity/agriculture-nutrition-rural-issues/for-i-was-hungry-cst-and-agriculture. cfm

276   Ibid, A Catholic Agenda for Action – Pursuing a More Just Agricultural System - Part 5, Stewardship of Creation (Washington, DC: United States Conference of Catholic Bishops, 2003). http://www.usccb.org/issues-and-action/human-life-and-dignity/agriculture-nutrition-rural-issues/for-i-was-hungry-catholic-agenda-for-action-part-5.cfm

- *Other Prayers for Animals*
  Hear our humble prayer, O God,
  for our friends the animals, your creatures.
  We pray especially for all that are suffering in any way:
  for the overworked and underfed,
  the hunted, lost, or hungry;
  for all in captivity or ill-treated,
  and for those that must be put to death.
  For those who deal with them,
  we ask a gentle heart of compassion,
  gentle hands, and kindly words.
  Make us all true friends to animals
  and worthy followers of our merciful Savior, Jesus Christ.
  R. Amen[277]

---

277   United States Conference of Catholic Bishops, "Other Prayers for Animals," Prayers to Care for Creation, accessed August 1, 2015. http://www.usccb.org/prayer-and-worship/prayers-and-devotions/prayers/prayers-to-care-for-creation.cfm

Seventh-day Adventist Church

General Information

The Seventh-day Adventist Church arose in the U.S. during a mid-19th century religious revival when expectations of the imminent return (advent) of Christ were high. Biblical passages led leaders to prophesize October 22, 1844 as the date of Christ's return, but when the date passed without incident, the day was reinterpreted as inaugurating "the last phase of [Christ's] atoning ministry in the heavenly sanctuary." The imminent advent of Christ remains a key tenet of the church, as do: the creation of the world in six days, with the seventh day (Saturday) set aside as the Sabbath; the Bible as inerrant and historically accurate and; the final destruction, rather than the eternal torment, of sinners.[278]

More information about the Seventh-day Adventist Church, including the church's beliefs, structure, and history, can be found by going to: http://www.adventist.org

Number of Members in the U.S.: 1.1 million[279]

Number of Members Worldwide: 18.5 million[280]

---

278   Seventh-day Adventist Church, "Information History," accessed August 1, 2015. http://www.adventist.org/en/information/history/

279   Seventh-day Adventist Church Office of Archives, "Statistics, and Research North American Division (1913-Present)," accessed August 1, 2015. http://www.adventiststatistics.org/view_Summary.asp?FieldID=D_NAD

280   Seventh-day Adventist Church, "Information Statistics: Seventh-day Adventist World Church Statistics 2014," accessed August 1, 2015. http://www.adventist.org/information/statistics/article/go/0/seventh-day-adventist-world-church-statistics-2014/

Official Statements on Animals

Human beings are "distinct...from all other creatures"
and "the crowning work of Creation"

In response to inquiries "from members, church pastors and the general public," the Seventh-day Adventist Church has developed a number of position papers on specific social, doctrinal, and theological issues. Within these official statements, the church affirms Genesis as a literal and accurate account of creation. In Genesis, says the church, we are told that creation took six days to complete, with the sixth day culminating in the creation of human beings. Humans, created in God's image and given dominion over the earth, "are distinct in kind and degree from all other earthly creatures" and are the "crowning work of Creation."

- God is Creator of all things, and has revealed in Scripture the authentic account of His creative activity. In six days the Lord made 'the heaven and the earth' and all living things upon the earth, and rested on the seventh day of that first week...The first man and woman were made in the image of God as the crowning work of Creation, given dominion over the world, and charged with responsibility to care for it.[281]

- Human beings, created in the image of God (Gen. 1:26, 27), are distinct in kind and degree from all other earthly creatures...[282]

---

281   Seventh-day Adventist Church, "Official Statements, Statements: An Affirmation of Creation" (2004), accessed August 1, 2015. http://www.adventist.org/information/official-statements/statements/article/go/o/affirmation-of-creation/6/

282   Seventh-day Adventist Church, "Official Statements, Documents: Human Gene Therapy" (2000), accessed August 1, 2015. http://www.adventist.org/information/official-statements/documents/article/go/o/human-gene-therapy/6/

***We are God's stewards on earth and are instructed to
safeguard and "esteem" his creatures***

According to the Seventh-day Adventist Church, "humankind was created in the image of God" and assigned the role
of "representing God as His stewards." Unfortunately, continues the church, "corruption and exploitation" have resulted in
"widespread suffering" rooted in "greed and refusal to practice
good and faithful stewardship within the divine boundaries of
creation." "Safeguarding God's creation," the church concludes,
requires "esteem for the…natural world with its countless species
of living creatures."

- Seventh-day Adventists believe that humankind was
  created in the image of God, thus representing God
  as His stewards, to rule the natural environment in a
  faithful and fruitful way.

  Unfortunately, corruption and exploitation have been
  brought into the management of the human domain
  of responsibility. Increasingly men and women have
  been involved in a megalomaniacal destruction of the
  earth's resources, resulting in widespread suffering,
  environmental disarray, and the threat of climate
  change…These problems are largely due to human
  selfishness and the egocentric pursuit of getting
  more and more…The ecological crisis is rooted in
  humankind's greed and refusal to practice good and
  faithful stewardship within the divine boundaries of
  creation.[283]

- The human decision to disobey God broke the
  original order of creation, resulting in a disharmony
  alien to His purposes. Thus our air and waters are
  polluted, forests and wildlife plundered, and natural
  resources exploited.[284]

---

283   *Seventh-day Adventist Church, "Official Statements, Statements:
Environment" (1995), accessed August 1, 2015. http://www.adventist.org/
information/official-statements/statements/article/go/0/environment/42/*
284   *Seventh-day Adventist Church, "Official Statements, Statements:*

- Safeguarding God's creation includes esteem for the diversity and ecological balance of the natural world with its countless species of living creatures (Gen. 1)... Exploitations and manipulations that would destroy natural balance or degrade God's created world should be prohibited.[285]

The Sabbath reminds us that all creatures are God's handiwork

God has set aside the seventh day of creation as a Sabbath, says the church, in order that we might have "a memorial and perpetual reminder of His creative act and establishment of the world" and as a way of underscoring "the importance of our integration with the total environment."

- God set aside the seventh-day Sabbath as a memorial and perpetual reminder of His creative act and establishment of the world. In resting on that day, Seventh-day Adventists reinforce the special sense of relationship with the Creator and His creation. Sabbath observance underscores the importance of our integration with the total environment.[286]

The "dignity of created life" calls for a wholesome lifestyle that promotes a vegetarian diet

Safeguarding God's creation requires us to live a wholesome lifestyle that reaffirms "the dignity of created life." In order to do this, says the church, we need to step off "the treadmill of unbridled consumerism," avoid "tobacco, alcohol and other drugs that harm the body," and "promote a simple vegetarian diet."

Caring for the Environment" (1992), accessed August 1, 2015. http://www.adventist.org/information/official-statements/statements/article/go/o/caring-for-the-environment/42/

285   Seventh-day Adventist Church, "Official Statements, Documents: Christian Principles for Genetic Interventions" (1995), accessed August 1, 2015. http://www.adventist.org/information/official-statements/documents/article/go/o/christian-principles-for-genetic-interventions/12/

286   Seventh-day Adventist, "Caring for the Environment."

- Seventh-day Adventists advocate a simple, wholesome lifestyle, where people do not step on the treadmill of unbridled consumerism, goods-getting, and production of waste. We call for respect of creation, restraint in the use of the world's resources, reevaluation of one's needs, and reaffirmation of the dignity of created life.[287]

- Because we recognize humans as part of God's creation, our concern for the environment extends to personal health and lifestyle. We advocate a wholesome manner of living and reject the use of substances such as tobacco, alcohol, and other drugs that harm the body and consume earth's resources; and we promote a simple vegetarian diet.[288]

Historical References on Animals

Ellen G. White: "Flesh food is not the right food for God's people"

Ellen G. White, one of the founders of the Seventh-day Adventist Church, was a prophet, visionary, and prolific writer whose works continue to be regarded by the church as an "authoritative source of truth which provide…comfort, guidance, instruction, and correction."[289] White's visions included warnings against the negative health effects of eating meat and predictions of a time when "it will not be safe to use anything that comes from the animal creation."

- Directions have been given to families that such articles as butter and the eating largely of flesh meats

287   *Seventh-day Adventist, "Environment."*

288   *Seventh-day Adventist, "Caring for the Environment."*

289   *Seventh-day Adventist Church, "Church Beliefs: The Gift of Prophecy," accessed July 31, 2015. http://www.adventist.org/en/beliefs/church/the-gift-of-prophecy/*

is not the best for physical and mental health. Fruits and grains and vegetables would, if cooked properly and eaten in moderate quantities, be proper articles of diet…I advise every Sabbath-keeping canvasser to avoid meat eating, not because it is regarded as sin to eat meat, but because it is not healthful. The animal creation is groaning.[290]

- The principles of healthful living mean a great deal to us individually and as a people. When the message of health reform first came to me, I was weak and feeble, subject to frequent fainting spells. I was pleading with God for help, and He opened before me the great subject of health reform. He instructed me that those who are keeping His commandments must be brought into sacred relation to Himself, and that by temperance in eating and drinking they must keep mind and body in the most favorable condition for service…

We do not mark out any precise line to be followed in diet; but we do say that in countries where there are fruits, grains, and nuts in abundance, flesh meat is not the right food for God's people…If meat eating was ever healthful, it is not safe now. Cancers, tumors, and pulmonary diseases are largely caused by meat eating.[291]

---

290   Ellen G. White, "MR No. 1209 - Counsels to Our Colporteurs Regarding Carefulness in Diet (Cir. 1889)," accessed August 1, 2015. All Ellen G. White quotations used by permission of the Ellen G. White Estate, Inc. http://egwtext.whiteestate.org/publication.php?pubtype=Book&bookCode=16MR&lang=en&collection=2&section=all&pagenumber=173
291   Ellen G. White, "Our Thinking is Affected by Our Eating, October 27" (1910), accessed August 1, 2015. http://egwtext.whiteestate.org/publication.php?pubtype=Book&bookCode=BLJ&lang=en&collection=2&section=all&pagenumber=316&QUERY=if+meat+eating+was+ever&resultId=1

- In many localities even fish is unwholesome, and ought not be used. This is especially so where fish come in contact with sewerage of large cities...[292]
- The Lord would bring his people into a position where they will not touch or taste the flesh of dead animals...There is no safety in the eating of the flesh of dead animals, and in a short time the milk of the cows will also be excluded from the diet of God's commandment-keeping people. In a short time it will not be safe to use anything that comes from the animal creation.[293]

Ellen G. White: Vegetarian diets improve body, mind, and soul

Although White focused primarily on the positive health effects of vegetarianism, she also taught that a vegetarian diet has positive effects on the mind and soul because mental, physical, and spiritual strength are interdependent.

- Since the mind and the soul find expression through the body, both mental and spiritual vigor are in great degree dependent upon physical strength and activity; whatever promotes physical health, promotes the development of a strong mind and a well-balanced character.[294]

292   Ellen G. White, "Healthful Living, Page 105," (1895), accessed August 1, 2015. http://egwtext.whiteestate.org/publication.php?pubtype=Book&bookCode=HL&lang=en&collection=2&section=all&pagenumber=105

293   Ellen G. White, "Testimony Studies on Diet and Foods, Page 71" (1926), accessed August 1, 2015. http://egwtext.whiteestate.org/publication.php?pubtype=Book&bookCode=TSDF&lang=en&collection=2&section=all&pagenumber=71&QUERY=In+a+short+time+it+will+not+be+safe&resultId=1

294   Ellen G. White, "Mind, Character, and Personality, Vol. 2, Page 406" (1905), accessed August 1, 2015. http://egwtext.whiteestate.org/publication.php?pubtype=Book&bookCode=2MCP&lang=en&collection=2&section=all&pagenumber=406&QUERY=since+the+mind+and+the+soul+find+expression&resultId=1

- I have been instructed that flesh food has a tendency to animalize the nature, to rob men and women of that love and sympathy which they should feel for everyone, and to give the lower passions control over the higher powers of the being.[295]

Ellen G. White: Meat eating is cruel to animals. A record of our cruelty "goes up to heaven"

White counseled Adventists to take the suffering of animals into consideration when making dietary choices. Although she never made vegetarianism a requirement of the faith, she did warn that: "A record goes up to heaven and a day is coming when judgment will be pronounced against those who abuse God's creatures."

- Think of the cruelty to animals that meat eating involves, and its effect on those who inflict and those who behold it. How it destroys the tenderness with which we should regard these creatures of God!

  The intelligence displayed by many dumb animals approaches so closely to human intelligence that it is a mystery. The animals see and hear and love and fear and suffer. They use their organs far more faithfully than many human beings use theirs. They manifest sympathy and tenderness toward their companions in suffering. Many animals show an affection for those who have charge of them, far superior to the affection shown by some of the human race. They form attachments for man which are not broken without great suffering to them.[296]

---

295   Ellen G. White, "Testimony Studies on Diet and Foods, Page 80" (1923), accessed August 1, 2015. http://egwtext.whiteestate.org/publication.php?pubtype=Book&bookCode=TSDF&lang=en&collection=2&section=all&pagenumber=80&QUERY=I+have+been+instructed+that+flesh-+food&resultId=1

296   Ellen G. White, "The Ministry of Healing, Page 315-316" (1905), accessed August 1, 2015. http://egwtext.whiteestate.org/publication.php?pubtype=Book&bookCode=MH&lang=en&collection=2&section=all&pa-

- He who will abuse animals because he has them in his power is both a coward and a tyrant. A disposition to cause pain, whether to our fellow men or to the brute creation, is satanic. Many do not realize that their cruelty will ever be known, because the poor dumb animals cannot reveal it. But could the eyes of these men be opened, as were those of Balaam, they would see an angel of God standing as a witness, to testify against them in the courts above. A record goes up to heaven, and a day is coming when judgment will be pronounced against those who abuse God's creatures.[297]

Contemporary Reflections on Animals

God cares about animals and has given humanity a "special obligation to be kind to creation"

Jo Ann Davidson, a professor of theology at the Seventh-day Adventist Theological Seminary, told readers of the weekly magazine *Adventist Review* that the Bible is filled with passages concerning God's care for animals and of humanity's "special obligation to be kind to creation."

- From the first chapter of Genesis to the end of the book of Revelation one finds an impressive doctrine of life.

  In the opening chapter of Genesis...both animals and human beings were created by God from the 'dust of the ground' and given the 'breath of life' (Gen. 2:7, 19) and identical blessings (Gen. 1:22, 28). This

genumber=315&QUERY=The+intelligence+displayed+by+many+dumb&resultId=1

297   *Ellen G. White, "Patriarchs and Prophets, Page 443" (1890), accessed August 1, 2015. http://egwtext.whiteestate.org/publication.php?pubtype=Book&bookCode=PP&lang=en&collection=2&section=all&pagenumber=443&QUERY=he+who+will+abuse+animals+because&resultId=1*

implies, at the very least, divine appreciation of them all. Humans and animals are given a vegetarian diet (Gen. 1:29, 30)...Later, Noah is told by God to take his family and animals into the ark 'to keep their kind alive on the face of all the earth' during a global catastrophe (Gen. 7:3)...After exiting the ark the animals are explicitly included in the divine covenant (Gen. 9:8-10; cf. Gen. 9:12, 15, 17)...

Later the children of Israel are led to the Promised Land and carefully instructed on creation care. They had an obligation to be kind to their animals...(Deut. 25:4)...Humans and animals along with the land are included in the stipulations for the weekly Sabbath and the sabbatical year (Ex. 23:10-12, cf. Ex. 20:8-11; Lev. 25:6, 7; Deut. 5:12-15)...God's providence for all life inspired many of the prayers and hymns in the Psalter, expressing how this reveals God's glory (see Ps. 148:7-13). The wisdom books invite appreciation for nonhuman life (Prov. 6:6)...

Jesus speaks of His affection for animals, stressing that even the lowliest of creatures is loved (Luke 12:6)...

In the final book of Scripture, the entire created world is dramatically encompassed with divine judgment (Rev. 7:1-3). After the seventh trumpet sounds in Revelation 11, the 24 elders cry out against those who have wreaked havoc on creation: 'You should reward Your servants the prophets and the saints...and should destroy those who destroy the earth' (Rev. 11:18).[298]

- Animals were to be treated humanely. For example, the Lord said that if you find a donkey that is staggering under a heavy load and has fallen, you must help it up—even if that donkey belongs to your enemy (Ex.

---

298   *Jo Ann Davidson, "Who Cares?: Environmental Ethics and the Christian," Adventist Review, Special Issue: Good Health—More than an Apple a Day, (2009), accessed August 1, 2015. http://archives.adventistreview.org/article/2681/archives/issue-2009-1518/who-cares*

23:5). Large work animals were not to be muzzled to prevent them from eating while assisting with the heavy work of agriculture (Deut. 25:4). They should be able to enjoy the fruits of the land that they are helping to reap. The Hebrew people had a distinctive obligation to be kind to creation.[299]

Factory farms damage the environment and treat animals with "violence and brutality"

In recent years, the *Adventist Review* has published several articles concerning meat eating and the industrialized farming of animals (also known as factory farming). According to these articles, the "meat industry" contributes to multiple environmental problems—including global warming, aquifer depletion, water pollution, and food shortages—and treats animals with dismaying "violence and brutality". "As children of our heavenly Father, who cares about even the sparrows," concludes one article, "it is our duty not to neglect [our stewardship] responsibilities and to speak for those, even of the animal kingdom, who are not able to speak for themselves."

- A plant-based diet is not only good for you but also an effective way to combat climate change, according to a new study by Loma Linda University Health.

  The research...found that a vegetarian diet results in nearly a third less greenhouse gas emissions than a diet with animal products...

  The takeaway message is that relatively small reductions in the consumption of animal products result in non-trivial environmental benefits...[300]

---

299   *Jo Ann Davidson, "And It Was Good: Stewardship of the Planet Isn't Just for Tree Huggers,"Adventist Review, August 21 (2008), accessed August 1, 2015. http://archives.adventistreview.org/issue.php?id=2030*
300   *Adventist Review Staff, "Vegetarian Diet Is Effective Tool against Climate Change, Study Finds,"Adventist Review, June 26 (2014), accessed August 1, 2015. http://www.adventistreview.org/church-news/vegetarian-diet-is-effective-tool-against-climate-change,-study-finds*

- [There are] critical ecological issues involved in eating flesh meat: the wasteful 'funnel effect' of many pounds of grain fed to a single steer, the same amount of grain feeding far more people; the huge amount of water used to grow fodder for feeding animals for slaughter. The same amount of water could serve a much larger community of people...[U]nderground water aquifers [are] being polluted by the seepage from immense amounts of...manure resulting from present methods of the animal 'industry'...

  These are but a few of the serious ecological issues related to the meat industry, let alone the frightful cruelty to animals involved, including the transport to slaughter and the horrifying slaughtering process itself. Common practices certainly do not model the biblical directive for a quick and painless slaughter out of respect for the animal. Very few have any conception of the violence and brutality that are inflicted on animals in order to gratify a carnivorous diet.[301]

- Millions of Americans recently watched news reports in dismay as video footage of grossly inhumane treatment of 'downer' cows at southern California's Westland/Hallmark Meat Company flashed across their television screens. Cows too sick or injured to stand were being shoved by forklifts or dragged with chains to the slaughterhouse chutes, where they were to be killed, then processed and sold for food. Other footage of the undercover video taken by the U.S. Humane Society included factory workers using electric prods and high-powered water hoses to force cows to stand, as well as kicking and heaving them to their feet. ...Tragically, this incident in inhumane treatment and total disregard for health standards is not an isolated one.

301   *Davidson, "Who Cares?"*

Having compassion for animals...as well as being good stewards of the environment in which we live...should not fall below our radar screens. As children of our heavenly Father, who cares about even the sparrows, it is our duty not to neglect these responsibilities and to speak for those, even of the animal kingdom, who are not able to speak for themselves.[302]

Research protocols should seek to "prevent or minimize pain and suffering to animals"

Facilities that perform experiments on animals should strive to obey God's biblical directive to "respect and care for animals," says an article in the Adventist *Dialogue* magazine. Although the article does not advocate the complete elimination of animal experiments, it does assert that animals should be used in experiments only when no other viable alternative is available, when protocols for minimizing animal suffering are strictly observed, and when research personnel are "trained with regard to principles of research ethics and animal welfare."

- While the Bible does not refer specifically to 'animal experimentation' as a permissible (or impermissible) activity, in the experimentation setting, the biblical imperative of respect and care for animals should translate into research protocol measures that would prevent or minimize pain and suffering to animals. Such measures could include analgesia, environmental temperature control, secure shelter, nutrition, hydration, and veterinary care. Physical handling of animals should be done in a manner that minimizes unnecessary stress. The number of animals used should be no more than needed to provide statistically defensible data. Animals should only be used in experiments that require them. Alternate models such as tissue culture or computer

302   Sandra Blackmer, "A Wake-up Call," Adventist Review, accessed July 31, 2015. http://archives.adventistreview.org/issue.php?id=1771&action=print

simulations should be used in place of animals as scientifically appropriate. Research protocols should be analyzed by an institutional review committee to ensure that the methodology is scientifically sound, and that measures are included that ensure animal welfare. Lastly, all research personnel should be trained with regard to principles of research ethics and animal welfare.[303]

"How we treat animals reveals our true natures." A Christ-like nature "protects the helpless"

We should care for all God's creatures, say recent Adventist magazine articles, because "how we treat animals reveals our true nature," because we align ourselves with Christ whenever we work to end "suffering and protect the helpless," because our "attitudes toward creation now will color attitudes we take toward the new creation," and because "those who destroy the earth will themselves be destroyed."

- How we treat animals reveals our true nature. When we have power over others, we display who has power over us. Satan's nature destroys, but Christ's nature ends suffering and protects the helpless...Whether our faith is theory or a living connection with Him will be felt by the people—*and the animals*—around us. It is our duty and joy to deny support to practices that harm others. Only then will we fully reflect Christ's love and peace.[304]

- Attitudes toward creation now will color attitudes we take toward the new creation. If we treat creation recklessly now, could we be expected to treat the renewed Earth differently? No wonder, Revelation

303   Katrina A. Branstedt, "Using Animals in Medical Research," College and University Dialogue: An International Journal of Faith, Thought, and Action, accessed July 31, 2015. http://dialogue.adventist.org/articles/15_2_bramstedt_e.htm

304   Matthew Priebe, "How We Treat Animals—Does God Care? Should We?" Adventist Review (2005), accessed August 1, 2015. http://archives.adventistreview.org/2005-1538/story3.html

11:18 says those who destroy Earth will themselves be destroyed.[305]

---

305   Henry Zuill, "The Environment: Should Christians Care? College and University Dialogue: An International Journal of Faith, Thought, and Action, accessed 7/31/15. http://dialogue.adventist.org/articles/19_1_zuill_e.htm

Southern Baptist Convention

General Information

The Southern Baptist Convention (SBC) is an alliance of autonomous Southern Baptist churches that "share a common bond of basic Biblical beliefs and a commitment to proclaim the Gospel of Jesus Christ to the entire world." Since its organization in 1845, the SBC has grown to be the largest Protestant denomination in the United States.[306]

More information about the Southern Baptist Convention, including the denomination's beliefs, structure, and history, can be found by going to: http://www.sbc.net

Number of Members in the U.S.: 15.7 million[307]

---

306   *Mission Education Team of the North American Mission Board, SBC, "Cooperative Missions: State and National Conventions" (Alpharetta: North American Mission Board, SBC, 2010), accessed August 1, 2015. https://www.google.com/url?q=http://www.namb.net/WorkArea/DownloadAsset.aspx%3Fid%3D8590000009&sa=U&ved=0CAQQFjAAahUKEwiH34ny6-nGAhWCbD4KHf8gAUc&client=internal-uds-cse&usg=AFQjCNFvsF3HSdBEVJAeISaaD9Gz3ifqAA*

307   *Timothy George, "Troubled Waters," First Things, June 2 (2014), accessed August 1, 2015. http://www.firstthings.com/web-exclusives/2014/06/troubled-waters*

Official Statements on Animals

Humanity is the crowning work of God's creation

The Southern Baptist Convention holds firmly to the principle that individual churches are independent and self-ruling. The SBC, therefore, does not issue "official statements" that are binding on member churches. The SBC, however, does post confessions of its faith, and it issues annual resolutions that have been voted on by member churches. While these confessions and resolutions are not binding, they are indicative of members' shared beliefs, opinions, and concerns. Among the SBC's confessions of faith is the assertion that humanity is "the special creation of God" and "the crowning work of His creation."

- Man is the special creation of God, in His own image. He created them male and female as the crowning work of His creation...The sacredness of human personality is evident in that God created man in His own image, and in that Christ died for man; therefore, every person of every race possesses dignity and is worthy of respect and Christian love.[308]

Animals may be used to serve human needs

Animals may be used to serve human needs as long as such uses do not violate the sanctity of human life, say various SBC resolutions. The SBC resolution on cloning, for example, permits the cloning of animals but not the cloning of human beings, while the SBC resolution on species-altering technologies permits the simple transfer of human cells into animals as long as the transfer does not result "in blurring the human-animal species barrier."

- *Resolved*, That, with the exception of cloning humans and human embryos, we do not oppose the use of nuclear transfer or other cloning techniques to

---

308   *Southern Baptist Convention, "Basic Beliefs: Man," accessed August 1, 2015. http://www.sbc.net/aboutus/basicbeliefs.asp*

produce molecules, DNA, cells, tissues, organs, plants, or animals...[309]

- *Resolved,* That while we support attempts at human somatic cell gene therapy for serious genetic illnesses if proper regard is given to informed consent, safety, efficacy, and the just allocation of available resources, we oppose any biotechnology that results in blurring the human-animal species barrier, such as the implantation of human brain cells into mice; and be it further

Resolved, That while we support the use of simple gene transfer from humans to animals for drug production (e.g., human insulin, human growth hormone, clotting factor VIII) and therapeutic human-animal technologies such as the use of pig heart valves in humans, we oppose any human germline genetic modification that results in the destruction of human embryos or their equivalent (e.g., totipotential cells).[310]

Although we may use animals and other "natural resources," human dominion has limitations

Human dominion over creation is intended for the benefit of present and future generations, says the SBC. Dominion, therefore, has limitations and must be subject "to higher standards than to profit alone."

- God has designed us with a dependence on the natural resources around us and has assigned us a dominion of stewardship and protection of those resources for future generations (Gen. 2:7-15)...Our God-given dominion over the creation is not unlimited, as though we were gods and not creatures, so therefore,

---

309   *Southern Baptist Convention, "Resolution: On Human Cloning"* (2001), *accessed August 1, 2015. http://www.sbc.net/resolutions/572/ on-human-cloning*

310   *Southern Baptist Convention, "Resolution: On Human Species-Altering Technology"* (2006), *accessed August 1, 2015. http://www.sbc.net/ resolutions/1158*

all persons and all industries are then accountable to higher standards than to profit alone.[311]

God has declared creation "good" and commanded humanity to "exercise caring stewardship" over it

In the beginning, God declared creation good and commanded humans to "exercise caring stewardship and dominion over the earth and environment," points out the SBC. Since the fall into sin, continues the church, humans "have often ignored the Creator...and...defiled the good creation." Christians, urges the church, should now "renew our commitment to God's command to exercise caring stewardship and wise dominion over the creation."

- *Whereas,* In the beginning God created the heavens and the earth (Genesis 1:1), declared it good (Genesis 1:4, 10, 12, 18, 21, 32), and it reveals His glory (Psalm 19:1-6); and *Whereas,* God created men and women in His image and likeness (Genesis 1:26-27), placing them in value above the rest of creation and commanding them to exercise caring stewardship and dominion over the earth and environment (Genesis 1:28; cf. Psalm 8); and...

  Whereas, Since the fall into sin, humans have often ignored the Creator, shirked their stewardship of the environment, and further defiled the good creation;... now, therefore, be it

  Resolved, That the messengers to the Southern Baptist Convention meeting in Greensboro, North Carolina, June 13-14, 2006, renew our commitment to God's command to exercise caring stewardship and wise dominion over the creation (Genesis 1:28); and be it further

  Resolved, That we urge all Southern Baptists toward the conservation and preservation of our natural

---

311   *Southern Baptist Convention, "Resolution: On the Gulf of Mexico Catastrophe (2010), accessed August 1, 2015. http://www.sbc.net/resolutions/1207*

resources for future generations while respecting ownership and property rights...[312]

Caring stewardship requires us to take into consideration vulnerable species and their habitats

In 2010, the explosion of the Deepwater Horizon oil rig in the Gulf of Mexico caused the largest marine oil spill in history. Lives and livelihoods were lost and the damage to fragile marine animals and eco-systems was extensive. The tragedy inspired the SBC to pass a resolution reminding members that God loves creation and wants us to "protect what God loves," including "the teeming life of the seas" and "the eco-systems of birds, shrimp, oysters, fish, and other life-forms... "

- *Whereas,* On April 20, 2010, the deadly explosion of the Deepwater Horizon oil rig in the Gulf of Mexico resulted in the deaths of eleven workers and touched off an underwater gusher of oil that has spewed millions of gallons of crude petroleum into the waters of the Gulf; and

  Whereas, This crisis is described already as the largest environmental calamity in American history; and

  Whereas, The oil spilling from the ocean's floor now poses a dire and immediate threat to the coastlands and inland estuaries, marshes, and waterways of the Gulf Coast of Louisiana, Mississippi, Alabama, and Florida, and to the eco-systems of birds, shrimp, oysters, fish, and other life-forms; and...

  Whereas, Holy Scripture tells us 'the earth is the Lord's and the fullness thereof' (Psalm 24:1, KJV),[313] and that God's wisdom and glory is seen in the teeming of life in the seas (Psalm 104:25); and

---

312   *Southern Baptist Convention, "On Environmentalism and Evangelicals" (2006), accessed August 1, 2015. http://www.sbc.net/resolutions/1159*

313   *Bible citations for all SBC statements come from the King James Version.*

Whereas, God has designed us with a dependence on the natural resources around us and has assigned us a dominion of stewardship and protection of those resources for future generations (Genesis 2:7-15);... now, therefore, be it...

Resolved, That we call on the governing authorities to act "determinatively and with undeterred resolve to end this crisis; to fortify our coastal defenses; to ensure full corporate accountability for damages, clean-up, and restoration; to ensure that government and private industry are not again caught without planning for such possibilities; and to promote future energy policies based on prudence, conservation, accountability, and safety; and be it further

Resolved, That we encourage persons, communities, industries, and governments to work together to find ways to lessen the potentiality of such tragic accidents and of such devastating pollution in order that we may protect what God loves and safeguard the lives, livelihoods, health, and well-being of our neighbors and of future generations; and be it further...

Resolved, That we acknowledge that this tragedy should remind us to testify to the love of God in His creation and to the hope, through the blood of Christ, of a fully restored creation in which the reign of God is seen 'on earth as it is in heaven' (Matthew 6:10).[314]

Contemporary Reflections on Animals

Billy Graham: God is interested in animal care

Billy Graham's radio, television, and newspaper ministries have made him one of the SBC's best-known members and,

---

314   SBC, *"On the Gulf of Mexico Catastrophe."*

according to a 1999 Gallup poll,[315] one of the most admired people of the 20th century. In 2010, Graham received a letter from a mother who worried that her daughter's desire to devote her life to animal care was not something God is "really interested in." Graham responded that the daughter "is doing a good thing in God's eyes" because God "is concerned with the way we treat animals."

- Yes, let me assure you that God is concerned about our care of every part of His creation—including the animals. After all, He made them, and ultimately they belong to Him. The Bible says, 'For every animal of the forest is mine, and the cattle on a thousand hills' (Psalm 50:10). And what your daughter is doing is a good thing in God's eyes, for He is concerned about the way we treat animals (especially those that depend on us). The Bible says, 'A righteous man cares for the needs of his animal' (Proverbs 12:10). On the day God made the animals, the Bible tells us that He pronounced it good (see Genesis 1:25).

  Should we ignore or treat cruelly something that God calls good? Of course not.

  Someone who is thoughtless or cruel to animals is also likely to be thoughtless or cruel to other people—who are made in God's image. Encourage your daughter to seek God's will for her life—and if she is convinced God is leading her in this way, be grateful for it and encourage her. On the other hand, caution her against loving animals more than she loves people (which can be easy to do—because people can be difficult to love!) Most of all, encourage your daughter to make Christ the center and foundation of her life, and to

---

315   Gallop/CNN/USA Today, "Greatest of the Century (and the Millennium): Gallop/CNN/USA Today Poll Dec. 20-21" (1999), accessed August 1, 2015. http://www.pollingreport.com/20th.htm

do everything for His glory—even if this doesn't turn
out to be her lifelong career.[316]

Billy Graham: When we treat animals with contempt, we treat God with contempt

Billy Graham received a letter asking if the Bible says anything about how humans should treat animals. Graham responded that "the Bible commands us to take care of animals. …In fact," said Graham, "the Bible says we must never treat any part of God's creation with contempt. When we do, we are indirectly treating our Creator with contempt."

- Yes, God made everything that lives on the earth—including animals. In the beginning, the Bible says, "God said, 'Let the land produce living creatures according to their kinds: livestock, creatures that move along the ground, and wild animals...'And it was so" (Genesis. 1:24).

  And yes, the Bible commands us to take care of the animals under our care. One of the signs of a righteous man, the Bible says, is that he takes care of his animals (see Proverbs 12:10). Even the animal of an enemy was to be treated kindly: 'If you come across your enemy's ox or donkey wandering off, be sure to take it back to him' (Exodus 23:4). One reason God commanded His people to rest one day out of seven was so their animals would be refreshed (see Exodus 23:12).

  In fact, the Bible says we must never treat any part of God's creation with contempt. When we do, we are indirectly treating our Creator with contempt. Instead, God calls us to be stewards or trustees of His creation, and the Bible reminds us that we are responsible to Him for the way we treat it. We've often forgotten this—but it's still true, and when we

---

316   Billy Graham, "Does God Care about Animals," *Answers by Billy Graham, May 13* (2010), accessed August 1, 2015. *http://billygraham.org/answer/does-god-care-about-animals/*

ignore it we not only hurt God's creation but we also hurt ourselves.

Most of all, however, God calls us to put Him first in our lives. He loves us, and our greatest calling is to respond to His love by opening our hearts and lives to His son, Jesus Christ.[317]

Millard J. Erickson: All creatures are part of God's plan

Millard J. Erickson is an ordained Baptist minister, professor of theology, and author of the acclaimed *Christian Theology*—a text that has been widely taught at Southern Baptist seminaries. According to Erickson, all creatures "have integrity as part of God's plan" so "we must not despise any part of God's creation." Humanity, says Erickson, has a special function within God's plan "to care for the rest of God's world."

- Everything that is has value. We must not regard something as illusory or insignificant simply because it is not divine. Everything that is, while it is not God, has been made by him. He made it because he was pleased to do so, and it was good in his sight. It was a wise plan that brought into being just what there is within the creation. Each part has its place, which is just what God intended for it to have. God loves all of his creation, not just certain parts of it. Thus we should also have concern for all of it, to preserve and guard and develop what God has made. We are part of the creation, but only a part. While God intended man to use the creation for his own needs, man is also to have dominion over it, to govern it for its good. We therefore have a large stake in the ecological concern. In fact, Christians should be at the very forefront of the concern for the preservation and welfare of the

317   Billy Graham, "Does the Bible Say Anything about How We Should Treat Animals?" Answers by Billy Graham, August 16 (2010), accessed August 1, 2015. http://billygraham.org/answer/does-the-bible-say-anything-about-how-we-should-treat-animals-god-made-them-also-didnt-he/

creation, for it is not merely something that is there; it is what God has made. Everything within creation has its function; that of man is to care for the rest of God's world. We must not despise any part of God's creation. As different as some creatures may be from us, they have integrity as part of Gods' plan.[318]

SBC Ethics and Religious Liberty Commission: Legislation should increase penalties for animal fighting

In March 2015, Russell D. Moore, president of the Southern Baptist Ethics and Religious Liberty Commission, wrote to the Tennessee legislature on behalf of the entire commission. Moore expressed "strong support" for a bill being considered by the legislature that would impose harsher penalties for animal fighting.

- On behalf of the Ethics and Religious Liberty Commission (ERLC) of the Southern Baptist convention, I am writing to express our strong support for HB 0962, a bill that will increase the deterrents for animal fighting. We respectfully request that HB 0962 be assigned to the Criminal Justice Committee.

  …With each passing year that the increased penalties fail to pass, we witness the incestuous relationship between animal fighting, gambling, and organized crime continues to grow. This is detrimental to many of our communities and the families that call them home. Unfortunately, Tennessee plays host to these conferences of nefarious activities because the punishment for dogfighting and cockfighting is a slap on the wrist in comparison to the payouts.

  …We are pleased to support this legislation and look forward to working with you to advance our mutual goals…[319]

---

318   Millard J. Erickson, Christian Theology (Grand Rapids: Baker Book House, 1990), 385.

319   Russell D. Moore, "Letter to Tennessee House Speaker Beth Harwell on Deterrents for Animal Fighting," March 2 (2015), accessed August 1, 2015. http://erlc.com/article/letter-to-tennessee-house-speaker-beth-har-

Barrett Duke: "Animals are not only worthy of our respect. They deserve it."

Dr. Barrett Duke, the SBC's Vice President for Public Policy and Research and Director of its Research Institute, published a recent article in which he enumerated biblical passages concerning animals. Duke concluded that these passages show that the Bible has long known what science is only now discovering: that animals are "much more complex than they at first appear to be...[and] are not only worthy of our respect. They deserve it."

- The Bible teaches us that God created animals. They aren't the product of happenstance or fortuitous natural processes any more than humans are...[W]e must abandon unbiblical notions about animals and embrace a more biblical view of our animal co-inhabitants. The Bible compels us to develop a better appreciation and respect for them. I'm glad science is revealing many enlightening truths about the animal world. But it is clear that Scripture has already revealed much of what science is discovering. Animals are much more complex than they at first appear to be. We should do all we can to better understand them and their place in God's creation. It will not only be good for them, but for us as well.

  God put animals on the planet and gave them a mandate as well. Part of the human calling is to help them fulfill this mandate in a way that enables them to reach their full potential in creation. They not only enrich our lives. They point to the creator of all things. Animals are not only worthy of our respect. They deserve it.[320]

---

well-on-deterrents-for-animal-fig

320   Barrett Duke, "10 Biblical Truths about Animals," The Ethics and Religious Liberty Commission of the Southern Baptist Convention, January 2 (2015), accessed August 1, 2015. http://erlc.com/article/10-biblical-truths-about-animals

United Church of Christ

General Information

The United Church of Christ (UCC) formed in 1957 when the Evangelical and Reformed Church and the Congregational Christian Churches merged into a single denomination. Through these formative branches, the UCC traces its history back to the Protestant Reformation and lays claim to a wide range of progressive firsts, including the first mainline Protestant denomination to: ordain an African-American (1785), ordain a woman (1853), ordain an openly gay person (1972), study the link between racial inequality and the placement of hazardous waste sites (1987), and affirm same-gender marriage equality (2005).[321]

More information about the United Church of Christ, including the church's beliefs, structure, and history, can be found by going to: http://www.ucc.org/

Number of Members in the U.S.: 1.1 million[322]

321   United Church of Christ, "Short Course in the History of the United Church of Christ," accessed July 31, 2015. http://d3n8a8pro7vhmx. cloudfront.net/unitedchurchofchrist/legacy_url/1175/shortcourse. pdf?1418424619

322   United Church of Christ, "About Us," accessed August 1, 2015. http://www.ucc.org/about-us/

Official Statements on Animals

Human beings have "a deep moral obligation to be good stewards" so that all creatures may thrive

The UCC holds a national convention every two years, known as the General Synod, where delegates consider and vote on official church resolutions. Over the years, these synods have repeatedly affirmed that human beings have a responsibility "to tend the earth" as "good stewards of God" in order that all God's creatures, both human and nonhuman, may thrive.

- [T]he biblical faith sees human beings as creatures of God, tenants in God's earth (Leviticus 25:23) and stewards of creation...[T]he biblical charge to 'have dominion over every living thing' (Genesis 1:28) has often been understood as placing human beings above creation instead of part of it, while the scriptures teach that we are creatures and that we are to tend the earth for its creatures (Genesis 2:15).[323]

- [A]s people of faith we answer a higher call, which is to have a deep moral obligation to be good stewards of God's creation so that all humans, other creatures and future generations may thrive...[324]

All "creatures deserve humane and respectful treatment because...it is their right in the eyes of God"

Scripture instructs us to treat all God's creatures with "wonder, reverence, love, and respect," says the UCC's General

---

323   *United Church of Christ, "Resolution: Respect for Animals," Minutes, Nineteenth General Synod, (1993), 54, accessed August 1, 2015. http://rescarta.ucc.org/jsp/RcWebImageViewer.jsp?doc_id=General%20Synod%20Minutes/ucoc0000/UD000001/00000020&page_name=00560054&view_width=10&rotation=0&view_session=28932&query1=&collection_filter=&search_doc=*

324   *United Church of Christ, "Resolution: Transition from Fossil Fuels to Renewable Energy," Thirtieth General Synod (2015), 1, accessed August 1, 2015.http://uccfiles.com/pdf/GS30-TRANSITION-FROM-FOSSIL-FUELS-TO-RENEWABLE-ENERGY.pdf*

Synod. "Compassion and decency," therefore, are to be extended not only to our fellow human beings but also to animals. "All living creatures," summarizes the synod, "deserve humane and respectful treatment because, as living creatures, it is their right in the eyes of God."

- [W]e understand scriptures compel us to act on our faith grounded in wonder, reverence, love, and respect for all God's creation...[W]e are called to spiritual and lifestyle transformation based on justice and reverence for all of God's creatures and creation.[325]
- [A]ll living creatures deserve humane and respectful treatment because, as living creatures, it is their right in the eyes of God...[H]uman compassion and decency require not only that we care for our fellow human beings, but that we treat no creature with cruelty or carelessness.[326]

"Our lives are to be filled with compassion, not cruelty, toward animals...wild and tame"

At the UCC's Nineteenth General Synod in 1993, delegates passed a resolution entitled Respect for Animals. In this resolution, the church affirmed that "our lives are to be filled with compassion, not cruelty, toward animals," regardless of whether the animal is wild or tame or used "in the laboratory and commercially." Although the resolution stopped short of recommending specific actions to be taken by individuals or congregations, it did recommend that members evaluate for themselves the morality of various human uses of animals and that the church gather and disseminate "educational and theological material on the place of animals" to help members answer difficult questions concerning "our place among all living creatures as God's creatures."

---

325 *United Church of Christ, "Resolution: Mountain Removal Coal Mining in Appalachia," Minutes, Twenty-ninth General Synod (2013), 70, accessed August 1, 2015. http://www.uccfiles.com/pdf/gs29minutes.pdf*
326 *UCC, "Resolution: Respect for Animals."*

- *Whereas,* the scriptures teach that our lives are to be filled with compassion, not cruelty, toward animals (Proverbs 12:10)...and

Whereas, a growing awareness of our environmental responsibility has led to a concern for the preservation and protection of animals, both in their wild and tame states, and the use of animals in the laboratory and commercially;

Therefore, Be It Resolved that the Nineteenth General Synod of the United Church of Christ commends to its members and congregations the consideration of our place among all living creatures as God's creatures, and invites them to evaluate human use of animals and resulting effects on the animals with questions such as these:

1. Are these animals treated justly, mercifully and with compassion and care?
2. Do these animals suffer unnecessary pain either in life or in death?
3. As a result of modern technology and advances, is there another, more humane way to supply our needs?
4. Does the benefit gained from the use of these animals outweigh the cost to them?
5. How does our current treatment of animals affect our spiritual development and welfare?
6. How does treatment of animals affect the diverse richness of God's creation?

Be it further resolved that the Nineteenth General Synod invites the Conferences, Associations, and congregations of the United Church of Christ to gather educational and theological material on the place of animals and to share this information among these entities with the assistance of the Office for

Church in Society so that our Church may study the relationships.[327]

Concentrated Animal Feeding Operations (CAFOs) "do not show respect for animals"

At the UCC's Twenty-eighth General Synod in 2011, the church again took up the issue of animals, this time with a specific focus on industrialized animal agriculture, also known as factory farms or CAFOs (Concentrated Animal Feeding Operations). The synod noted that CAFOs not only negatively impact animal welfare but also damage the environment, are associated with high rates of worker injury and mistreatment, and are linked to a variety of human health problems. For these and other reasons, the synod recommended that the UCC "develop curricula for all ages that compassionately and respectfully explore…our food choices."

- *Whereas*, our dietary choices reflect many…social, environmental, and economic justice issues, and

  Whereas, modern intensive farming is a leading cause of land, water, and energy consumption; worldwide animal agriculture contributes more to global warming (18% of greenhouse gases) than all forms of transportation combined (14 percent)…; and long-distance transport of food further increases the impact of our diets on the environment; and

  Whereas, the high injury rates and mistreatment of slaughterhouse workers has been well-documented… and

  Whereas, the intensive crowding and unhealthy living conditions that typify concentrated animal feeding operations (CAFOs) do not show respect for animals, and

  Whereas, animal and human welfare issues are intricately linked in numerous other ways, such as 1) pollution problems caused by CAFOs…; 2) bacterial resistance to antibiotics caused by the routine feeding

---

327   *Ibid.*

of antibiotics to animals; 3) 'Mad Cow Disease,' bird flu, and other human health risks associated with intensive animal agricultural practices; 4) a wide range of medical disorders linked to the typical American diet, including heart disease, obesity, diabetes, arthritis, and certain cancers...; and 5) the negative impact of CAFOs on small family farms and thus on rural life, culture, and community, and

Whereas, people have different nutritional needs, financial situations, and degrees of access to food, such that a mindful and faithful diet for one person at one location might be very different from a mindful and faithful diet for another person at another location...

Therefore Be It Resolved that the Twenty-eighth General Synod encourages Conferences, Associations, congregations and individuals to explore ways in which our food choices can be mindful and faithful, so that, to the best of our abilities, what we eat reflects our values and beliefs; and

Be It Further Resolved that the UCC Covenanted Ministries identify and/or develop curricula for all ages that compassionately and respectfully explore the ways in which our diets impact our ecological 'footprint' on the earth, human and animal welfare concerns, healthy nourishment for our bodies, and the needs and concerns of workers. These curricula would further explore ways that our food choices affect food security and the equitable availability of food for all God's children.[328]

---

328   *United Church of Christ, "Resolution: Mindful and Faithful Eating," Twenty-eighth General Synod(2011), 47-48, accessed August 1, 2015. http://uccfiles.com/pdf/gs28minutes.pdf*

Historical References on Animals

The United Church of Christ was formed too recently to have references on animals that can be considered "historical." The church, however, was formed through the merger of older denominations that trace their history through several well-known Protestant reformers, including John Calvin and Martin Luther. Statements by Calvin concerning animals can be found in the Presbyterian Church (U.S.A.) entry, above, while statements by Luther can be found in both the Evangelical Lutheran Church in American and The Lutheran Church–Missouri Synod entries, above.[329]

Contemporary Reflections on Animals

"Dominion does not mean domination. [It] means responsibility and gratitude for the gift of life itself."

We exist in a "profound kinship" with all creatures, says a statement by the UCC's Environmental Ministries, and "every living thing [is] part of the total gift" of God's universe. Humanity has been granted dominion over this gift, says the UCC, but we have made the mistake of equating dominion with domination. Instead, we must see that "dominion means responsibility and gratitude for the gift of life itself."

- Humanity is asked to answer a call of stewardship understood as care for and solidarity with God's good creation. The distinction between human and other created things begins to soften, inviting a profound kinship, all participating in a creation community.[330]

329   More information about the history of the UCC can be found in "Short Course in the History of the United Church of Christ."

330   United Church of Christ Environmental Ministries, "Why Should People of Faith Care about the Environment?," accessed July 31, 2015.

- Our Biblical heritage tells us that God created the entire universe and gifted humankind with the responsibility to maintain and honor the gift. If we see creation as a gift and not an entitlement—or an object to be dominated and controlled—then we practice respect and love for both the Giver and the gift. Dominion does not mean domination. Dominion means responsibility and gratitude for the gift of life itself. In this way, we see every creature and every living thing as a part of the total gift and necessary to sustain life for the next generations to come.

People of faith are called to be humble stewards of the natural systems of which they are a part. As the dominant specie[s] that has the opportunity for both harm to creation and care of creation, humans are challenged to examine their place in a holistic view of creation and ask themselves if they are humbly respectful or arrogantly harmful to God's creation. Every generation and every person has the ethical responsibility to determine their own and their community's own response to God's gift of creation and to see if their daily practices hurt or enhance what God has given to all.[331]

Each creature "mutually co-exist(s)," "expresses the divine image," and has a "sacred" inherent worth

In a pastoral letter on faith and the environment, the UCC affirmed that each and every creature co-exists "in an ever evolving symphony of praise to their Creator." All creatures, whether human or nonhuman, express "the divine image," says the letter, and each creature "embodies an inherent worth that is indeed sacred and good..."

---

http://www.ucc.org/environmental-ministries

331   *United Church of Christ Environmental Ministries, "Biodiversity," accessed August 1, 2015). http://www.ucc.org/environmental-ministries_ biodiversity*

- Light and darkness, water and land, sea creatures, earth creatures, birds, plants, herbs, fruit trees, the sky with its stars, moon, and sun! All mutually co-exist in an ever evolving symphony of praise to their Creator. Indeed, the creating, redeeming, and sustaining presence of our God weaves the fabric of creation. Together we sing a hymn of holy love for the beauty of the earth as it evolves and we with it, in relationship with one who has called us to love the world...

Each species and habitat, each culture and region, each place and people in the world expresses the divine image. Each embodies an inherent worth that is indeed sacred and good, worthy not only of care, but also of celebration and appreciation in the living of our days.[332]

CAFOs perpetuate the twin evils of ecological and racial injustice

In 1987, the UCC released a landmark study entitled *Toxic Wastes and Race* that revealed a chronic and systematic connection between racial injustice and environmental degradation. In 2007, the church released a follow-up study that concluded little had changed in the 20 years since the first study had been released. Both studies found that "environmental racism" reaches across a wide spectrum of government agencies and private industries, including industries that directly impact animals. CAFOs were identified as particularly "egregious perpetrators of environmental racism," with "corporate hog farms" singled out for special condemnation. CAFOs, said the study, routinely locate themselves "in or near communities of color" and produce "tremendous amounts of animal wastes" which pollute ground water and sicken both wildlife and human communities.

332   *United Church of Christ Collegium of Officers with the Environmental and Energy Task Force, And Indeed It Is Very Good. A Pastoral Letter on Faith and Environment: Living in Community with God's Creation* (Cleveland: United Church of Christ, 2008). *http://d3n8a8pro7vhmx. cloudfront.net/unitedchurchofchrist/legacy_url/264/pastoral_letter-on- faith-and-the-environment.pdf?1418423623*

- Many...corporate [animal] farms are located in or near communities of color. Corporate hog farms are some of the most egregious perpetrators of environmental racism. These hog farms create tremendous amounts of animal wastes. Factory-farm operations throughout North America have millions of gallons of liquefied animal feces stored in open lagoons that emit more than 400 different volatile, dangerous compounds into the atmosphere. These 'sewerless cities' generate so much surplus manure that it cannot be stored or disposed of safely. Some large hog farms produce volumes of untreated hog manure equivalent to the human waste of a city of 360,000 people. One hog farming operation in North Carolina carelessly allowed tons of untreated wastes to leach into groundwater sources. During a severe storm, the wastes ran off into rivers and killed wildlife and contaminated drinking water sources. The community affected was predominantly African American.[333]

God speaks through every living creature. We need to listen to "God's voice...in the world around us"

The UCC's commitment to creation-care and animal-protection is reflected in its liturgical materials. Prayers developed by the UCC's Justice and Witness Ministries remind members that God speaks through all creatures and entreats us to listen "to God's voice...speaking...when every living creature on earth breathes."

- Perhaps our doubting of God's presence in creation is what hinders our 'ecological outreach.' If we stopped to realize that God's presence is in every blade of grass, every cloud, then maybe we would do

333   United Church of Christ Justice and Witness Ministries, Toxic Wastes and Race at Twenty 1987-2007: A Report Prepared for the United Church of Christ Justice & Witness Ministries (Cleveland: United Church of Christ, 2007), 118. http://www.ucc.org/environmental-ministries_toxic-waste-20

better at cherishing the gift we have been given. On Integrity of Creation Sunday and on Earth Day, the United Church of Christ expresses its commitment to ecological justice and the earth as teacher. In this simple prayer, we contemplate a classic Easter Bible story in a new way—listening to God's voice of peace in the world around us.

One: God speaks through rocks and trees and water,

People: And the words 'peace be with you' are heard.

One: God speaks through budding flowers and twinkling stars,

People: And surely 'peace be with you' is heard.

One: God speaks, and is still speaking, when every living creature on earth breathes:

People: 'Peace be with you. Peace be with you.' (pause)

One: But some do not hear the words.

People: Some do not hear God speaking through the land or the sea or the air.

One: They doubt.

People: God speaks, but they do not hear.[334]

We must repent and reform our past "wanton and reckless" treatment of animals and the earth

In a prayer developed by the UCC's Environmental Justice Program, the church confesses that "instead of acting compassionately and gently toward all forms of life, humanity had behaved wantonly and recklessly." The prayer asks God's forgiveness and entreats the Lord to "help us to change."

• Reader 1: God you created our planet, the birds, fish and other animals and you saw that all created things were good.

---

334   *United Church of Christ Justice and Witness Ministries, "God Speaks, Earth Speaks: A Contemplative Prayer Based on John 20:19-31, Integrity of Creation Sunday, Second Sunday of Easter, April 18, 2004, or Earth Day, April 22, 2004 (2003), accessed August 1, 2015. http://www.eco-justice.org/godspeak.pdf*

Reader 2: God of life, You also created us, the human family to be your viceroys and to act compassionately and gently towards all forms of life.

People: Remind us, O God, and help us to change.

Reader 1: We confess that we often forget that we are utterly dependent upon you and interdependent with the rest of your creation.

Reader 2: God of creation, we confess that instead of acting compassionately and gently toward all forms of life, humanity had behaved wantonly and recklessly.

People: Forgive us, O God, and help us to change.

Reader 1: God of compassion, our land lies polluted under our feet, and we see members of the animal kingdom, on land and in sea, dying as a result of the contamination that we have created.

Reader 2: God of grace, we confess that we are damaging the earth, the home that you have given us through our consumerism and the use of products that are constantly polluting our air, land, and water, harming wildlife and endangering human health.

People: Forgive us, O God, and help us to change.

Reader 1: God of wisdom, help us understand that whatever we do to the web of life we do to ourselves.

Reader 2: God of power, help us acknowledge that we must act now and wake up to our moral obligations and that the future of our beautiful planet is in our hands.

People: Forgive us, O God, and help us to change.[335]

---

335   *United Church of Christ Environmental Justice Ministry, "A*

Litany of an Environmental Confession," accessed August 1, 2015. http://
d3n8a8pro7vhmx.cloudfront.net/unitedchurchofchrist/legacy_url/6375/a_
litany_of.pdf?1418430896

The United Methodist Church

General Information

The United Methodist Church (UMC) traces its origins to the lives and ministries of John Wesley (1703-1791) and his brother Charles (1707-1788). Following the Wesleyan dictum, "As to all opinions which do not strike at the root of Christianity, we think and let think," the church permits members to hold divergent opinions about a wide range of religious and social issues but also teaches that there is a "living core of Christian truth that stands revealed in Scripture, illumined by tradition, vivified in personal and corporate experience, and confirmed by reason."[336]

More information about the UMC, including the church's beliefs, structure, and history, can be found by going to: http://www.umc.org/

Number of Members in the U.S.: 7.3 million

Number of Members Worldwide: 12.8 million[337]

336   The United Methodist Church, "Basics of Our Faith: Section 2: Our Doctrinal History," accessed July 31, 2015. http://www.umc.org/what-we-believe/section-2-our-doctrinal-history

337   The United Methodist Church, "United Methodists At-a-Glance: United Methodists around the World," accessed August 1, 2015. http://www.umc.org/news-and-media/united-methodists-at-a-glance

Official Statements on Animals

God desires us to put our faith into action, protecting His world and the animals in it

Official positions of The United Methodist Church are contained in two books: *The Book of Resolutions* and *The Book of Discipline*. These texts teach that salvation is an unmerited gift from God but that it also "evidences itself in good works." As a result of this emphasis on faith put into action, the church has a strong commitment to social justice and a long history of involvement in contemporary social issues including issues that impact animals and their habitats. "We cannot just be observers," says the UMC, but instead must actively promote the well-being of all God's creatures. All lives, including animals' lives, are "to be valued and conserved because they are God's and not solely because they are useful to human beings."

- Faith is the only response essential for salvation. However, the General Rules remind us that salvation evidences itself in good works.[338]
- The United Methodist Church believes God's love for the world is an active and engaged love, a love seeking justice and liberty. We cannot just be observers. So we care enough about people's lives to risk interpreting God's love, to take a stand, to call each of us into a response, no matter how controversial or complex.[339]
- All creation is the Lord's, and we are responsible for the ways in which we use and abuse it. Water, air, soil, minerals, energy resources, plants, animal life, and

---

338   United Methodist Church, *The Book of Discipline of The United Methodist Church* (Nashville: The United Methodist Publishing House, 2012), 51. http://issuu.com/abingdonpress/docs/9781426718120_online_part1?e=1213442/1091664

339   United Methodist Church, *The Book of Resolutions of The United Methodist Church* (Nashville: The United Methodist Publishing House, 2012), 27-28. http://issuu.com/abingdonpress/docs/9781426757877_online_part1

space are to be valued and conserved because they are God's creation and not solely because they are useful to human beings.[340]

"God chose to give human beings a divine image...so we would be recognized as stewards of God"

In *The Book of Resolutions*, the UMC repeatedly affirms that human beings have been "created in God's image." But, says the church, "God chose to give human beings a divine image not so we would exploit creation to our own ends, but so we would be recognized as stewards of God." As stewards, warns the church, we are expected to act as caretakers of "what belongs to another."

- In Genesis 1:26, the Bible affirms that every person is created in God's image. But this gift brings with it a unique responsibility. Being created in God's image brings with it the responsibility to care for God's creation. God chose to give human beings a divine image not so we would exploit creation to our own ends, but so we would be recognized as stewards of God. To have dominion over the earth is a trusteeship, a sign that God cares for creation and has entrusted it to our stewardship.[341]

- Humankind enjoys a unique place in God's universe. On the one hand, we are simply one of God's many finite creatures, made from the 'topsoil of the fertile land,' bounded in time and space, fallible in judgment, limited in control, dependent upon our Creator, and interdependent with all other creatures. On the other hand, we are created in the very image of God, with the divine Spirit breathed into us, and entrusted to 'take charge of' God's creation (Genesis 2:7; 1:26, 28; see Psalm 8:6). We are simultaneously caretakers with God of the world in which we live.[342]

---

340   UMC, *The Book of Discipline*, 105.
341   UMC, *The Book of Resolutions*, 81.
342   *Ibid*, 49.

- In the Bible, a steward is one given responsibility for what belongs to another. The Greek word we translated as steward is *oikonomous*, one who cares for the household or acts as a trustee. The word *oikos*, meaning household, is used to describe the world as God's household. Christians, then, are to be stewards of the whole household (creation) of God.[343]

Faithful stewardship requires us to respect God's covenant with all creatures

"The earth is the LORD's," affirms *The Book of Resolutions*, and we "are entrusted to care for God's beautiful creation." Unfortunately, says the church, we too often have confused our stewardship responsibilities with "a license to abuse" creation. It is now time for us to "repent of our devastation of the physical and nonhuman world," to remind ourselves that God's redemptive "covenant is with all creatures," and to proclaim the "good news...that Jesus Christ came to redeem all creation."

- 'The earth is the LORD's, and the everything in it' (Psalm 24:1). We are entrusted to care for God's beautiful creation (Genesis 2:15; Psalm 8) and to notice and praise God for its diversity of creatures (Psalm 148). Cosmic redemption includes all the created order (Colossians 1:19-20), which after all bears witness to God (Romans 1:20). We have failed, however, to care for God's creation. Too often we have interpreted God's invitation to subdue and take charge of creation (Genesis 1:28) as license to abuse it.[344]
- We are called to repent of our devastation of the physical and nonhuman world, because this world is God's creation and is therefore to be valued and conserved.[345]

---

343   *Ibid*, 81.

344   *Ibid*, 67-68.

345   *Ibid*, 88.

- We have misused God's good creation. We have denied that God's covenant is with all living creatures (Genesis 9:9)...We forget that the good news that we are called to proclaim includes the promise that Jesus Christ came to redeem all creation (Colossians 1:15-20).[346]

Faithful stewardship requires actions that support a higher quality of life for all creatures

In order for us to become faithful stewards, says the UMC, we must learn that we live in an interdependent world where seemingly private choices can have widespread consequences. These choices extend to all areas of life, including the economic, political, social, and technological. "Therefore," says the UMC, "let us recognize the responsibility of the church and its members to place a high priority on changes in economic, political, social, and technological lifestyles to support a more ecologically equitable and sustainable world leading to a higher quality of life for all God's creation." Failure to accept this responsibility, says the church, is the same as "rejecting or ignoring accountability to God and interdependency with the whole of creation [which] is the essence of sin."

- All creation is under the authority of God and all creation is interdependent.[347]
- Economic, political, social, and technological developments have increased our human numbers, and lengthened and enriched our lives. However, these developments have led to regional defoliation, dramatic extinction of species, massive human suffering, overpopulation, and misuse and overconsumption of natural and nonrenewable resources, particularly by industrialized societies. This continued course of action jeopardizes the natural heritage that God has entrusted to all generations. Therefore, let us recognize the responsibility of the

---

346   *Ibid, 68.*

347   *Ibid, 80.*

church and its members to place a high priority on changes in economic, political, social, and technological lifestyles to support a more ecologically equitable and sustainable world leading to a higher quality of life for all of God's creation.[348]

- Failure to accept limits by rejecting or ignoring accountability to God and interdependency with the whole of creation is the essence of sin.[349]

Agricultural animals are to be treated humanely & given conditions as close to natural as possible

In *The Book of Discipline*, the UMC gives its support to agricultural practices that preserve species diversity and that treat animals "humanely...where their living conditions are as close to natural systems as possible."

- Sustainable agriculture requires a global evaluation of the impact of agriculture on food and raw material production, the preservation of animal breeds and plant varieties, and the preservation and development of the cultivated landscape.[350]

- We support a sustainable agricultural system that will maintain and support the natural fertility of agricultural soil, promote the diversity of flora and fauna, and adapt to regional conditions and structures—a system where agricultural animals are treated humanely and where their living conditions are as close to natural systems as possible. We aspire to an effective agricultural system where plant, livestock, and poultry production maintains the natural ecological cycles, conserves energy, and reduces chemical input to a minimum.[351]

---

348   *UMC, The Book of Discipline,* 105

349   *UMC, The Book of Resolutions,* 300.

350   *UMC, The Book of Discipline,* 123-124.

351   *Ibid,* 123.

***Regulations that protect pets, research animals, and
endangered species are to be supported***

The UMC supports the protection of endangered species, including the "imperiled habitats" on which these species
depend. The UMC further supports "regulations that protect the life and health of animals, including those ensuring the
humane treatment of pets and other domestic animals, animals
used in research, and the painless slaughtering of meat animals,
fish, and fowl."

- We believe that the wondrous diversity of nature is
  a key part of God's plan for creation. Therefore, we
  oppose measures which would eliminate diversity in
  plant and animal varieties, eliminate species, or destroy
  habitats critical to the survival of endangered species
  or varieties. We support national and international
  efforts to protect endangered species and imperiled
  habitats.[352]

- We support regulations that protect the life and
  health of animals, including those ensuring the
  humane treatment of pets and other domestic
  animals, animals used in research, and the painless
  slaughtering of meat animals, fish, and fowl. We
  recognize unmanaged and managed commercial,
  multinational, and corporate exploitation of wildlife
  and the destruction of the ecosystems on which
  they depend threatens the balance of natural
  systems, compromises biodiversity, reduces resilience,
  and threatens ecosystem services. We encourage
  commitment to effective implementation of national
  and international governmental and business
  regulations and guidelines for the conservation of all
  animal species with particular support to safeguard
  those threatened with extinction.[353]

---

352   UMC, *The Book of Resolutions*, 85.

353   UMC, *The Book of Discipline*, 106-107.

"The task of the steward is to seek shalom": wholeness and healing for all creation

According to *The Book of Resolutions*, the ultimate "task of the steward is to seek shalom." This term, "often translated 'peace,' [has] the broader meaning of...wholeness...Shalom is best understood when we experience wholeness and harmony as human beings with God, with others, and with creation itself," bringing about "the healing of all creation."

- The Old Testament relates...the vision of shalom. Often translated 'peace,' the broader meaning of shalom is wholeness. In the Old Testament, shalom is used to characterize the wholeness of a faithful life lived in relationship to God. Shalom is best understood when we experience wholeness and harmony as human beings with God, with others, and with creation itself. The task of the steward is to seek shalom.[354]

- The coming of God's reign is the guiding hope for all creation. Hebrew Scripture and the life, teaching, death, and resurrection of Jesus Christ affirm that God's reign is characterized by liberation from all forms of oppression, justice in all relationships, peace and good will among all peoples, and the healing of all creation."[355]

Historical References on Animals

John Wesley: God extended his mercy to animals in Eden and will deliver them to a future paradise

The UMC can trace its concern for animals back to the teachings of the denomination's founder, John Wesley.

---

354   *UMC, The Book of Resolutions, 81.*
355   *Ibid, 301.*

According to Wesley, God blessed both man and animal in Eden and will deliver both to a future paradise where they will have their full portion of immortality and "happiness...without alloy, without interruption, and without end."

- All the beasts of the field, and all the fowls of the air, were with Adam in paradise. And there is no question but their state was...paradisiacal; perfectly happy. Undoubtedly, it bore a near resemblance to the state of man himself...And they too were immortal...[356]

- (God) seeth 'the earnest expectation' wherewith the whole animated creation 'waiteth for' that final 'manifestation of the sons of God;' in which 'they themselves also shall be delivered' (not by annihilation; annihilation is not deliverance) 'from the' present 'bondage of corruption, into' a measure of the 'the glorious liberty of the children of God.'... Thus, in that day, all the vanity to which they are now helplessly subject will be abolished; they will suffer no more, either from within or without; the days of their groaning are ended...In the new earth, as well as the new heavens, there will be nothing to give pain, but everything that the wisdom and goodness of God can create to give happiness. As a recompence for what they once suffered, while under the 'bondage of corruption,' when God has 'renewed the face of the earth,' and their corruptible body has put on incorruption, they shall enjoy happiness suited to their state, without alloy, without interruption, and without end.[357]

John Wesley: God's tender mercy to animals "directs us...to show mercy to these also"

---

356   John Wesley, "Sermon 60: The General Deliverance," *The Works of the Rev. John Wesley, AM, Vol. VI.* John Emory, ed. (London: Wesleyan Conference Office, 1878), 242, 245.

357   *Ibid*, 248-250.

According to Wesley, God's mercy "is over all his works" and "directs us to be tender of even the meaner creatures; to show mercy to these also."

- Nothing is more sure, than that as 'the Lord is loving to every man,' so 'his mercy is over all his works;' all that have sense, all that are capable of pleasure or pain, of happiness or misery. In consequence to this, 'He openeth his hand, and filleth all things living with plenteousness. He prepareth food for cattle,' as well as 'herbs for the children of men.' He provideth for the fowls of the air, 'feeding the young ravens when they cry unto him.' 'He sendeth the springs into the rivers, that run among the hills, to give drink to every beast of the field,' and that even 'the wild asses may quench their thirst.' And, suitably to this, he directs us to be tender of even the meaner creatures; to show mercy to these also.[358]

John Wesley: A diet without meat is good for one's health but is not a requirement of the faith

Wesley was criticized by his detractors for his diet, which frequently was devoid of "wine and animal food" (the word "vegetarian" did not enter the English language until the 19th century). One of these detractors, the Bishop of London, claimed that Wesley made this diet a requirement of the Methodist faith. Wesley explained in a letter to the bishop that refraining from eating "flesh" is not a religious requirement but it is good for one's health.

- By 'extraordinary strictness and severities,' I presume your lordship means, the abstaining from wine and animal food; which, it is sure, Christianity does not require. But if you do, I fear your lordship is not thoroughly informed of the matter of fact. I began to do this about twelve years ago…But I resumed the use of them both, about two years after, for the sake of some who thought I made it a point of conscience;

---

358   *Ibid*, 241.

telling them 'I *will* eat flesh while the world standeth,' rather than 'make my brother to offend.' Dr. Cheyne advised me to leave them off again, assuring me, 'Till you do, you will never be free from fevers.' And since I have taken his advice, I have been free (blessed be God!) from all bodily disorders. (I continued this about two years). Would to God I knew any method of being equally free from all 'follies of indiscretions!' But this I never expect to attain till my spirit returns to God.[359]

Contemporary Reflections on Animals

Animals do not have souls or go to heaven but they are our friends and deserve our care

Although the UMC's official texts, *The Book of Discipline* and *The Book of Resolutions*, do not address the issue of animals in heaven, the issue is addressed in a section of the UMC website entitled "What We Believe." In this section, Rev. Dan Benedict of the UMC's General Board of Discipleship states that "United Methodists do not teach that animals have souls and therefore need redemption and forgiveness or heaven in the same way that humans do." However, continues Benedict, the UMC does teach that all animals belong to God "and therefore we are responsible for the ways in which we use and abuse" them. "We see animals," concludes Benedict, "as companions and 'friends' to humans."

- With other Catholic and Protestant denominations, we United Methodists do not teach that animals have souls and therefore need redemption and forgiveness or heaven in the same way that humans do. However, we do teach that 'All creation is the Lord's, and therefore we are responsible for the ways in which we

359   John Wesley, "Letter to the Bishop of London," *The Works of the Reverend John Wesley, AM, Vol V. John Emory, ed. (New York: T. Mason & G. Lane, 1839), 345.*

use and abuse it (including the animals and diverse forms of life on the planet).'...[W]e see animals as companions and 'friends' to humans and believe that all of them belong to God.[360]

The bond between human and animal is "almost a kind of an embodiment of God's grace"

The UMC's commitment to the compassionate steward-ship of animals can be seen in several initiatives implemented by Methodist schools and churches. The Methodist Theological School in Ohio, for instance, has registered its concern about the treatment of animals in factory farms by purchasing its "meat and dairy...from nearby family farms with high animal wel-fare standards." The deacon of an Oklahoma church began a program that finds foster homes for the pets of people entering hospice care as a way of easing "the transition for the patient and the pet." And a retired pastor teaches theological and min-isterial lessons to other UMC pastors in California with the help of therapy horses. In the words of one UMC religious leader, the human-animal bond is "a hugely, deeply theological thing... It's almost a kind of embodiment of God's grace."

- *Factory farms*: Over the last 50 years, our system of agriculture has shifted dramatically from small and moderate-sized family farms to industrial-scale factory farms, characterized by a vertically integrated production system. These changes have come at enormous costs to the farmers, land and animal. Once upon a time, animals were raised. Now, they are referred to as 'production units' on these large industrial farms. Factory farms deny animals their natural behaviors and tendencies, and eliminate the sacred bond that exists between the farmer, his land and the animals. Industrial agriculture is also the leading contributor to greenhouse gases.

360   Rev. Dan Benedict, "What We Believe: Do United Methodists believe that animals have souls and go to heaven?" accessed August 1, 2015. http://www.umc.org/what-we-believe/do-united-methodists-believe-that-animals-have-souls-and-go-to-heaven

Yet, there are beacons of hope on the American landscape. This June, I had the privilege of visiting the Methodist Theological School in Ohio. [T]he meat and dairy the school purchases are procured from nearby family farms with high animal welfare standards.[361]

- *Hospice pets*: When pet owners have to go into hospice care, they can worry a great deal about the fate of their pets. A program called Pet Peace of Mind helps find foster families for these animals, and helps ease the transition for the patient and the pet.

  …Rev. Delana Taylor McNac…a deacon with Haikey Chapel Indian United Methodist Church here in Tulsa, Oklahoma…started the Pet Peace of Mind program back in 2007. The program works with non-profit hospices to try to find either a foster home or permanent adoptive home for a patient's pet during their end of life journey.

  These volunteers are saving the lives of these animals. About the only other choice for them is to be taken to Animal Control and there's only so many days they get and then they're euthanized…You really want that dog or animal to have a place to go, you really do. I'm sure the gentleman [going into hospice] is at peace. I have a feeling he knows the dog is in a good home.[362]

- *Therapy horses*: So, what can a pastor learn from a horse? Quite a bit, according to the Rev. Robert Wagener, a

361   Reasa Currier, "Commentary: Methodist Theological School 'Cares for Creation'," The United Methodist Church Newsdesk June 30 (2015), accessed August 1, 2015. http://www.umc.org/news-and-media/method-ist-theological-seminary-farm-cares-for-creation

362   Staff, "Volunteers Adopt Hospice Pets," The United Methodist Church Newsdesk, June 9 (2011), accessed August 1, 2015. http://www.umc.org/news-and-media/volunteers-adopt-hospice-pets

retired [UMC] pastor. Wagener...has seen firsthand the benefits of Equine-Facilitated Therapy. It was his idea...to structure a session specifically for pastors and he is excited about the possibilities. For Wagener, working with horses 'teaches you to be in connection with your people. And if you're truly connected with them, they'll follow you.'

Watching horses...he has seen how the lead horse guides rather than dominates the herd, and, for Wagener, that concept applies to pastors. 'I am your leader and I want you to follow me. And as you follow me I want you to trust me that I would never harm or hurt you.'

Wagener, who brought the scriptural passage of the lion and the lamb to share at the beginning of the day, asks the group how one's communication style might impact another person's sense of trust...[I]t's pretty clear that a predatory leadership style is not going to work well with horses—but it's 'probably not going to work well with people either.'

'You bond with these horses,' observes [one pastor], 'and you become, I can't explain it in any other way, a part of their herd. That's a hugely, deeply theological thing, to be a part of the family, a part of the group. It's almost a kind of an embodiment of God's grace.'[363]

Animal fighting is inhumane and should be banned

In April 2007, Louisiana UMC Bishop William W. Hutchinson joined with The Humane Society of the United States to call for a ban on cockfighting. Thanks in part to the work of Bishop Hutchinson, the ban was passed by the Louisiana legislature in June 2007 and took effect in August 2008.

- I join with others in support of SB 39, the ban of cockfighting. This is an inhumane practice that

---

363   'Laurens Glass, "What Can a Horse Teach a Pastor?," A UMC.org Feature, February 19 (2014), accessed August 1, 2015. http://www.umc.org/what-we-believe/what-can-a-horse-teach-a-pastor

leads to the ill treatment of animals as well as fuels an unhealthy atmosphere in which gambling runs rampant. I encourage the immediate passage of this bill.

The United Methodist Church has taken a clear stand on the issue of Animal Life...It is past time for this cruel and inhumane practice to end.[364]

---

364   William W. Hutchinson, "Bishop Speaks Out Against Cockfighting" (Washington, DC: The Humane Society of the United States, 2007). http://www.humanesociety.org/about/departments/faith/facts/bishop_hutchinson_statement.html

Bibliography

Assemblies of God

Assemblies of God. *AG ACMR and Related U.S. Statistics, 2004-2014*. http://bit.ly/1JrVoa5

---.. *AG Worldwide Churches and Adherents, 1987-2014*. http://bit.ly/1JrVoqw

---. *Brief History of the Assemblies of God*. http://bit.ly/1JrVoqH

---. "Home page". http://ag.org/top/

Brandon, Rose McCormick. "The Gift of a Loyal Pet." *Pentecostal Evangel*, July 13 (2008). http://bit.ly/1JrVrmb

Colson, Chuck. "Are Animals Persons?" *For Every Woman: Resources, Advice, and Guidance for Today's Woman* (2004). http://bit.ly/1JrVEG2.

Commission on Doctrinal Purity and the Executive Presbytery of the Assemblies of God. "Genetic Alteration and Cloning." http://bit.ly/1JrVE8Y.

---. "Environmental Protection." http://bit.ly/1JrVEpt.

General Council of the Assemblies of God. *Position Paper: The Doctrine of Creation*. Springfield: The General Council of the Assemblies of God. Revised 2014 http://bit.ly/1J172Hm.

Horn, Ken. "Vantage Point: Creation Evangelism." *Pentecostal Evangel*. 2008. http://bit.ly/1q4m8fT

Pentecostal Evangel. "Conversation: Tri Robinson, Creation Stewardship." *Pentecostal Evangel*, September 9 (2007). http://bit.ly/1JrVFtN

Powell, M.H. "Biotechnology: Becoming Responsible Stewards of Knowledge." *Enrichment Journal: Enriching and Equipping Spirit-Filled Ministries.* (2011). http://bit.ly/1JrVGoO

---. "More Valuable than Sparrows: Measuring Human Worth." *Enrichment Journal: Enriching and Equipping Spirit-Filled Ministries.*

Springfield: The General Council of the Assemblies of God (2012). http://bit.ly/1KbEagD.

Quick, Christina. "AG News: Bible Believers Join Environmentalism Discussion." *Pentecostal Evangel*, August 29 (2013). http://bit.ly/1JrVGOi

---. "Go Inside and Play: Today's Kids Favor Nintendo over Nature." *Pentecostal Evangel* (2007). http://bit.ly/1JrVIpm

Richardson, William E. "After You Say 'Amen.'" *Pentecostal Evangel*. March 15 (2007). http://bit.ly/1JrVKgX

Senior Adult Ministries. "Adopt a Pet." *Primeline: Practical Living*. http://bit.ly/1J17ghY

Sparks, Nicole and Darrin J. Rodgers. "John McConnell, Jr. and the Pentecostal Origins of Earth Day. *Assemblies of God Heritage, Vol 30* (2010). http://bit.ly/1JrVIWp

Church of God in Christ

Blake, Charles E., Sr. "The Centennial Proclamation: An Apostolic Missive, September 2007."

Brooks, P.A. and Charles Hawthorne. *Understanding Bible Doctrine As Taught In The Church Of God In Christ, Centennial Edition*. Detroit: Church of God in Christ (2002).

Church of God in Christ. "Home page." http://www.cogic.org/

---. "The Founder & Church History." http://bit.ly/1JrVMoY

---. "Our Foundation." http://bit.ly/1JrVOgw

---. "What We Believe." http://bit.ly/1JrVOx5

Evangelical Environmental Network. "Evangelical Climate Initiative (2006). http://bit.ly/1JrVPkG

United Nations. "The Millennium Development Goals Report." New York: United Nations (2008). http://bit.ly/1JrVRZQ

United Nations International Interfaith Network for Development and Reproductive Health. *A Faith-Filled Commitment to Development Includes a Commitment to Women's Rights and Reproductive Health: Religious Reflections on the Millennium Development Goals*. Washington, D.C.: International Interfaith Network for Development and Reproductive Health (2005). http://bit.ly/1JrVSxo

World Council of Churches. "2008 Faith in Human Rights Statement" (2008). http://bit.ly/1JrVSNz.

Church of Jesus Christ of Latter-day Saints, The

Church of Jesus Christ of Latter-day Saints, The. ed. *The Doctrine & Covenants of The Church of Jesus Christ of Latter-day Saints Containing Revelations Given to Joseph Smith, the Prophet with Some Additions by His Successors in the Presidency of the Church.* Salt Lake City: The Church of Jesus Christ of Latter-day Saints (2013). http://bit.ly/1JrVRsO

---. "Home Page." http://bit.ly/1JrVQVN

---. *The Pearl of Great Price: A Selection from the Revelations, Translations, and Narrations of Joseph Smith First Prophet, Seer, and Revelator to The Church of Jesus Christ of Latter-day Saints.* Salt Lake: The Church of Jesus Christ of Latter-day Saints (2015). http://bit.ly/1JrVTRt.

Jones, Gerald E. "The Gospel and Animals." *Ensign.* August (1972). http://bit.ly/1JrVRJq

Kimball, Spencer W. "Fundamental Principles to Ponder and Live." *Ensign.* November (1978). http://bit.ly/1JrVXk4

Smith, Joseph. *History of the Church of Jesus Christ of Latter-day Saints: Period 1, History of Joseph Smith, the Prophet, Vol. II.* B. H. Roberts, ed. Salt Lake City: Deseret News (1904).

---. *History of the Church of Jesus Christ of Latter-day Saints: Period 1, History of Joseph Smith, the Prophet, Vol. V.* B.H. Roberts, ed. Salt Lake City: Deseret News (1909).

Smith, Joseph Fielding. *Gospel Doctrine: Selections from the Sermons and Writings of Joseph F. Smith.* Salt Lake City: The Desert News (1919).

Stratton, Richard D. *Kindness to Animals and Caring for the Earth: Selections from the Sermons and Writings of Latter-day Saint Church Leaders.* Portland: Inkwater Press (2004).

Young, Brigham. *Journal of Discourses: Delivered by President Brigham Young, His Two Counsellors, the Twelve Apostles, and Others*, Vol. 8. G.D. Watt and J.V. Long, ed. Liverpool: George Q. Cannon (1861).

---. *Journal of Discourses: Delivered by President Brigham Young, His Two Counsellors, the Twelve Apostles, and Others*, Vol. 9, G.D. Watt and J.V. Long, ed. Liverpool: George Q. Cannon (1862).

---. *Journal of Discourses: Delivered by President Brigham Young, His Two Counsellors, and the Twelve Apostles*, Vol. 12, G.D. Watt and J.V. Long, ed. Liverpool: Albert Carrington (1869).

---. *Journals, April 4 – July 31, 1847*. Excerpted by Heritage Gateways, Utah Education Network. http://bit.ly/1JrVVsE

Episcopal Church, The

Domestic and Foreign Missionary Society of the Protestant Episcopal Church, *Catechism of Creation: An Episcopal Understanding*, First Edition, Revised (2005). http://bit.ly/1JrVYoa

Episcopal Church, The. *The Book of Common Prayer: and Administration of the Sacraments and Other Rites and Ceremonies of the Church Together with The Psalms of David According to the Use of The Episcopal Church.* New York: Church Publishing Incorporated (1979).

---. "History of the American Church." (1999) http://bit.ly/1ogtnlb.

---. "Home Page." http://bit.ly/1LNXNlp

---. *St. Francis Day Resources*. http://bit.ly/1JrVYVn

Episcopal Church Executive Council Committee on Science, Technology and Faith, The. *Catechism of Creation: An Episcopal Understanding*, First Edition, Revised (2005). http://bit.ly/1JrVYoa

---. *Environmental Stewardship*. New York: The Episcopal Church (1994). http://bit.ly/1JrW13y

Episcopal Church General Convention, The. "Resolution #2003-D016: Support Ethical Care of Animals." *Journal of the General Convention of...The Episcopal Church, Minneapolis, 2003*. New York: General Convention (2004). http://bit.ly/1JrW3IE

---. "Resolution #2009-C078: Direct the Development of Liturgies for the Loss of a Companion Animal." *Journal of the*

General Convention of…The Episcopal Church, Anaheim, 2009. New York: General Convention (2009). http://bit.ly/1JrW1jO

---. "Resolution #2009-D015: Urge Dioceses to Educate on Environmental Decisions Affecting Animal Species. *Journal of the General Convention of…The Episcopal Church, Anaheim, 2009.* New York: General Convention (2009). http://bit.ly/1JrW1k2

---. "Resolution #2012-A012: Urge Governments to Follow Principles in Adopting Trade Policies. *Journal of the General Convention of…The Episcopal Church, Indianapolis, 2012.* New York: General Convention (2012). http://bit.ly/1JrW1Ao

---. "Resolution #2012-A054: Authorize Rites for Care of Animals." *Journal of the General Convention of…The Episcopal Church, Indianapolis, 2012.* New York: General Convention (2012). http://bit.ly/1JrW4fu

Episcopal Church House of Bishops, The. *House of Bishops calls upon U.S. Senate to protect Arctic National Wildlife Refuge.* March 14 (2005). http://www.episcopalchurch.org/library/article/house-bishops-calls-us-senate-protect-arctic-national-wildlife-refuge

Episcopal News Service. "World's largest climate action march: Episcopalians protest for change." September 23. New York: The Episcopal Church (2014). http://bit.ly/1JrW4fC

Executive Council and The Environmental Stewardship Team of The Episcopal Church. Environmental Stewardship. (1994). http://bit.ly/1JrW13y

Fuller, Thomas. *The Holy State and the Profane State.* London: William Pickering (1840). http://bit.ly/1JrW4MO

Gryboski, Michael. "Episcopal Church Continues Downward Trend According to Report." *The Christian Post,* November 1 (2013). http://bit.ly/1JrW53e

Inge, W.R. "The Idea of Progress," 1-34. *The Romanes Lecture 1920: The Idea of Progress.* Oxford: At the Clarendon Press (1920).

Macaulay, James. *Plea for Mercy to Animals.* London: The Religious Tract Society (1875).

Protestant Episcopal Church in the United States of America. *Journal of the Proceedings of the Bishops, Clergy, and Laity, of the Protestant Episcopal Church in the United States of America, Assembled in a General Convention, Held in St. John's Chapel, in the City of New York, From October 6th to October 28th, Inclusive, in the Year of Our Lord 1847.* New York: Daniel Dana, Jr. (1847). http://bit.ly/1JrW7YZ

---. *Debates of the House of Deputies in the General Convention of the Protestant Church in the United States of America, Held in New York City, October, A.D. 1874.* Hartford: M.H. Mallory and Company, Printers (1874).

---. *Journal of the General Convention of the Protestant Episcopal Church in the United States of America, Held in the City of Portland from September Sixth to September Twenty-Third, inclusive, in the Year of Our Lord 1922.* New York: The Abbott Press (1923).

Schori, Katharine Jefferts. *Healing Our Planet Earth: Stewardship of the Earth.* April 12 (2008). http://bit.ly/1JrW92R

---. "Keynote Address." *The Climate Change Crisis* (2015). http://bit.ly/1JrW9zU

---. "Presiding Bishop's Message for Easter 2008." March 11 (2008). http://bit.ly/1O477ir

Evangelical Lutheran Church in America

Cooper, Aaron and David Rhoads. "The Season of Creation." *Living Lutheran: Lively Engagement in Faith & Life.* (2012). http://bit.ly/1JrW7rL

Evangelical Lutheran Church in America. *Animals and Hunger: Hunger Education Toolkits* http://bit.ly/1iAF9ku

---. "ELCA Facts." http://bit.ly/1JrWaDY

---. "History." http://bit.ly/1O475a7

---. "A Social Statement on Caring for Creation: Vision, Hope, Justice" (1993) http://bit.ly/1JrWbb3

---. "A Social Statement on Genetics, Faith and Responsibility." (2011). http://bit.ly/1JrWbrB

---. "A Social Statement on Sufficient, Sustainable Livelihood for All." (1999). http://bit.ly/1JrWbIe

---. "Social Statements." http://bit.ly/1JrWbIe

Hanson, Mark S. "A Commentary." *Awakening to God's Call to Earthkeeping* (2006). http://bit.ly/1JrWenk

Living Lutheran. "Blessing of the Animals." *Living Lutheran: Lively Engagement in Faith & Life.* (2013). http://bit.ly/1JrWcf5

Luther, Martin. *Commentary on the Sermon on the Mount.* Charles A. Hay, translator. Philadelphia: Lutheran Publication Society (1892).

---. *Luther's Epistle Sermons: Trinity Sunday to Advent, Vol III.* John Nicholas Lenker, translator. Minneapolis: The Luther Press (1909).

---. *Luther's Works, Vol. 37.* Helmut T. Lehmann, editor. Philadelphia: Muhlenbert Press (1959).

---. *The Table Talk of Martin Luther.* William Hazlitt, translator. New York: HG Bohn (1857).

Lutz, Charles. "Loving My Neighbor in the Whole of God's Creation." *Journal of Lutheran Ethics*, Vol. 3, Issue 3. (2003). http://bit.ly/1JrWcfd

Maczik, Brandi. "Caring for Animals." *Living Lutheran: Lively Engagement in Faith & Life.* Chicago: ELCA Churchwide Ministries (2013). http://bit.ly/1JrWcvv

Michaelis, Nancy. "Eat Less Meat." *ELCA Blogs.* http://bit.ly/1JrWcvA

Murphy, George L. *The Blessing of Farm Animals: An Occasional Liturgical Resource.* The Lutheran Alliance for Faith, Science and Technology. Reprinted by Evangelical Lutheran Church of America http://bit.ly/1JrWeDQ

Rasmussen, Larry L. "Extinction and Sin." *Journal of Lutheran Ethics*, Volume 3, Issue 9. (2003). http://bit.ly/1JrWcMe

Lutheran Church– Missouri Synod, The

Luther, Martin. *Commentary on the Sermon on the Mount.* Charles A. Hay, translator. Philadelphia: Lutheran Publication Society (1892).

---. *Luther's Epistle Sermons: Trinity Sunday to Advent Vol III*. John Nicholas Lenker, translator. Minneapolis: The Luther Press (1909).

---. *The Table Talk of Martin Luther*. William Hazlitt, translator. New York: HG Bohn (1857).

Lutheran Church–Missouri Synod, The. "A Brief Statement of the Doctrinal Position of the Missouri Synod." *Belief and Practice* (1932). http://bit.ly/1JrWfaE

---. "Frequently Asked Questions/LCMS views: The Bible FAQS." *Belief and Practice*. http://bit.ly/1JrWfaQ

---. "History of the LCMS." http://bit.ly/1JrWgMo

---. "Home Page." http://www.lcms.org/

---. "A Statement of Scriptural and Confessional Principles." (1973). http://bit.ly/1JrWh2t

---. "Synod Stats: Membership drops, giving increases." September 28 (2011). http://bit.ly/1JrWjao

Lutheran Church–Missouri Synod Commission on Theology and Church Relations, The. *Creation in Biblical Perspective: Report of the Commission on Theology and Church Relations*. St Louis: The Lutheran Church–Missouri Synod (1970). http://bit.ly/1JrWjaB

---. *Together with All Creatures: Caring for God's Living Earth, A Report of the Commission on Theology and Church Relations*. St. Louis: The Lutheran Church–Missouri Synod (2010). http://bit.ly/1O477yU

Presbyterian Church (U.S.A.)

202nd General Assembly. Presbyterian Church (U.S.A.). *Restoring Creation for Ecology and Justice*. Louisville: Office of the General Assembly, Presbyterian Church (U.S.A.) (1990). http://bit.ly/1JrWjaF

Calvin, John. *Commentary on the Epistles of Paul the Apostle to the Corinthians, Vol 1*. John Pringle, translator. Edinburgh: The Calvin Translation Society (1848).

---. *Institutes of the Christian Religion, Vol I*. Henry Beveridge, translator. Edinburgh: The Calvin Translation Society. (1845).

---. *Institutes of the Christian Religion, Vol I*. Henry Beveridge, translator. Edinburgh: T&T Clark (1863).

---. *Institutes of the Christian Religion, Vol II*. Henry Beveridge, translator. Edinburgh: T&T Clark (1863).

---. *The Library of Christian Classics, Vol. XXII. Calvin: Theological Treatises*. J.K.S. Reid, translator. Philadelphia: The Westminster Press (1954).

Presbyterian Church (U.S.A.). *Book of Order 2015-2017*. Louisville: The Office of the General Assembly (2015).

---. "PC(USA) Congregations and Membership, 2001-2012, Table 1." http://bit.ly/1Q4jwnc

---. "Presbyterian 101: A General Guide to Facts about the Presbyterian Church (U.S.A.)." http://bit.ly/1JrVlej

---. "Presbyterian 101: Presbyterian Distinctives." http://www.pcusa.org/ministries/101/distinctives/

Presbyterian Church (U.S.A.) Committee on Social Witness in Cooperation with Stewardship Communication Development Ministry Unit and Social Justice and Peacemaking Ministry Unit. *Restoring Creation for Ecology and Justice: Responding to the Cry of Creation for Healing and Justice, Leader's Guide* http://bit.ly/1KHAHgh

Presbyterian Church (U.S.A.) Office of the General Assembly. "GA Minutes: The Dialogue between Theology and Science" (1982). http://bit.ly/1JrWjHC

---. "General Assembly of the PC(U.S.A.)." http://bit.ly/1VQQnzu.

Presbyterian Hunger Program. *Just Eating? Practicing Our Faith at the Table: Readings for Reflection and Actions*. http://bit.ly/1JrWi6B

Roman Catholic Church, The

Aquinas, Thomas. *The 'Summa Theologica' of St. Thomas Aquinas, Part I*. Father of the English Dominican Province, translator. London: R&T Washbourne, Ltd. (1912).

Celano, Thomas of. *The Lives of S. Francis of Assisi*. A.G. Ferrers Howell, translator. London: Methuen & Co. (1908).

Center for Applied Research in the Apostolate, "Frequently Requested Church Statistics: United States Data Over Time." http://bit.ly/1JrWket

Holy See, The. *Catechism of the Catholic Church*. Vatican City: Libreria Editrice Vaticana (1993). http://bit.ly/1JrWkeE

---. Home Page, English. http://bit.ly/1JrVn6b

International Theological Commission. "Communion and Stewardship: Human Persons Created in the Image of God." Vatican City: Libreria Editrice Vaticana (2002). http://bit.ly/1JrWliF

Pope Francis. *Apostolic Exhortation, Evangelii Gaudium, of the Holy Father Francis to the Bishops, Clergy, Consecrated Persons and the Lay Faithful on the Proclamation of the Gospel in Today's World*. Vatican City: Libreria Editrice Vaticana (2013). http://bit.ly/1JrWlzc

---. *Encyclical Letter Laudato si' of the Holy Father Francis On Care for Our Common Home*. Vatican City: Libreria Editrice Vaticana (2015). http://bit.ly/1Q4jA6h

Pope John Paul II. "Common Declaration on Environmental Ethics: Common Declaration of John Paul II and the Ecumenical Patriarch His Holiness Bartholomew I. Monday 10 June 2002." Vatican City: Libreria Editrice Vaticana (2002). http://bit.ly/1JrWlPA

---. *The Creative Action of the Divine Spirit. General Audience, January 7, 1990*. Vatican City: Libreria Editrice Vaticana (1990). http://bit.ly/1JrWmDe

---. "Message of His Holiness Pope John Paul II for the Celebration of the World Day of Peace: 1 January 1990: Peace with God the Creator, Peace with all of Creation." Vatican City: Libreria Editrice Vaticana (2002). http://bit.ly/1JrWmTO

Ratzinger, Joseph Cardinal. *God and the World: A Conversation with Peter Seewald*. San Francisco: Ignatius Press (2002).

United States Conference of Catholic Bishops. *Prayers to Care for Creation* (2015). http://bit.ly/1JrWp1Y

United States Conference of Catholic Bishops Committee on Domestic Policy. *For I Was Hungry and You Gave Me Food: Catholic Reflections of Food, Farmers, and Farmworkers*. Washington, DC:

United States Conference of Catholic Bishops (2003). http://bit.ly/1JrWpil

Seventh-day Adventist Church

Adventist Review Staff. "Vegetarian Diet Is Effective Tool against Climate Change, Study Finds." *Adventist Review.* June 26 (2014). http://bit.ly/1O477Pk

Blackmer, Sandra. "A Wake-up Call." *Adventist Review* . http://bit.ly/1O477Pm

Branstedt, Katrina A. "Using Animals in Medical Research." *College and University Dialogue: An International Journal of Faith, Thought, and Action* http://bit.ly/1JrWqTB

Davidson, JoAnn. "And It Was Good: Stewardship of the Planet Isn't Just for Tree Huggers," August 21 (2008). http://bit.ly/1JrWqTF

---. "Who Cares? Environmental Ethics and the Christian." *Adventist Review, Special Issue: Good Health—More than an Apple a Day.* (2009). http://bit.ly/1JrWtie

Priebe, Matthew. "How We Treat Animals—Does God Care? Should We?" *Adventist Review* (2005). http://bit.ly/1KbFekx.

Seventh-day Adventist Church. "Church Beliefs: The Gift of Prophecy." http://bit.ly/1JrWrqr

---. "Home Page." http://bit.ly/1JrVnmC

---. "Information History." http://bit.ly/1JrWtP3

---. "Information Statistics: Seventh-day Adventist World Church Statistics 2014." http://bit.ly/1JrWsuu

---. "Official Statements. Documents: Christian Principles for Genetic Interventions" (1995). http://bit.ly/1JrWsL8

---. "Official Statements. Documents: Human Gene Therapy" (2000). http://bit.ly/1JrWvXq

---. "Official Statements. Statements: An Affirmation of Creation" (2004). http://bit.ly/1JrWv9M

---. "Official Statement. Statements: Caring for the Environment" (1992). http://bit.ly1KdkdZR

---. "Official Statements. Statements: Environment" (1995). http://bit.ly/1JrWvqe

Seventh-day Adventist Church Office of Archives. "Statistics, and Research North American Division (1913-Present)." http://bit.ly/1JrWwKL

Ellen G. White. "Healthful Living," (1895). http://bit.ly/1JrWvGW

---. "Mind, Character, and Personality, Vol. 2," (1905). http://bit.ly/1JrWyCz

---. "The Ministry of Healing," (1905). http://bit.ly/1JrWySV

---. "MR No. 1209 - Counsels to Our Colporteurs Regarding Carefulness in Diet (Cir. 1889)" http://bit.ly/1JrWzpV

---. "Our Thinking is Affected by Our Eating, October 27" (1910). http://bit.ly/1JrWAdI

---. "Patriarchs and Prophets," (1890). http://bit.ly/1JrWAu3

---. "Testimony Studies on Diet and Foods," (1923). http://bit.ly/1JrWC5k.

---. "Testimony Studies on Diet and Foods," (1926). http://bit.ly/1JrWCIJ.

Zuill, Henry. "The Environment: Should Christians Care?" *College and University Dialogue: An International Journal of Faith, Thought, and Action* http://bit.ly/1JrWDpP

Southern Baptist Convention

Duke, Barrett. "10 Biblical Truths about Animals." *The Ethics and Religious Liberty Commission of the Southern Baptist Convention.* January 2 (2015). http://bit.ly/1UFrdGV

Erickson, Millard J. *Christian Theology.* Grand Rapids: Baker Book House (1990)

Gallop/CNN/*USA Today.* "Greatest of the Century (and the Millennium): Gallop/CNN/*USA Today* Poll Dec. 20-21" (1999). http://bit.ly/1JrWFxR

George, Timothy. "Troubled Waters," *First Things.* June 2 (2014). http://bit.ly/1JrWGSu

Graham, Billy. "Does the Bible Say Anything about How We Should Treat Animals?" *Answers by Billy Graham.* August 16 (2010). http://bit.ly/1JrWG4W

---. "Does God Care About Animals," *Answers by Billy Graham*, May 13 (2010). http://billygraham.org/answer/does-god-care-about-animals/

Mission Education Team of the North American Mission Board, SBC. "Cooperative Missions: State and National Conventions." Alpharetta: North American Mission Board, SBC. (2010). http://bit.ly/1JrWHWy

Moore, Russell D. "Letter to Tennessee House Speaker Beth Harwell on Deterrents for Animal Fighting." March 2 (2015). http://bit.ly/1JrWIcY

Southern Baptist Convention. "Basic Beliefs." http://bit.ly/1JrWJO1

---. "Home Page." http://www.sbc.net

---. "Resolution: On Environmentalism and Evangelicals" (2006). http://bit.ly/1JrWitD

---. "Resolution: On Human Cloning" (2001). http://bit.ly/1JrWKl5

---. "Resolution: On Human Species-Altering Technology" (2006). http://bit.ly/1JrWJou

---. "Resolution: On the Gulf of Mexico Catastrophe" (2010). http://bit.ly/1JrWKSe.

United Church of Christ

United Church of Christ. "About Us." http://bit.ly/1JrWLWl

---. "Home Page." http://www.ucc.org/

---. "Minutes." *Nineteenth General Synod* (1993). http://bit.ly/1JrWMcG

---. "Minutes." *Twenty-eighth General Synod* (2011). http://bit.ly/1JrWMcL

---. "Minutes." *Twenty-ninth General Synod* (2013). http://bit.ly/1JrWLpm

---. "Resolution: Transition from Fossil Fuels to Renewable Energy," *Thirtieth General Synod* (2015). http://bit.ly/1JrWLFI

---. "Short Course in the History of the United Church of Christ." http://bit.ly/1JrWMtt

United Church of Christ Collegium of Officers with the Environmental and Energy Task Force. *And Indeed It Is Very Good. A Pastoral Letter on Faith and Environment: Living in Community with God's Creation.* Cleveland: United Church of Christ (2008). http://bit.ly/1JrWMJQ

United Church of Christ Environmental Justice Ministry. "A Litany of Environmental Confession." http://bit.ly/1JrWNod

United Church of Christ Environmental Ministries. "Biodiversity." http://bit.ly/1JrWNov

---. "Why Should People of Faith Care about the Environment?" (2015). http://bit.ly/1JrWNxh

United Church of Christ Justice and Witness Ministries. "God Speaks, Earth Speaks: A Contemplative Prayer Based on John 20:19-31. Integrity of Creation Sunday, Second Sunday of Easter, April 18, 2004, or Earth Day, April 22, 2004" (2003). http://bit.ly/1JrWNxt

---. *Toxic Wastes and Race at Twenty 1987-2007.* Cleveland: United Church of Christ (2007). http://bit.ly/1JYC44v

United Methodist Church, The

Benedict, Dan. "What We Believe: Do United Methodists believe that animals have souls and go to heaven?" http://bit.ly/1JrWNNT

Currier, Reasa. "Commentary: Methodist Theological School 'Cares for Creation.'" The United Methodist Church Newsdesk. June 30 (2015). http://bit.ly/1JrWPW7

Glass, Laurens. "What Can a Horse Teach a Pastor?" *A UMC. org Feature.* February 19 (2014). http://bit.ly/1JrWRx8

Hutchinson, William W. "Bishop Speaks Out Against Cockfighting." Washington, D.C.: The Humane Society of the United States (2007). http://bit.ly/1JrWTVD

United Methodist Church, The. "Basics of Our Faith: Section 2: Our Doctrinal History." http://bit.ly/1KHCfa1

---. "Home Page." http://www.umc.org/

---. *The Book of Discipline of The United Methodist Church.* Nashville: The United Methodist Publishing House (2012). http://bit.ly/1JrWSRD

---. *The Book of Resolutions of The United Methodist Church.* Nashville: The United Methodist Publishing House (2012). http://bit.ly/1JrWTFj

---. "United Methodists At-a-Glance: United Methodists around the World." http://bit.ly/1JrWWRp

United Methodist Church Newsdesk, The. "Volunteers Adopt Hospice Pets," June 9 (2011). http://bit.ly/1JrWW3P

Wesley, John. *The Works of the Reverend John Wesley, A.M, Vol. V.* John Emory, editor. New York: T. Mason & G. Lane (1839).

---. *The Works of the Reverend John Wesley, A.M, Vol VI.* John Emory, editor. London: Wesleyan Conference Office (1878).

About Us

THE HUMANE SOCIETY of the United States (HSUS) is the nation's largest animal protection organization. Hands-on care and services to more than 100,000 animals is provided each year by us and our affiliates, and we professionalize the field through education and training for local organizations. We are driving transformational change in the U.S. and around the world by combating large-scale cruelties such as puppy mills, animal fighting, factory farming, seal slaughter, horse cruelty, captive hunts and the wildlife trade. Our mission statement: **Celebrating animals, Confronting Cruelty.** Our website: http://www.humanesociety.org.

The HSUS Faith Outreach program seeks to engage people and institutions of faith with animal protection issues, on the premise that religious values call upon us all to act in a kind and merciful way towards all creatures. We have a national Faith Volunteer and Ally Program and several ongoing and seasonal campaigns to connect faith communities with resources and tools to help animals. We also host meetings for faith leaders to explore animal welfare issues and we seek their counsel and guidance on the full scope of HSUS priorities. Visit http://www.humanesociety.org/faith.

The HSUS has two faith councils, which provide critical and strategic guidance and support. The Faith Advisory Council is composed of leading scholars and representatives from a range of religious denominations, faiths and backgrounds. The Dharmic Leadership Council includes doctors, attorneys, executives in the field of nonprofit advocacy, technology and industry, and other activists and creative individuals. Council members play a leading role in reminding people of their own longstanding scriptural and other traditions of human responsibility and compassion toward all animals. Each council member serves as an ambassador for The HSUS in his or her community, including providing spiritual support for leaders who have taken a stand on animal protection issues in their region.

Members of The HSUS Faith Advisory Council:

Imam Muhammad Hagmagid Ali, president, Islamic Society of North America, Washington, D.C.

Dr. Charles Arand, chair, systematic theology, Concordia University, St. Louis, Missouri

Bishop John Bryson Chane, eighth bishop of Washington in the Episcopal Church, Washington, D.C.

Dr. Matthew Halteman, professor of philosophy, Calvin College, Grand Rapids, Michigan

Father Daniel Kroger, CEO, Franciscan Media, Cincinnati, Ohio

Dr. Aaron Gross, professor of theology and religious studies with a focus on contemporary Jewish traditions, UC San Diego; founder and CEO, Farm Forward, San Diego, California

Dr. Seyyed Hossein Nasr, professor of Islamic Studies, George Washington University, Washington, D.C.

Rev. Dr. Laura Hobgood-Oster, chair, Department of Religion, Southwestern University, Georgetown, Texas

Dr. Karen Swallow Prior, professor of English, Liberty University, Lynchburg, Virginia

Dr. Jerry Root, professor and associate director, Billy Graham Institute for Strategic Evangelism; director, Wheaton Evangelism Institute, Wheaton College, Wheaton, Illinois

Rabbi David Wolpe, rabbi, Sinai Temple, Los Angeles, California

Dr. Paul Waldau, chair, Department of Anthrozoology, Canisius College, Massachusetts

Marianne Williamson, author, speaker and spiritual teacher, Los Angeles, California

Members of The HSUS Dharmic Leadership Council:

Shuvya Arakali, financial analyst, J.P. Morgan; executive committee member, Lakshmi Cow and Animal Sanctuary

Vandhana Bala, general counsel, Mercy for Animals

Anju Bhargava, president, Hindu American Seva Communities

Dr. Sonya V. Chawla, medical director, Med-Star Medical Group, Foxhall Square

Bushan Deodhar, president, Sumeru Software Solutions; CEO, Shankara Skincare; director, U.S. Office for Sri Sri Ravi Shankar

Retired Navy Capt. (Dr.) Sushil Jain, president and CEO, Jain Healthcare Professionals; past president, JAINA (Federation of Jain Associations in North America)

Sai Santosh Kumar Kolluru, law student; executive committee member, Lakshmi Cow and Animal Sanctuary

Allen Lalwani, president, American Spray Tech; committee member, Sadhu Vaswani Center of New Jersey

Shekar Natarajan, vice president, Supply Chain and Logistics Strategy, Walmart

Suhag Shukla, executive director, legal counsel and co-founder, Hindu American Foundation

Kirti Vaswani, co-founder, EQLearn and Indian Business Solutions, LLC

Hemant K. Wadhwani, president, Hanuman Capital Initiative

Note: Institutional affiliations are listed for identification purposes only.

Appendix 1

IN 2OI4, THE HSUS released a video series, "Living Legacy: Faith Voices on Animal Protection," highlighting historical faith leaders who made critical contributions to the animal welfare movement.

Below is an excerpt from, "A Humane Nation," the blog of The HSUS president and CEO, Wayne Pacelle:

> Our Faith Outreach program at The HSUS partners with people of faith to fight animal cruelty, spread kindness, and highlight the rich history of compassion for animals in all the world's major religious traditions. From the Dalai Lama to the Episcopal bishop of Washington to Dada Vaswani, I've had the good fortune of meeting many remarkable people of faith who share my deep conviction that it's our human responsibility to be merciful toward all of God's creatures.
>
> Reaching into the past, to those people whose faith drove them to protect animals from cruelty, can be just as inspiring. Some of the most notable names that come to mind are 19th-century reformer William Wilberforce, evangelical author and social activist Hannah More, and 20th-century writer C.S. Lewis. That is why I am pleased to announce that we are releasing this week a 12-part video series, "Living Legacy: Faith Voices on Animal Welfare," to honor

these three pioneers.

Wilberforce was an English Parliamentarian best known for his heroic efforts to end slavery. He was passionately committed to animal welfare and instrumental in establishing the Royal Society for the Prevention of Cruelty to Animals (RSPCA), the world's first animal welfare charity.

More, an evangelical and writer, wrote stories that combined biblical themes with popular entertainment—stories that included kindness to animals.

Lewis was an academic, a force of nature and the author of dozens of popular books, including the beloved Narnia series. For him, pain, including animal pain, was understood best from a biblical perspective, and the videos reveal that he became an anti-vivisectionist because he believed that God makes every living creature for a purpose.

In the videos, these striking historic personalities are discussed by three influential voices: Eric Metaxas, author of *Amazing Grace: William Wilberforce and the Heroic Campaign to End Slavery*, Dr. Karen Swallow Prior, professor of English at Liberty University and author of *Fierce Convictions: The Extraordinary Life of Hannah More*, and Dr. Jerry Root, associate professor at Wheaton College, director of the Wheaton Evangelism Initiative and the Billy Graham Center for Evangelism, and a C.S. Lewis scholar.

We hope these videos will give animal lovers a historical perspective into the long relationship between faith and animal welfare, and the widespread support that exists for animal protection among people of faith.

View the videos at http://bit.ly/1JrWZN6.

C. S. Lewis as an Advocate for Animals

Abstract

C. S. Lewis was a magnanimous man and had a love of animals as well as a passion for the advocacy for the ethical and moral treatment of animals. He employs many literary genres to make a case for man's responsibility for the animals, these include his: Letters, Literary Criticism, Fiction, Christian Apologetics, and Essays (especially a specific essay written in opposition of "Vivisection"). It is instructive to see where Lewis is successful in his advocacy and also where he is weak. Furthermore, Lewis provides a model for advocacy on behalf of animals whenever fresh challenges occur, which can be helpful to those who share his concerns. Lewis's method of argumentation is rooted in objectivity pursued and guarded by the checks and balances of authority, reason, and experience.

Introduction: C. S. Lewis as advocate for the animals

The Oxford scholar and Cambridge Professor, C. S. Lewis, was deeply concerned about human responsibility for animals. This concern grew out of a general magnanimity that was characteristic of much of his life. Anecdotes about Lewis abound. He was almost bigger than life. I received a letter many years ago from the Oxford Chaucer scholar and friend of Lewis, Neville Coghill, who described his fellow *Inkling* this way:

> He [Lewis] was a great medieval and classical scholar who also wrote about Christianity to which he

became a convert to the Anglican Communion, he also wrote a number of books about an imaginary country called Narnia, mainly for children, but very readable. He was kind and good and a splendid talker, in many ways rather like Dr. Johnson—in bulk as well as in wit and learning. Personal letter dated 15 February 1974 (a copy is in the Marion Wade Center at Wheaton College).

Certainly, Lewis was much like Dr. Johnson; perhaps this is why people remembered stories about Lewis and wrote them down in the same way James Boswell wrote down stories about Dr. Johnson. And many of these stories reveal that he was magnanimous almost to a fault. He gave away two-thirds of all his royalty income which included the money he made from his preaching and Christian apologetic work.[365] Lewis's friend, Owen Barfield set up the Agape Trust through which Lewis distributed funds to those in need. This was all done anonymously. Professor Clyde S. Kilby says in the Preface to Letters to an American Lady that Lewis gave away two thirds of all his income.[366]

If panhandlers approached Lewis and asked him for money he always emptied his pockets and gave whatever might be found there. Once, this occurred while Lewis was accompanied by a friend. When the warning was sounded, "Why did you give that money to that man? He will just go and drink it." Lewis responded, "Yes, but if I kept it I would drink it!"[367] He was more ready to hold his own motives up to scrutiny than those of others. This kind of good heartedness was seamlessly evident in Lewis's treatment of animals and his advocacy on their behalf.

The Kilns, Lewis's home in the Risinghurst neighborhood of Headington just outside of Oxford was virtually a hotel for animals. Cats and dogs were always part of the assembly under that

---

365   HOOPER, Walter. C. S. Lewis: Companion & Guide. London: Harper Collins, 1996. Pp. 32, 623, 747.

366   Lewis, C. S. Letters to an American Lady, Edited by Clyde S. Kilby. Grand Rapids, Michigan: William B. Eerdmans, 1971. P. 9

367   LEWIS, C. S. Letters to an American Lady. P. 108

roof. Lewis even confided in one letter that while his neighbors were known to trap the mice in their houses. Lewis's own practice was to feed them. In fact, on one occasion he told a bursar at Magdalene College, Cambridge that the bursar mustn't try to trap a mouse seen in college for it could be somebody's mother.[368] And, there is one well known story told by Lewis's former student and long time friend and biographer, George Sayer, which summarizes Lewis's compassion for the animals and the lengths he would go, personally to protect them. While on a walk with Lewis in the woods, Sayer recounts that a bedraggled fox bounded out of the thicket right before them looking worn and weary. The energy of the fox was seemingly spent as it staggered away. Moments later mounted fox hunters came galloping up and Lewis asked if they were looking for a fox. When the hunters responded in the affirmative Lewis sent them in a direction opposite to the one the fox had taken.[369] Lewis was an outrageous lover of animals and, whenever the need arose, advocated on their behalf.

Literary genres where Lewis makes a case for man's responsibility for the animals

Lewis's breadth as a writer is evident by 73 titles that bear his name and these fall in eleven different literary genres. In many of these genres his interest in animals percolates to the surface whether he wrote letters, literary criticism, poetry, fiction, Christian apologetics, or essays his love of animals and interests on their behalf is evident.

---

368   *Told to me by Michael Ward, Lewis scholar and author of* Planet Narnia

369   SAYER, George. —Jack on Holiday in C. S. Lewis at the Breakfast Table, *James Como, editor. New York: Macmillian, 1979. P. 207*

Letters

Lewis's letters contain numerous examples where he is writing to his correspondents about animals, making it clear that he often was observant of the beasts around him and reflected on them in his thoughts.

Letters to children

In his letters to children Lewis drops his guard and speaks of things almost innocently and childlike himself; this is especially so when it comes to animals. He tells one child of a rabbit in the gardens at Magdalen College, Oxford he has named Baron Biscuit. Lewis would feed this rabbit from his hand and even wrote a poem about him and sent it to his young correspondant.[370]

Lewis wrote to another child that he had with him at the Kilns a dog named Bruce, and cats named Kitty-koo and Pushkin.[371] It was in these letters that Lewis confided he never set traps for mice and in fact he had many living in his rooms at Oxford.[372] He clearly noticed the animals in his world and he loved to tell children about them.

The Collected Letters of C. S. Lewis

In The Collected Letters of C. S. Lewis there are numerous references to animals and Lewis's observations of them as well as his thoughts and speculations about them. Representative of these letters is one he wrote to a Mrs. Allen expressing his disdain at the experimentation taking place using monkeys: "I read with interest and indignation your story of the experiment on the monkeys; there seems no end to the folly and wickedness

---

370   LEWIS, C. S. Letters to Children. Lyle Dorsett and Marjorie Lamp Mead, editors. New York: Macmillan, 1985. Pp. 21-22

371   Ibid. February 11, 1945. P. 23

372   Ibid. June 3, 1953. P. 32

of this world."[373] He also speculated about animal pain in these letters: "I find however that the problem of animal pain is just as tough when I concentrate on creatures I dislike as ones I cd. [could] make pets of...I loathe hens. But my conscience would say the same things if I forgot to feed them as if I forgot to feed the cat..."[374]

Letters to an American Lady

In his thirteen-year correspondence with an American Lady, Lewis clarified that he was still holding to a controversial position on animal immortality right up to the months before his own death.

> My stuff about animals came long ago in *The Problem of Pain*. I ventured the supposal—it could be nothing more—that as we are raised in Christ, so at least some animals are raised *in* us. Who knows, indeed, but that a great deal even of the inanimate creation is raised *in* the redeemed souls who have, during this life, taken its beauty into themselves. That may be the way in which the—new heaven and the new earth are formed. Of course we can only guess and wonder. But these particular guesses arise in me, I trust, from taking seriously the resurrection of the body: a doctrine which now-a-days is very soft pedaled by nearly all the faithful—to our great impoverishment. Not that you and I have now much reason to rejoice in having bodies! Like old automobiles, aren't they where all sorts of apparently different things keep going wrong, but what they add up to is the plain fact that the machine is wearing out. Well, it was not meant to last forever. Still, I have a kindly feeling for the old rattle-trap. Through it God showed me that

373   LEWIS, C. S. The Collected Letters of C. S. Lewis. Volume III. Walter Hooper, editor. 28 December, 1950. San Francisco: Harper Collins, 2007. Pp. 77-78.

374   Ibid. 29 Dec. 1961. P. 1308

whole side of His beauty which is embodied in colour, sound, smell and size. No doubt it has often led me astray: but not half so often, I suspect, as my soul has led *it* astray. For the spiritual evils which we share with the devils (pride, spite) are far worse than what we share with the beasts: and sensuality really arises more from the imagination than from the appetites; which, if left merely to their own animal strength, and not elaborated by our imagination, would be fairly easily managed. But this is turning into a sermon![375]

Literary Criticism

Lewis's work on the backgrounds of medieval literature, *The Discarded Image*, reveals once more his attention to the place of animals in the thought and imagination of the middle ages. Lewis discusses the medieval zoology as it comes down to us through the literature of the time. He observes that there is little talk of the animals proximate to the agrarian experience of a person of that age even though everyone in that period was far more familiar with cows and goats and sheep and horses and hawking and stags than we whose domestic life is defined by urbanization. Nevertheless, the Bestiaries of the day contained a wider variety of animals more interesting to the medieval imagination. Lewis notes, "The written zoology of their period is mainly a mass of cock-and-bull stories about creatures the authors have never seen, and often about creatures that never existed."[376] These stories and descriptions were often embellishments, "They are usually handing on what was received from the ancients."[377]

---

375   LEWIS, C. S., *Letters to an American Lady. Clyde Kilby*, editor. (26 November 1962). *Grand Rapids, Michigan: Eerdmans, 1967. Pp. 110–111*

376   LEWIS, C. S. *The Discarded Image. Cambridge: Cambridge University Press, 1964. P.147*

377   *Ibid.*

Lewis also speculates, had Aristotle's "Genuinely scientific zoology...been known first and followed exclusively we might have had no bestiaries."[378]

The classical authors simply passed on to the medieval authors their material. Lewis says that it was Phadrus (1st Century A.D.) who gave us the dragon of Germanic, Anglo-Saxon and Norse notoriety.

"In two thousand years western humanity has neither got tired of it nor improved it. Beowulf's Dragon and Wagner's dragon are unmistakably the dragon of Phadrus."[379] Furthermore, Centaurs, Lewis believed were born out of projecting human characteristics onto the horse. The Unicorns, the Phoenix, and so forth are also derived from classical sources and embellished in the hands of the medieval authors.[380] Some animals more proximate to actual medieval observation and experience, such as the pelican have attributed to them myths of varying significance. It was believed the pelican plucked at its own breast and gave life to its young by feeding them its own blood. The myth became a symbol for Christ.[381] All of this is mentioned to make two points. First, Lewis is able to underscore the fact that wonder relative to animals (whether mythological or actual) has always leant itself to the lore of literature, it has been part and parcel of human history from time in memoriam. Second, human history has always had its accuracies and its myths relative to these mysterious creatures who share life with us on this planet.

Lewis concludes the section on the beasts in *The Discarded Image* with these words, "If, a Platonism taught...the visible world is made after an invisible pattern, if things below the Moon are all derived from things above her, the expectation that an anagogical or moral sense will have been built into the nature and behavior of the creatures would not be a priori unreasonable. To us an account of animal behavior would seem improbable if it

---

378   *Ibid.*

379   *Ibid. P.148*

380   *Ibid. P. 148-49*

381   *The crest of Corpus Christi College at Oxford University has the symbol of the Pelican for this reason*

suggested too obvious a moral. Not so to them. Their premises were different."[382] While a close read of Lewis's corpus reveals he was neither a Platonist nor an Aristotelian, though he borrowed from both, he allowed his borrowing, in this case, to be in the interest of the animals. He makes similar use of fiction to advocate on behalf of animals as well.

Fiction

Lewis saw the value of fiction as a rhetorical tool. Lewis the logician often debated his beliefs propositionally with clear, cogent and coherent arguments still he recognized that some points are likely to be made by other means. Lewis uses fiction in order to persuade as well as logic. He was a lover of stories and he and his friend J. R. R. Tolkien together committed themselves to write the kinds of stories they liked to read, and they made brush strokes on the canvases of their work that clearly supported their personal interests. Tolkien's love of trees and forests along with a general sense of human responsibility for the environment is woven into the fabric of Middle-earth. Similarly Lewis clearly advocated for the animals in his Narnian books and his science fiction trilogy.

The talking beasts of Narnia are afforded equal rights with the humans of that world; albeit the Narnian animals possess reason and personhood. Lewis allows his fiction to open the eyes of his readers that they might see and appreciate the beasts and all they bring even to the discovery of human dignity in the just treatment of these mysterious creatures. In a sense he uses these books to fulfill the longing he expressed in the Epilogue of *An Experiment in Criticism*. In that book Lewis wrote that his own eyes were not enough for him he longed to see what others have seen. Even that was not enough he longed to read what they have imagined. Still, he was not satisfied, he regretted that the brutes could not write books for he wished he could see how the world presented itself to the eyes of a mouse or a bee, or how it came charged to the olfactory sense of a dog. While Lewis's Narnia

---

382   *Ibid.* P. 152

books cannot give us this precisely, he certainly sets the hearts of his readers to wondering. The books are written to tell specific stories, they are stories where children enter the world of animals. Seeing animals there, with dignity and grace, there are more likely to see better in their own world when they return from the adventure. The great lion Aslan, the Christ figure of Narnia, tells Lucy that he lives in her world too only there he goes by a different name. She has been brought to Narnia to know him in Narnia for a short while that she might come to know him better in her world. Similarly, in seeing the animals of Narnia in a fresh way, every animal in our world is seen with a renewed sense of wonder and awe.

Lewis's science fiction books look at the matter of animals in a different light. The animals are not central to the stories *per se*, though they do play a major role in the conclusion of the trilogy and bring about justice and judgment to that world. Nevertheless, their primary role is one of background, yet the point is constantly (and consistently) made that those who are good in these books have a love for animals and always make room for them. The Manor, where Ransom, the hero of the science fiction books, holds sway, is a menagerie of animals. And they are treated with kindness and make up the hominess of that world. By contrast, the evil characters with their nefarious designs that make up the N. I.C. E. (the National Institute of Coordinated Experiments) are all vivisectionists. While it is not explicitly stated, Lewis makes a clear link in these books between evil characters and the ill treatment of animals. In fact, perhaps the most evil character in all of his fiction, Weston, whose evil reduces Lewis simply to call him "the unman" is a vivisectionist. The loss of his humanity is seen in his disregard of the animals. This linkage is also seen in other evil characters in Lewis's fiction. Evil Uncle Andrew, in *The Magician's Nephew*, performs experiments on Guinea Pigs and eventually performs experiments on the children Polly and Digory. The Magician, in Lewis's narrative poem *Dymer*, shoots a lark and then, in time, turns his gun on Dymer. Jadis Queen of Charn, who becomes the White Witch of Narnia, is identified by her characteristic cruelty to animals.

In all of this Lewis is making rhetorical points on behalf of the animals. It is a mark of evil to treat animals poorly; it is a sign of goodness to treat them well. A just person assumes responsibility for the animals. But Lewis is not dependent solely on fiction to make this point.

Lewis's Christian Apologetics

Lewis's Apologetics work is where he directs his attention most clearly to the questions of animals. He is sometimes unsuccessful in his rhetoric and sometimes successful. Evident is his love of animals and his sense of responsibility to advocate on their behalf. Lewis wrote *The Problem of Pain* in an attempt to present traditional Christian answers to the problem of suffering and evil. He draws from the tradition of Augustine and Boethius to present a "free-will theodicy" that says evil is the result of the ill-use of free will and that this is the main spring of evil and suffering in the world. Here his approach is predominately a philosophical one. Lewis also draws from the tradition that flows out of Irenaeus and is known as a "soul- making theodicy." Though evil and suffering have been allowed by God in the world, God uses suffering as a means to cultivate virtue in the life of the sufferer. He writes, "Innocence is not goodness; even Divine nature even in her prime cannot make of virtue a gift."[383] This summary of Lewis's argument in *The Problem of Pain* may sound too sparse and underdeveloped—and it is—my reason for giving this brief explanation is merely to situate Lewis's application of this argument to the question of animal pain and suffering.

In Lewis theodicy it is the matter of animal pain that poses the most difficulty for him. Over and over again he notes that his thoughts are speculative due, in part, to the mystery animals are to him. All of his sympathies are with the animals; his good intentions to understand their pain and reconcile their suffering into a coherent apology for the Christian faith go without

---

383   LEWIS, C. S. *The Allegory of Love.* Oxford: Oxford University Press, 1936. P. 60

question. Nevertheless, his work in theodicy seems to lack sophistication when it comes to the animals and all they endure and suffer in this fallen world. If animals have no wills, they cannot be responsible for suffering due to rebellion and sin.

Anything relative to a free-will theodicy does not seem to apply to them. That is, animals do not suffer due to evil choices on their part though they do suffer due to bad choices on the part of humans. Furthermore, if animals have no souls they are incapable of virtue and suffering will not improve their character. Soul-making theodicy cannot be used to explain how suffering might benefit the animals. Lewis realizes traditional Christian arguments applied to the topic of human pain and suffering cannot be strictly applied to animals. He seeks a probable explanation for animal pain; it is a subject that matters to him, in part because of his deep love of animals. He concedes the importance of the issue, but stresses it is not a matter about which we can have certainty since "It is outside of the range of our knowledge."[384]

Lewis does not believe animals exhibit signs of possessing a soul or self-consciousness and consequently, pain for animals will be experienced differently than it is for humans. Lewis's argument flows along these lines, he asks his readers to distinguish between sentience and consciousness.[385] He argues that the feeling of sensations does not imply consciousness. To have sensation (a) followed by sensation (b) followed by sensation (c), and so on, is not to experience these things; it is merely to sense them. The experience of these sensations would demand that we are able to look at them sequentially. In order to do this, there must be something in us outside the sequence of the sensations themselves, which can perceive when each sensation begins and ends. Lewis believes that "this something is…Consciousness or Soul and the process I have just described is one of the proofs that the soul, though experiencing time, is not itself completely

384   LEWIS, C. S. *The Problem of Pain*. London, Fount Paperbacks, 1977. p. 103
385   *Ibid., p. 105*

timeful."[386] If an animal has no soul, then its experience of these sensations will be without a sense of succession. Lewis writes:

> The correct description would be Pain is taking place in this animal'; not, as we commonly
>
> say, this animal feels pain', for the words this' and
>
> feels' really smuggle in the assumption that it is a self' or soul' or
>
> consciousness' standing above the sensations and organizing them into an experience' as
>
> [humans] do.[387]

What Lewis has written here neglects the fact that animals seem to remember suffering pain and take care to avoid it. Why do animals from dogs to donkeys tend to flinch if a hand moves swiftly near its head? Is this a mere startle or is the animal protecting itself in a way that indicates a possible awareness of a potential for pain? It may be nothing more than startle in which case Lewis may be right. On the other hand, it may indicate a reaction that draws on stored memory and the flinch is an expression of fear and anxiety. If the latter is the case then Lewis's argument begins to unravel. In a response to this argument, philosopher C. E. M. Joad, agreed with Lewis that a robust theodicy must take into account the problem of animal suffering. Nevertheless, Joad disagreed with Lewis on the matter of pain being a less significant matter if the animal has no soul. Joad objected that, "the fact that pain is felt, no matter who or what feels it…that demands explanation."[388] Lewis concedes Joad's point but responds, "But it surely does matter how far the sufferer is capable of what we can recognize as misery" and Lewis believes that misery is a state that demands soulish, self-awareness.[389]

---

386   *Ibid., p. 105*
387   *Ibid., p. 106*
388   LEWIS, C. S. *God in the Dock: Essays in Theology and Ethics.*
Grand Rapids, Michigan: Errdmans, 1970. P. 168
389   *Ibid., P. 168*

Sadly, while Lewis's overall thesis in *The Problem of Pain* has value within the narrow focus he has carved for himself, the issue of animal suffering is clearly outside the scope of his argument. He drifts towards subjectivism in order to fit animal pain into his system. I do think, however, there is a way Lewis might have brought the animal issue into his argument without having to reconcile it with free-will and still maintain his objectivist commitments.

In *The Problem of Pain*, Lewis mentions that humans experience some pain simply because they come in conflict with "a relatively independent and inexorable' Nature."[390]

Those conflicts do not necessarily signify acts of rebellion against Nature. Certainly we can suffer because we make misjudgments concerning the world around us. We can just as easily drink from a stream where we think the water is good, only to find through the tasting that it is bitter and unhealthy. The relative pain of a bitter taste acts for us as a kind of warning device to move on and avoid grave consequences. Without even bringing up the issue of free-will, we may argue that animals may have been given the capacity of pain for reasons similar to these. If an animal finds that the thicket has thorns that tear at its fur, the animal experiencing pain goes around another way. Pains, in this way, may prescribe limits which, if heeded, can add to whatever quality of life might be available to animals. Lewis might have developed his argument along these lines and still brought it into the realm of his particular focus.

As to the question of justice, Lewis recognizes that though animal pain may not be "God's handiwork,"[391] even so, "if God has not caused it, he has permitted it, and once again, what shall be done for these innocents?"[392] Here he directs his attention to "animal immortality," and engages in the most highly speculative portion of his discussion of animal suffering. It is his belief that an animal may gain something like self-consciousness in

---

390   *The Problem of Pain*, p. 23
391   *Ibid.*, p. 109
392   *Ibid.*, p. 109

response and submission to its master. Just as man is redeemed in Christ, so too, the animal can be redeemed in man.[393]

A reader familiar with Lewis's work can only assume that here he is not at his best. Philosopher, Evelyn Underhill, who otherwise liked *The Problem of Pain*, was shocked to read such things in Lewis and thought it her duty to tell him about it. She wrote, "I feel your concept of God would be improved by just a touch of wildness."[394] Furthermore, Lewis's friend, Austin Farrer, the Oxford philosopher and fellow *Inkling*, generally liked Lewis's ability to reason and debate; but, on this matter he wrote that Lewis's "Imagination has slipped from the leash of reason."[395] And, as has been noted, in *Letters to an American Lady*, shortly before he died, Lewis is still holding to the possibility of this position about animals as he originally described it in *The Problem of Pain* some 20-plus years earlier.[396]

Lewis does not deny that he writes full of doubts, and acknowledges that all the while, "When we are speaking of creatures so removed from us as wild beasts, and prehistoric beasts, we hardly know what we are talking about."[397] Though he usually writes with clarity, this chapter is full of obscurity. He would have been wiser to have refined his thoughts, in this section of the book, before publication, or left it out completely since it distracts from the strong portions of the book and diminishes Lewis's rhetoric.

Since he did not, he must face further problems. Lewis's failure to deal adequately with the problem of animal pain, and the fact that his argument, if properly adjusted, can be strengthened,

---

393   *Ibid., pp.* 111-113.

394   UNDERHILL, Evelyn. *The Letters of Evelyn Underhill, Charles Williams, editor.* London: Longmans, Green and C., 1944. P. 302. *Also note Colin Duriez's observation in Tolkien and C. S. Lewis: The Gift of Friendship. Mahwah, New Jersey: Hidden Spring, 2003. Pp.* 138-39

395   Farrer, Austin, —*The Christian Apologist in Light on C. S. Lewis, Jocelyn Gibb, editor.* New York: Harcourt, Brace & World, 1965. P. 42

396   LEWIS, *Letters to an American Lady. Letter dated:* 26 November '62. P. 110-111.*Ibid., p.* 113

397   *Ibid., p.* 113.

reveals once again that his argument is a work in progress and not a last word. Even a relatively sound rhetorician such as Lewis does not always argue infallibly. There is always room for further discursive thought.

Rehabilitating Lewis's theodicy with respect for animals.

Lewis's failure to fit animals into his theodicy in a reasoned way does not mean that a successful Christian defense for the problem of animal pain is impossible. Philosopher Austin Farrer, addresses this issue much more convincingly, and his contribution is helpful in seeing how Lewis might have modified his own argument. Farrer's argument runs something like this: While some suffering among men is certainly justifiable due to guilt, animal suffering could have no such justification.[398] Human suffering can produce growth in character such as "heroic endurance," "moral wisdom," and sacrifice for the sake of others; animals cannot benefit in this way, and therefore animal suffering cannot be justified in this way.[399] Furthermore, animal irrationality aggravates the problem, for "the power of reason can render physical sufferings endurable."[400] Understanding the dentist's motives makes it possible to endure his drill. Animals, lacking reason, do not possess this advantage. Farrer also notes that because animals cannot communicate their pains, they are likely to suffer longer before their needs are tended to.[401]

Farrer observes that there is a common element running through each of the items mentioned above; it is that animal pain is "sheer pain", and as such, it appears to be "an

---

398   FARRER, Austin, 1966. Love Almighty and Ills Unlimited. London: Collins/ The Fontana Library, p. 84. (Hereafter cited as FARRER,Love Almighty)

399   Ibid., p. 85

400   Ibid., p. 85

401   Ibid., p. 86

unmitigated evil, incapable of justification."[402] Here, he asks the question: Would animals be better off if they had no pains at all?[403] It would seem that they would not be better off if they had no capacity to feel pain, for animal pain is necessary to animal consciousness, and without it they would have no chance for survival. He argues that "the working of animal pain has the rough effect of defending the species and promoting evolutionary development."[404] And Farrer believes the whole process has been creatively guided.[405] God cares for each individual creature by his providence and compassion. It appears that the Christian argument can be developed much further, and certainly Farrer is more satisfying than Lewis. In fact, Lewis's unsuccessful treatment of animal pain stems from his failure to develop a satisfactory resolution for the problem of natural evil and weakens the effectiveness of his rhetoric.

His argument does not seem to bother much with physical or natural evil, and when it does, Lewis's attempts to address it are unsatisfactory. When natural evils are discussed at all, they are seen as the product of a malevolent supernatural being. Lewis writes of the "Satanic corruption of the beasts," evidenced by "the fact that animals, or some animals, live by destroying each other."[406] Later, he adds that "it is possible to believe that animal pain is not God's handiwork but begun by Satan's malice and perpetuated by man's desertion of his post."[407] Since Lewis believes the Scriptures lack a system of nature, he does not see, as a Christian apologist, that it is incumbent upon him to supply one.[408] He acts as an apologist charged with the task to defend what he believes is present in Scripture and nothing more. He is the apologist of *Mere Christianity*. Even so, he seems to be inconsistent, picking and choosing when and where he will develop an

---

402   *Ibid., p. 86*

403   *Ibid., p. 86*

404   *Ibid., p. 97*

405   *Ibid., p.95*

406   *LEWIS, Pain, p. 108*

407   *Ibid., p. 109*

408   *Ibid., p. 109*

idea in an imaginative way in order to provide probable solutions to particular problems. As to the problem of natural evil, he avoids doing any imaginative speculation as to what might be helpful in resolving certain difficulties beyond the data supplied by the texts of Scripture. It could even be argued that Lewis misreads the Scriptures here. Certainly enough data can be found in the Bible to begin the work of natural theology, and with it develop probable resolutions to the questions of natural evil, which others have, in fact, done.[409] It is also odd that Lewis, who is quit successful in the use of his imagination in a host of other places, would neglect the opportunity at this point, to venture an attempt at some kind of explanation.

On a related note, Cambridge scientist and theologian John Polkinghorne has suggested that theology could address the issue of natural evil (what he terms physical evil) along the lines of what he calls a "free process defence." God has created the universe unfinished and has permitted the created order to develop over time:

> A world allowed to make itself through the evolutionary exploration of its potentiality is a better world than one produced ready-made by fiat. In such an evolving world there must be malfunctions and blind alleys. The same biochemical processes that enable some cells to mutate and produce new forms of life will allow other cells to mutate and become malignant. [410]

While God sustains history in a single timeless act—there is, therefore, only a general providence—"God is in the overall necessity, but the detailed happenstance of actual historical

409   See POLKINGHORNE, John, 1998. Science and Theology: An Introduction. London: SPCK/ Fortress Press. pp. 93-95. (Hereafter cited as POLKINGHORNE, Science and Theology) WARD, Keith, 1998. God, Faith & the New Millennium: Christian Belief in an Age of Science. Oxford: One World. Chapter 8. Creation, Suffering and the Divine Purpose, pp. 91-108. (Hereafter cited as WARD, God, Faith & the New Millenium) FARRER, Love Almighty, pp. 77-105

410   POLKINGHORNE, Science and Theology, p. 9446

process is just how it all chances to work out."[411] Polkinghorne believes, perhaps too strongly, that "the integrity of modern science would be breached in an arbitrary way by any other suggestion.[412] Polkinghorne's judgment may be premature. Other suggestions might become necessary by virtue of the fact that science is often developing new probabilities to account for new discoveries. Nevertheless, as a Christian, Polkinghorne seeks to absolve the Divine will for actual evil and suffering in creation, thus relieving Him from responsibility for it. The question still remains: Why did God not take a more active role in the developing creation? To this, Polkinghorne simply replies, "The stronger one's account of Divine action, the more pressing becomes the problem of theodicy."[413] While Polkinghorne does not develop the argument as fully as one might hope, he moves in a direction that Lewis might have taken, but does not.

A similar view is held by Oxford theologian Keith Ward, but he develops it further:

> It seems probable, for example, that a universe that is truly emergent is one in which some measure of conflict and suffering will necessarily exist. Old forms have to die away, to make room for new. And it may be partly through competition and conflict that new forms come into existence. In this way, the distinctive values that only an emergent, evolutionary universe can realise—values of courage, tenacity, creative adventure, as well as values of compassion, co-operation and self- sacrifice—will not be able to exist without the existence of some sort of suffering that God does not directly intend.
>
> We might say that God intends the values, the goods, that only such a process can realise. Therefore God does generate the whole process intentionally. Yet God does not intend the suffering and conflict that the process entails, or at least makes unpreventable

411   *Ibid., p. 85*
412   *Ibid., p. 85*
413   *Ibid., p. 86*

by God.[414]

Thus, God may have permitted nature to take its own course of development, just as He permitted man to go his own way. If development can be observed in nature even through a process of suffering, perhaps an apologetic can be informed, in part, by natural revelation, as well as through special revelation. In this way, even the Fall of man could be seen as developmentally necessary. Lewis's argument could benefit from discoveries related to natural development. So too scientists can benefit from theology when it suggests that providence provides an explanation for the good observed by the positive development of species through a process that includes suffering and survival in nature. These insights suggest ways that an apologetic might be developed with respect to natural evil. Lewis is not unaware of these things; by the time he writes *Miracles*, his thinking has progressed along lines such as these. He believes that nature was not created perfectly. He does not believe it to be created evil, thus involving himself in all the difficulties of ascribing evil in creation to the work of a good God. Instead, he believes that God created the universe imperfectly, in the sense that it was immature and undergoing a process towards some kind of maturity. Creation, like man, was made innocent, and like man reveals that it experiences corruption. How does it come "to be in this condition," asks Lewis?

> By which question we may mean either how she comes to be imperfect— to leave room for improvement' as the school masters say in their reports—or else, how she comes to be positively depraved. If we ask the question in the first sense, the Christian answer (I think) is that God, from the first, created her such as to reach her perfection by a process in time. He made an Earth at first without form and void' and brought it by degrees to its perfection...In that sense a certain degree of evolutionism' or developmentalism' is inherent in Christianity. Her positive depravity calls for a very different explanation. According to

414   WARD, *God, Faith and the New Millennium*, p. 93

the Christians this is all due to sin: the sin both of men and of powerful, non- human beings, supernatural but created.[415]

One wonders where Lewis might go with this idea if he would tease it out further. However, he keeps coming back to the belief that all the difficulties of natural evil have for their cause fallen beings, either men or devils, and it appears that this position hinders him from making a fuller development of his contribution to the problem of evil. His failure occurs because he does not accommodate himself, as well as he might, to objective reality; and to the degree that he fails in this regard, he also fails rhetorically.

Lewis's essays

Another literary form where one can observe Lewis's advocacy on behalf of the animals is in his essays, particularly in his essay written against the practice of vivisection. Lewis was an uncompromising antivivisectionist. He had a deep love of animals; nevertheless, his antivivisectionist position was arrived at by conviction not by mere sentiment. Lewis's views regarding human responsibility for the animals grew as much out of his theological principles as his philosophical conclusions. Lewis's article *Vivisection* reveals careful precision by virtue of his clear definitions, his coherent inferences, and his power to make a solid and convincing argument. What sense can we make about Lewis's views regarding animals? And, does Lewis say anything from a faith perspective that might help us work our way through the complex labyrinth of man in relation with these otherwise mysterious creatures who occupy both time and space with mankind on this wonderful planet?

---

415   *LEWIS, Miracles, p. 146*

The argument of *Vivisection*

In 1947, Lewis published an article for the New England Anti-vivisection Society.[416] Vivisection is defined as the act or practice of cutting into or otherwise injuring living animals, especially for the purpose of scientific research. I will try to reproduce the skeletal structure of his argument against vivisection.

First, Lewis argues that emotion may make it difficult to enter into a rational discussion about vivisection.[417] One the one hand: those who oppose experiments on animals may be accused of having their reason clouded due to sentimentality towards the animals. But, Lewis argues, on the other hand, those in favor of vivisection may be equally accused of sentimentality. Their arguments may be caught up in sentimentality directed towards human suffering and therefore their advocacy for practices in favor of animal experimentation may be driven by emotion on behalf of the sufferings endured by humans. When arguments for either side drift towards sentiment the matter becomes clouded. Lewis, seeking to be fair, notes: "The one appeal, quite as clearly as the other, is addressed to emotion, to the particular emotion we call pity. And neither appeal proves anything. If the thing is right—and if right at all, it is a duty—then pity for the animal is one of the temptations we must resist in order to perform that duty. If the thing is wrong, then pity for human suffering is precisely the temptation which will most probably lure us into doing that wrong thing. But the real question—whether it is right or wrong—remains meanwhile just where it is."[418]

---

416   *Lewis's argument on Vivisection, can also be found in God in the Dock: Essays in Theology and Ethics. Part II, Chapter 9 —Vivisection (originally published by the New England Anti-Vivisection Society in 1947, and later republished in C. S. Lewis: The Grand Miracle and Other Selected Essays on Theology and Ethics from God and the Dock. New York: Ballantine, 1983. Pp. 137- 141 (from which the excerpts for this paper were taken)*

417   LEWIS, *—Vivisection p. 137*

418   *Ibid.*

Second, Lewis argues that "A rational discussion of this subject begins by inquiring whether pain is, or is not, an evil."[419] If pain is not an evil, the case against vivisection falls. To be fair, Lewis also recognizes that if this is the case the argument for vivisection also fails: if the practice of animal experimentation is not defended as a means to reduce human suffering then by what means can vivisection ever be defended?[420] No right thinking, or right feeling, individual would ever inflict pain on another creature unnecessarily. Furthermore, Lewis also recognizes that if pain is not evil per se, then why should we seek to reduce human suffering in the first place? At this moment in his argument Lewis begins with what he considers an assumption necessary to the whole question that is, that pain is an evil.[421]

Third, Lewis argues, "if pain is an evil then the infliction of pain, considered in itself, must clearly be an evil act. But there are such things as necessary evils. Some acts which would be bad, simply in themselves, may be excusable and even laudable when they are the means to a greater good."[422] Examples to support Lewis's contention are readily available. Suicide is considered bad not only for the taking of life but also for the grief caused to those who are left behind; nevertheless, a soldier who muffles a hand grenade with his own body in order to save his fellow soldiers does something heroic. Furthermore, starving oneself is bad; but, a mother's willingness to deny herself food in order to make sure her children are fed is heroic. Therefore, Lewis writes, "In saying that the infliction of pain, simply in itself, is bad, we are not saying that pain ought never to be inflicted."[423] Surgeons apply scalpels to the bodies of their patients in order to cut away tumors that could end life; dentists apply their drills to cavities; coaches and physical therapists may drive those committed to their charge to real physical pain in order to achieve maximal results. Some pain inflicted may produce great good and can

---

419   *Ibid.*

420   *Ibid.*

421   *Ibid.*

422   *Ibid.*

423   *Ibid.*

be compatible with good intention. Nevertheless, Lewis rightly argues, whenever pain is inflicted it requires justification.[424]

This is, in fact, a point Lewis is constantly making in his critical essays regarding ethical acts; that is, *all judgments imply a standard*.[425] If a standard is self-referential it will often become utilitarian, that is, it operates without an overarching rule or governing principle that applies to the one inflicting pain as well as the one who is injured. If a standard of judgment can be found that is objective and has universal application—that is a transcendent standard—how would one know he had arrived at a proper understanding of that which is fundamentally rooted in something outside of himself? The epistemological questions must always be addressed and we will see how Lewis addresses these later.

In his argument against vivisection Lewis continues, "If we find a man giving pleasure it is for us to prove (if we criticize him) that his action is wrong. But if we find a man inflicting pain it is for him to prove that his action is right. If he cannot he is a wicked man."[426] A bad act in itself may not be an evil act, per se unless it is a knowing evil. Lewis has already argued that inflicted pain is bad if it cannot be soundly justified. In the case where inflicting pain cannot be reasonably justified the person inflicting pain commits an evil act.

Fourth, Lewis explores what might be considered by some as a possible Christian support for vivisection. He argues, "Now vivisection can only be defended by showing it to be right that one species should suffer in order that another species should be happier."[427] At this point a divide in the argument occurs and two strains of thought are considered. I will call them point 4a and point 4b.

---

424   *Ibid*. P. 138

425   LEWIS, C. S. *De Futilitatel Christian Reflections*, Walter Hooper, editor. *Grand Rapids, Michigan: Eerdmans. 1967. Pp. 65-66.*

426   LEWIS, —*Vivisection p. 138.*

427   *Ibid*.

Point 4a says that a Christian defender of vivisection may argue for the practice because animals have no souls.[428] Lewis believes this may well be the case; nevertheless, he considers it a matter of opinion. While opinions are not certainties they must be based on probability or they are reduced to mere prejudice. Therefore, opinions are subject to doubt, and reasonable people may differ on matters of opinion. Furthermore, a point is not established by an opinion. Probability is significant but without conclusive proof one must remain open to further considerations. Opinions keep one engaged in dialogue while searching for the truth of a matter, and must never be dismissive of an opponent. Lewis asserts that there are some things about the animals that simply remain a mystery to us; one of these is that we cannot assert with certainty whether or not animals have souls. Therefore, he argues that in the absence of certainty we must exercise restraint when it comes to inflicting pain on animals.[429] Furthermore, if by the absence of a soul one means that animals have no moral responsibilities—that is they are not morally responsible for their acts—then they should not be punished for their behavior. If animals are not able to develop morally then they should not have to suffer in a process that leads to maturity and moral development. Nevertheless, Lewis asserts that, "animals cannot deserve pain, nor profit morally by the discipline of pain, nor be recompensed by happiness in another life for suffering in this."[430] If anything, Lewis argues, the animals' lack of moral responsibility must awaken in man the moral responsibility to protect and care for them.

When the argument diverges towards what I am calling point 4b then the Christian defender of vivisection is reduced to one line of reason: "That the superiority of man over beast is a real objective fact, guaranteed by revelation, and that the property of sacrificing beast to man is a logical consequence. We are worth more than many sparrows' (Matthew 10:31)."[431] But,

---

428   Ibid. P. 138
429   Ibid.
430   Ibid.
431   Ibid.

Lewis notes, this position is more complex than it appears on the surface. The argument for vivisection which appeals to conformity with a hierarchical order created by God is precarious.[432] If hierarchy is used to justify the human act of inflicting pain upon animals then, argues Lewis, what counts against the angelic order inflicting pain on humans simply because of hierarchical privilege?[433] In fact superiority of hierarchal position may demand that those above protect those dependent upon them. Of course, again, much of this discussion is within the realm of opinion and must operate within those limits. Nevertheless, Lewis acknowledges that within the limits of opinion it might be probable to suggest that a Christian pathologist could find it necessary to vivisect and do so "with scrupulous care to avoid the least dram or scruple of unnecessary pain, in a trembling awe of the high mode in which human life must be lived if it is to justify the sacrifices made for it, then (whether we agree with him or not) we can respect his point of view."[434] But Lewis acknowledges most vivisectors do not come from those who operate out of Christian assumptions about the universe and the created order. Most, he believes come from the realm operating from naturalism and Darwinian assumptions.[435]

Turning now to his fifth point, Lewis's gives a stern warning against the assumptions of naturalism and Darwinianism as a means to justify vivisection. He calls attention to this alarming fact: "The very same people who will most contemptuously brush aside any consideration of animal suffering if it stands in the way of 'research' will also, on another context, most vehemently deny there is any radical difference between man and the other animals."[436] In light of this Lewis makes the following inference, "We sacrifice other species to our own not because it has any objective metaphysical privileged over others, but simply

---

432   *Ibid. p. 139*

433   *Ibid.*

434   *Ibid.*

435   *Ibid. p. 139*

436   *Ibid.*

because it is ours."[437] Lewis warns against this view on three counts. First, lacking in any objective standard it is nothing more than sentimentality. We have an emotional allegiance and loyalty to our race, our party, or our creed, is only valid if our race, party, or creed is in the right. If it is not such loyalty is unjustifiable. Second, lacking any objective standard Lewis notes this "sinister" feature of such a justification for vivisection: "If a mere sentiment justifies cruelty, why stop at a sentiment for the whole human race?"[438] Lewis notes that such an allowance as this—a position rooted in sentiment to one's particular party without doing the hard work of analysis as to whether or not our party's position is right, justifiable, and can stand up to scrutiny—can be used to justify the strong against the weak, the majority race against the minority, the ruling class or party against others, "superior men" against their "inferiors" and we might even add here, the living against the unborn. Third, Lewis goes so far as to say the reason we do not hear an outcry against the ethics of naturalism and Darwinianism is because he believes these assumptions have already won in our culture and they are held unthinkingly as to their validity or their applications.[439]

Lewis concludes his essay with this prophetic warning: "The victory of vivisection marks a great advance in the triumph of ruthless, non-moral utilitarianism over the old world of ethical law; a triumph in which we, as well as animals, are already the victims, and of which Dachu and Hiroshima mark the more recent achievements. In justifying cruelty to animals we put ourselves also on the animal level. We chose the jungle and must abide by our choice."[440] Lewis's conclusion is a searing one, made like a prophet crying in the wilderness to a world grown deaf through its rationalized behaviors. Nevertheless, Lewis makes his points as if to say, "Let him who still has hears to hear, hear."

---

437   *Ibid.*
438   *Ibid. Pp. 139-40*
439   *Ibid. Pp. 140-41*
440   *Ibid. P. 141*

This essay on Vivisection reveals Lewis, the logician making a robust and fair-minded argument on behalf of the animals. If, however, he believes there will be more battles to fight, then those who would seek to craft convincing arguments in the midst of fresh challenges might also benefit by a quick course in Lewisian epistemology which informs his homiletics. For the shaping and making of arguments that appeal to reality, as best it can be known, was very much a part of Lewis's academic life as well as his public one.

Lewis as an objectivist

Lewis was an objectivist and believed all convincing arguments must begin with an appeal to reality. When the appeal is false, reality is the corrective. Perhaps a story might clarify the point. During his later years at Oxford University, Lewis was the president of the debating society appropriately called the Oxford Socratic Club. The late Princeton University Professor Erik Routley, a student at Oxford at the time, recalls an evening where Lewis was confronted by one who was deeply affected by Positivist Philosophy. Lewis was asked, "Well, how can you prove anything? I mean, how can you prove there isn't a blue cow sitting on that piano?" To which Lewis replied, "Well, in what sense blue?"[441] Nothing can be confirmed without objects to which one might refer (either a material object, or an object of thought contained within a definition and developed with inferential care and precision). I once came out of a stall in the men's lavatory only to find a woman fixing her makeup at the mirror. When she saw me she chided me for being in the women's rest room. In response I simply pointed to objects in the room and uttered a single word, "Urinals." She screamed and left the room. It was a debate simply won. Clarifying reality ended all discussion. Of course not all reality is as easily established as that, nevertheless, these examples do make clear what is necessary to argue any point well. Lewis believed that judgments have

---

441   ROUTLEY, Erik, —A Prophet C. S. Lewis at the Breakfast Table, James Como, editor. P. 35

no meaning without a standard; they must be tethered to: something transcendent; something defined; or some material object.

Lewis's guidelines for making any kind of sound argument

In *The Abolition of Man* Lewis argues that reality exists independent of those who have the capacity to know about it. He uses the word "Tao" as a kind of shorthand for what he calls, "The Doctrine of Objective Value, the belief that certain attitudes are really true, and others really false, to the kind of thing the universe is and the kind of things we are."[442] This is not a matter of whim or wishful thinking. All thought, feeling, and volition, ought to conform to reality. Lewis, unapologetically and narrowly asserts that the Tao, "is the sole source of all value judgments."[443] In words that echo his argument in *Vivisection*, he wrote "Only the Tao provides a common human law of action which can over-arch rulers and ruled alike. A dogmatic belief in objective value is necessary to the very idea of a rule which is not tyranny or an obedience which is not slavery."[444] In *The Abolition of Man*, Lewis asserts there is an objective universe which is inexorable. He suggests that it is incumbent upon men and women to adjust the scoliosis of their thinking, and their moral and emotional selves to this objective reality. Seldom do we understand our world exactly as it is, so we do well to benefit from the perspectives of others in dialectically safe community. This objective world, and the wide range of ways to express what can be known about that world, guides Lewis in making aesthetic judgments, moral judgments, literary critical judgments, as well as judgments concerning man's responsibility to nature and the animal world. With respect of this, Lewis seeks to reason in ways that are integrated and coherent. Furthermore, due to

---

442   Lewis, C. S. *The Abolition of Man* San Francisco: Harper Collins Edition, 2001. P. 18

443   *Ibid.* P. 43

444   *Ibid,* P. 73

human limitation Lewis recognized some form of check and balance was necessary for human thought if one was to reason well.

Lewis's epistemological checks and balances: authority, reason, and experience

The finite as well as morally flawed condition evident in human thinking and experience will require some kind of device to minimize the hazards of thought and maximize attempts at better approximations to know and understand. Some kind of system of checks and balances on all levels of human thinking is necessary to get somewhere near success in the endeavor. Lewis certainly recognizes this, and his belief that truth is objective encourages him in the effort to find checks on his own thought processes. Drawing on the conventions of Classical and Scholastic thought Lewis found these checks in: "Authority, Reason and Experience." He writes, "Authority, reason, experience; on these three, mixed in varying proportion all our knowledge depends."[445] He sees this triad in use throughout history and

445 LEWIS, *Christian Reflections, p. 41. The use of authority, reason and experience to confirm a matter occurs, not infrequently, in Lewis's work. His essay, Why I Am Not a Pacifist. The Weight of Glory: and Other Addresses. New York: Touchstone/Simon and Schuster. 1996. pp. 53-71 (Hereafter cited as LEWIS, Weight of Glory), is developed throughout on a practical application of authority, reason and experience. Lewis writes that affirmations in literary criticism come from history, i.e., authority; scholarship, i.e., reason; and experience. They are aids to Enable the reader to enter more fully into the author's intentions. LEWIS, C. S., 1969. The Anthropological Approach. Selected Literary Essays. Walter Hooper, ed. Cambridge: Cambridge University Press, p. 307. (Hereafter cited as LEWIS, Selected Literary Essays) In The Discarded Image, he writes, In the Middle Ages, there are three kinds of proof: from Reason, from Authority, and from Experience. We establish a geometrical truth by reason; an historical truth, by authority, by auctours. We learn by experience that oysters do or do not agree with us. p. 189. In the portion of The Discarded Image on The*

employs it himself with confidence, encouraging his readers to do the same.

Authority

Regarding Authority, Lewis writes, "Believing things on authority only means believing them because you have been told them by someone you think trustworthy."[446]

He believes that ninety-nine percent of the facts with which our reason works come to us by means of some kind of authority, "Of every hundred facts upon which to reason, ninety-nine depend on authority."[447]

He also writes, "Ninety-nine percent of the things you believe are believed on authority. I believe there is such a place as New York. I have not seen it myself. I could not prove it by abstract reasoning that there must be such a place. I believe it because reliable people have told me so. The ordinary man believes in the Solar System, atoms, evolution, and the circulation of the blood on authority—because the scientists say so. Every historical statement in the world is believed on authority. None of us has seen the Norman Conquest or the defeat of the Spanish Armada. None of us could prove them by pure logic as you prove a thing in mathematics. We believe them simply because people who did see them have left writings that tell us about

---

Seven Liberal Arts, specifically the section on Dialectic, Lewis clarifies that Dialectic in the Medieval sense of the word has nothing to do with The modern Marxist sense...Hegelian in origin. p. 189. Lewis clarifies that the Dialectic he speaks of Is concerned with proving, and sets forth three kinds of proof: reason, authority and experience. p. 189. Certainly one of the most well known applications of this triad by Lewis grows out of his development of the aut Deus aut malus homo argument for the Deity of Christ. LEWIS, God in the Dock. p. 101. In Mere Christianity, Lewis supports the argument with authority, reason and experience. First, Jesus claimed to be God (authority); second, his life and teaching appeared to confirm it (experience); third, it appears that he couldn't be mad or evil (reason). p. 4281

446   LEWIS, Mere Christianity. Book II. 5, p. 49
447   LEWIS, The Weight of Glory, p. 54.

them: in fact, on authority."[448] and that "few of us have followed the reasoning on which even ten percent of the truths we believe are based."[449] Therefore, Lewis recognizes, "A man who jibbed at authority in other things as some people do in religion would have to be content to know nothing all his life."[450] Ultimately, Lewis believes that Authority is vested in the God who reveals Himself and his purposes. In this regard Lewis believes that the Christian faith is an objective faith for it accounts for a revealed and objective world. Furthermore, if creatures are ever to know their creator, the initiative[451] can never rest on the side of the creature. The creator will have to reveal Himself (or creaturely knowledge of Him will be impossible), and these revelations will have authoritative value. Lewis believes that God reveals Himself several ways: generally in Nature and in the Laws of Nature;[452] in human conscience and the Moral Law;[453] and also in other human beings.[454] Natural revelation also presents itself for human speculation in what can be known about creatures other than man; that is in the animals something of the creativity and purpose of God can be studied. Furthermore, God reveals Himself specifically in several ways also: the Word of God Incarnate; in the Word of God written; and, in some ways, through individual inspiration.[455]

---

448   LEWIS, Mere Christianity. Book II. 5. p. 49.

449   LEWIS, The Weight of Glory , p. 55

450   LEWIS, Mere Christianity. Book II. 5, pp. 49-50

451   LEWIS, Surprised By Joy , p. 227

452   LEWIS, Christian Reflections, pp. 78-81

453   LEWIS, Mere Christianity. Book I. 4-5, pp. 19-25

454   LEWIS, The Weight of Glory, p. 40. Lewis writes, "Next to the Blessed Sacrament itself, your neighbour is the holiest object presented to your senses. If he is your Christian Neighbour, he is holy in almost the same way, for in him also Christ vere latitat— the glorifier and the glorified, Glory Himself, is truly hidden."

455   Of Bunyan's particular genius Lewis observes, "It came'. I doubt if we shall ever know more of the process called inspiration' than those two monosyllables tell us." LEWIS, Selected Literary Essays, p. 147

Even though Lewis believes that God has revealed Himself in many ways, he also believes it is possible for the revelation of God to be abused. Anyone can attach the words "Thus saith the Lord" to his own opinions, invoking divine authority to sustain his own views and produce a kind of tyranny.[456] This cannot be held as an objection against authority per se, but only to the misuse of authority. Lewis often quoted the maxim from Plato's Laws, "An abuse does not nullify a proper use." Abuse occurs when Divine authority is used to buttress the opinions of manipulators and power mongers. Thus, though authority is of vital importance in knowing, to be of value it must be checked by reason and experience.

Reason

Lewis recognizes that "all possible knowledge...depends on the validity of reasoning."[457] Lewis also writes,"We may state it as a rule that no thought is valid if it can be fully explained as the result of irrational causes.[458] He thinks that there is a rationality existing in the universe from which all human rationality is derived; it is objective, not merely a consequence of projecting onto the universe what is not there intrinsically. "Unless all that we take to be knowledge is an illusion, we must hold that in

456 *Lewis writes, "On those who add Thus saith the Lord' to their merely human utterances descends the doom of conscience that seems clearer the more it is loaded with sin. All this comes from pretending that God has spoken when He has not". Meditations on the Third Commandment. LEWIS, God in the Dock , p. 198. Lewis also recognizes, "Even for adults, it is sweet, sweet, sweet poison' to feel able to imply Thus saith the Lord' at the end of every expression of our pet aversions." LEWIS, Christian Reflections, p. 31. He adds, 'The danger of mistaking our merely natural, though perhaps legitimate enthusiasms for holy zeal, is always great'. LEWIS, God in the Dock, p. 198. It is a kind of borderline blasphemy. I say borderline because when this is done, I hardly believe that it is done as an act of intentional blasphemy. Nonetheless, it is done all too often, and has its own kind of negative consequence in both the doer and the one done by*

457 *LEWIS, Miracles, p. 19.*

458 *Ibid., pp. 20-21*

thinking we are not reading rationality into an irrational universe, but responding to a rationality with which the universe has always been saturated."[459] For Lewis, Reason involves three aspects: 1) the reception of facts; 2) the perception of self-evident truths and axioms; and 3) "the art or skill of arranging the facts so as to yield a series of such intuitions which linked together produce a proof of the truth or falsehood of the proposition we are considering."[460] This last aim is a rhetorical one, for it employs invention and arranges the argument for persuasive ends. Furthermore, Lewis believes, for instance, that "primary moral principles on which all others depend are rationally perceived."[461] "We just see that there is no reason why my neighbour's happiness should be sacrificed to my own, as we just see that things which are equal to the same thing are equal to one another." Lewis adds, "If we cannot prove either axiom, that is not because they are irrational but because they are self-evident and all proofs depend on them. Their intrinsic reasonableness shines by its own light."[462] This leads him to conclude, "It is because all morality is based on such self-evident principles that we say to a man, when we would recall him to right conduct, be reasonable."[463] He believes that wrong conduct has something in it that is unreasonable. Therefore, it is a precursor to that form of subjectivism which is untethered from objective reality.

Lest he be misunderstood, it must also be noted that, for Lewis, moral failure is not synonymous with utter moral blindness or rational lapse, as he explains:

> As regards the Fall, I submit that the general tenor of scripture does not encourage us to believe that our knowledge of the Law has been depraved in the same degree as our power to fulfill it....our perceptions of right...may, no doubt, be impaired; but there is a difference between imperfect sight and blindness. A

459   *LEWIS, Christian Reflections, p.* 65
460   *Ibid., p.* 54
461   *LEWIS, Miracles, p.* 35
462   *Ibid*
463   *Ibid*

theology which goes about to represent our practical reason as radically unsound is headed for disaster.[464]

If we are utterly blind, morally, we can never be judged for our moral lapses. The blind man must be treated with sympathy when he stumbles, not with contempt. He cannot help himself. However, if one can judge the moral failures he observes in others, he is not in the same condition as the blind man. Our own failures are without excuse, especially when we find ourselves doing the very thing we have condemned in others. Of course, it may be that our judgments against others are not as refined as we first suppose. If we can be blind to our own lapses and misunderstand how morally shortsighted we are, then it is possible that we might misjudge the actions and intentions of others as well. We might condemn a relatively innocent behavior simply because we misunderstand it or find ourselves inconvenienced by it. If this can be the case, then we will have to admit the possibility that cosmic activity can also be misunderstood and misjudged.

Lewis observes, "Unless we allow ultimate reality to be moral we cannot morally condemn it."[465] He understands that "our very condemnation of reality carries in its heart an unconscious act of allegiance to that same reality as the source of our moral standards."[466] Consequently, "The pell-mell of phenomena, as we first observe them, seems to be full of anomalies and irregularities; but being assured that reality is logical we go on framing and trying out hypotheses to show the apparent irregularities are not really irregular at all."[467] Lewis writes, "The process whereby, having admitted that reality in the last resort must be moral, we attempt to explain evil, is the history of theology."[468] Reason, despite its deficiencies in its work with available and ever expanding data, allows for approximate answers to the problem of evil (whether it be evil of man against man, or man against animals), and should constantly be used for bet-

---

464   LEWIS, *Christian Reflections*, p. 79

465   *Ibid.*, p. 70

466   *Ibid.*

467   *Ibid.*, pp. 70-71

468   *Ibid.*, p. 71

ter and better approximations. Reason, as helpful as it is, cannot give a final word on any matter because of the limitations under which it operates. There are too many variables. Good attempts at dealing with the issues of evil generally, and animal suffering specifically, may be judged by their scope and the degree to which they account for the complexities involved. It is enough for some critics to see evidence in the problem of evil and suffering to conclude that God (at least the Christian God) cannot exist. One wonders if the complexities of knowledge, generally, and the issues relating to the limits of reason, justify such a definitive position on the matter. Furthermore, one wonders if the numbers of problems created by denying the existence of God, as well as the problems that occur in attempts to try and explain the phenomena of evil and suffering without a belief in God, can be surmounted. It would appear that the most substantial work done on this matter (with the most reasonable approaches) has been done by those who take the existence of God as valid, and the many problems of evil, including the matter of animal suffering, as matters which must be tackled. Lewis is among those who believe that reason is necessary for working through issues essential to these problems, but reason cannot properly function in isolation from authority and experience.

Experience

Lewis believes that experience, despite all of its benefits, should not be trusted on its own. It needs the checks of authority and reason. Hume argues, "The *ultimate* standard by which we determine *all* disputes...is *always* derived from experience and observation [italics mine]."[469] Lewis takes issue with this kind of thought. He writes, "We never start from a *tabula rasa*: if we did, we should end, ethically speaking, with a *tabula rasa*."[470]

The *tabula rasa*, like a movie screen, cannot retain any of the images projected on it unless it has some power to retain those

---

469   HUME, David. An Inquiry Concerning Human Understanding. Sec. X. Of Miracles. Part I. p. 490

470   LEWIS, Christian Reflections, p. 53

images. It can never make sense of the images retained unless it has some capacity to sort, classify, compare, and contrast those images. The power to retain and to sort must be a power that precedes the experience itself. Thus, to make any sense of experience *a posteriori*, there must exist something *a priori*. As William James observes, "Without selective interest, experience is an utter chaos."[471] Experience must operate with the checks and balances of reason and authority, or it seems destined to fall into various forms of subjectivism or skepticism.

Lewis writes, "The senses are not infallible."[472] He says further, Experience by itself proves nothing.[473] And, Experience proves this, or that, according to the preconceptions we bring to it.[474] While he sees the risks of emphasizing experience over reason and authority, he also recognizes the value of experience as part of a whole epistemological operation. In his autobiography, Lewis notes the valuable part that experience played in his own thinking. "What I like about experience is that it is such an honest thing." Then he adds, "You may take any number of wrong turnings; but keep your eyes open and you will not be allowed to go very far before warning signs appear. You may have deceived yourself, but experience is not trying to deceive you. The universe rings true wherever you fairly test it."[475] The fair test, for Lewis, includes the checks and balances of authority, reason, and experience. In his attempts to resolve the problems of objectivity, Lewis, whether successful or not, sought to respect this balance.

---

471   *Psychology. William James. XI. Mark Twain writes, "We should be careful to get out of an experience only the wisdom that is in it—and stop there; lest we be like the cat that sits down on a hot stove-lid. She will never sit on a hot stove-lid again—and that is well; but also she will never sit down on a cold one anymore." Pudd'nhead Wilson's New Calendar. XI. Lewis writes, "consciousness is, from the outset, selective, and ceases when selection ceases...not to attend to one part of our experience at the expense of the rest, is to be asleep." LEWIS, Preface to Paradise Lost, p. 136*

472   *LEWIS, God in the Dock, p. 25.*

473   *Ibid., pp. 25-26*

474   *Ibid., p. 26*

475   *LEWIS, Surprised By Joy, p. 177*

Those who seek to advocate on behalf of the animals in the face of every fresh challenge would do well to benefit from Lewis's approach.

The fundamental soundness of Lewis's epistemology can be tested and applied not scientifically but by virtue of its internal coherence and reasonableness. His system holds water. The potential for leaks can be plugged by virtue of its checks and balances and its capacity to eliminate self-referentialism. Why is this important in the manner of considering man's responsibility to the animals, nature, the environment, the unborn, matters of social justice, the education of children, and so forth? Because if one's arguments fail at the point of objectivity they lose the power to convince. This does not mean all arguments classified as truly objective will convince. Other variables may be at play in the hearts and minds of one's hearers. Nevertheless, if an argument hopes to persuade and maintain the capacity to remain convincing it must be rooted in objective reality. This approach of Lewis's then must be of significant interest to all who would persuade others of man's responsibility for animals.

One potential objection to Lewis's approach must also be considered due to a present contempt for objectivity that is grossly misinformed. Some wrongly suppose that all interest in objective thought is associated with the Enlightenment rationalism used to support Western conquest, colonialism, and even vivisection. Lewis's source for objectivity was older, more robust than anything suggested by the Enlightenment. His sources are Classical, Scholastic, Eastern and Western. Lewis was deliberate to use the word Tao to describe objective value. He wanted an Eastern word. The Appendix of *The Abolition of Man* is full of sources both Eastern and Western to illustrate that Lewis's thought on the matter of objectivity has a life that transcends anything suggested by the Enlightenment.

Conclusion

Lewis was persuasive when it came to advocacy on behalf of human responsibility for the animals. Where his arguments

are strong they reflect a mind skilled in argument and persua-
sion. Furthermore, he wrote significantly about reality and the
description of things as they are rather than how we might long
for those things to be. He also wrote with a relative interper-
sonal security that did not become defensive when bested in an
argument. He stayed engaged and grew stronger in his understanding of various matters as well as in his rhetorical skill. This
material is also useful for all who would engage in crafting fresh
arguments whenever new challenges arise; much can be learned
from Lewis by contagion as well as by instruction. Nevertheless, in this article it was discovered that Lewis's writing about
animals is uneven. Some places he seems to be more concerned
with emotional features surrounding the question and at other
times his reason appears to be scintillating and very convincing
given the precision of his reason and his capacity for rhetorical
clarity. The principles that guide his thinking reveal a man well
trained in classical and scholastic logic. Nevertheless, though
there are rules to reason as there are rules to the game of chess,
knowing the rules is no guarantee a contestant will win every
time he or she sits down to play the game. So too, the best of
thinkers, whose knowledge of the game of reason and rhetoric
is well honed and disciplined may at times reason poorly. This
is not stated as a critique merely a reminder lest we too should
begin to think we will reason flawlessly every time we sit down
to consider seriously some matter put before us. Issues may be at
play in each of us that can blind us to deep-seated inclinations
that feed our assumptions and predispose us to see only what
we want to see. Philosopher John Locke once observed, "What-
soever credit or authority we give to any proposition more than
it receives from the principles and proofs it supports itself on, is
owing to our inclination that way."[476] Something can be said
about Lewis, helpful for all who wrestle seriously with the matter of animals, he kept working on deepening his grasp of this
theme he considered so important. The matter of the mystery

---

476   KER, Ian and Alan Hill, editors. Newman after a Hundred Years.
John Locke quoted by Basil Mitchell in —Newman as Philosopher Oxford:
Clarendon, 1990. P. 223

of animals, the matter of sharing life with them on this planet, the matter of animal pain, and human responsibility for the animals are all topics that call for serious attention; certainly Lewis thought so. Some of his earliest work in Christian apologetics concerned itself with the matter and some of his last letters are still addressing the topic. This is a subject of great importance and the time given to wrestling with each feature of it is well worth the investment. Consistent with a major theme running through all of his writing, "Reality is Iconoclastic," Lewis acknowledges that no last word on any matter is likely to be discovered, nevertheless, sure words are accessible. Working from the known, Lewis is always willing to employ both reason and the imagination to push the envelope of understanding further and further along into the regions of the yet unknown but hopefully accessible. Whatever one may think of his conclusions Lewis, as a scholar of his stature, must be taken seriously. Perhaps the most convincing feature of all he wrote about animals was his willingness to stay with the topic. In this regard he is an ally to all who feel the moral responsibility to concern themselves with the welfare of the animals and to engage in rhetoric for their defense and care.

—*Gerald Root, Ph.D* .

Hannah More:
Burdened for
the Beasts

(Excerpted and adapted from *Fierce Convictions—The Extraordinary Life of Hannah More: Poet, Reformer, Abolitionist* by Karen Swallow Prior, Nelson Books, 2014)

Although largely forgotten today, the British poet and dramatist Hannah More (1745-1833) was well known during her lifetime for her widespread efforts at reform across all of society. While not a central focus of her efforts, animal welfare was a concern for her. More was a close friend of William Wilberforce, the abolitionist who also helped begin England's first society for prevention of animal cruelty, and she joined him in advocating, even if less prominently, mercy and kindness toward animals.

The culture into which More was born was one that imagined, and had imagined for many centuries, that all of creation, from top to bottom, was bonded together from heaven to earth like the links of a chain. Every category of creation was seen as a link on this great chain of being, as it was called. Human beings were the middle links, each order of angels ascended as the upward links, and each order of animal, plants and minerals descended along the lower ones. This hierarchical view extended into the general categories as well. Within the category of human beings all were hierarchically arranged by class, with royalty and nobility on the links above commoners, and so on.

This image of the great chain of being held powerful sway over the image by which More's society viewed the relationships of human beings with one another and the rest of creation. People were only beginning to imagine a world that did not consist of rigid, hierarchical boundaries.

From today's vantage point, one in which equality is valued, the problems with such a controlling image are readily apparent. Yet the strength of such a view of the order of creation was the belief that each link, whether placed high or low on the chain, was equally important to the strength of the entire chain. The well-being of society as a whole depended on the well-being of each link in the chain and on maintaining each link's proper place in the chain. While members of More's society found it difficult to envision a form of equality that would not upend all order, they valued the importance of each link in the chain.

The understanding that on the great chain humans held a higher place than animals had a twofold implication for reform efforts by More and her friends. First, human beings were understood as superior in moral significance and value in the chain of being; however, their elevated place on the chain was accompanied by great responsibility toward the lower creatures. By the same thinking, the upper classes were likewise responsible for the well-being of the lower classes. More and her like-minded reformers, therefore, saw the reform of one part of society as having ripple effects for all of society. The work More undertook in educating the poor was not an endeavor separate from her attempts to elevate the morals of the upper class. Nor were these efforts separate from her quieter endeavors to promote kindness toward animals. In strengthening the separate links, each of these activities served to strengthen the entire chain.

The image of the great chain of being made the interconnectedness of all creation impossible to ignore to minds of moral clarity and integrity. A famous series of engravings printed in 1751 by the eighteenth-century artist William Hogarth dramatically portrayed this kind of interconnectedness within the scales of both creation and morality. "The Four Stages of Cruelty" depicts a central figure that goes from torturing small animals as a boy, to beating a fallen horse as a corrupt coachman, to murdering his lover and finally to receiving his just reward of public dissection after being tried, convicted and hanged. Each print is highly detailed (including the depiction of various acts of horrific cruelty perpetrated on animals), expanding the story as unfolded through the sequence of pictures and creating a visual narrative that sets forth a holistic moral vision. While in the previous century, Descartes and his followers had viewed animals as mere machines to be used by humans with no regard in the name of science, Hogarth's work reflects a shifting attitude. Kindness toward animals was a growing concern in the eighteenth century.

The evolution of More's own views on animal welfare reflects both this societal shift and her own strengthening faith convictions. In her earlier literary career, More criticized poetic expressions of sentimentality toward animals as a form of rhetorical excess and emotional self-indulgence, especially in her poem "Sensibility," published in 1782 in the same volume as *Sacred Dramas*. During the so-called "long eighteenth century," 1660-1830, a "cult of sensibility" arose which exalted the outward manifestations of emotional sensitivity—weeping, fainting and the like—as the marks of morality and refined character, to the point that signs of sensibility became more important than benevolent or moral action. In addressing the virtues and limits of sensibility in the poem, More cautioned against the hypocrisy of an overly sentimental view of animals that neglects higher moral obligations:

> There are, who fill with brilliant plaints the page,
>
> If a poor linnet meet the gunner's rage;
>
> There are, who for a dying fawn deplore,
>
> As if friend, parent, country, were no more;

Who boast, quick rapture trembling in their eye,

If from the spider's snare they snatch a fly;

There are, whose well-sung plaints each breast inflame,

And break all hearts--but his from whom they came.

He, scorning life's low duties to attend,

Writes odes on friendship, while he cheats his friend...
(lines 267-276)[477]

When More's interests and work later shifted in response to her growing Christian conviction, her view toward animal welfare underwent a parallel expansion. Despite the excesses of sensibility which concerned More, it was sensibility that helped foster the growing opposition toward cruelty in all forms, whether that of slavery, prison and labor conditions or animal mistreatment. Sensibility was part of a larger social and theological framework that encompassed all of society and creation. This meant that the welfare of animals was an important issue for the reformers. "England is a paradise for women and hell for horses," Robert Burton, the famous seventeenth-century Oxford scholar, had written as far back as 1621 in *The Anatomy of Melancholy*. More was joining others in attesting the truth of the latter point.

William Cowper—the poet More described as one she could read on Sunday and coauthor with John Newton's of the *Olney Hymns*—reflected both emotional sensibility and Evangelical conviction in his poetic treatment of animals. Indeed, Cowper has been called the "eighteenth-century poet of animal welfare"[478]

for his poetic (and personal) identification with suffering animals, most famously in *The Task*. Here Cowper likens his own pain to that of a struck deer, which he then links to the crucified Christ:

    I was a stricken deer that left the herd

477   *Hannah More, Works vol. 5*

478   *Emma Major, Madam Britannia: Women, Church, and Nation 1712--1812. Oxford University Press, 2011, p.74*

Long since; with many an arrow deep infixt

My panting side was charged when I withdrew

To seek a tranquil death in distant shades.

There was I found by one who had himself

Been hurt by th' archers. In his side he bore

And in his hands and feet the cruel scars.[479]

Such cultivation of the moral imagination through art and literature undergirded the efforts of the reformers across a range of concerns. The same empathy for slaves that More and her friends sought to develop through a moral imagination ran along the entire chain of being, all the way down to the brutes. The abolitionists' inclusion of animal welfare in their attempts to cultivate benevolence across society went back at least to More's friend and fellow abolitionist Margaret Middleton, who was an early role model to Hannah in the animal welfare concern. More said of Middleton that "her kindness, which you would think must needs be exhausted on the negroes, extends to the suffering of every animal."[480] Imaginative identification with others illuminated, More and her friends believed, the relationship of humanity in relationship to God.

In the view of reformers like More, a society that mistreated animals presented a distorted image of God's relationship to his human creation.

---

479   William Cowper, *The Task, Book III. http://www.gutenberg.org/cache/epub/3698/pg3698.html]*

480   *Qtd. in Ann Stott, Hannah More: The First Victorian. Oxford University Press, 2003, p. 87*

Amazing Grace: The Work of William Wilberforce

Amazing Grace, A film biography of William Wilberforce, anti-slavery crusader and co-founder of the world's oldest anti-cruelty society, captures Wilberforce's deep devotion to animals and his determination to end the cruelty and suffering imposed upon them in the late 18th and early 19th centuries.

The film, which came out in American theaters in February 2007, was exactly 200 years after Wilberforce's 20-year fight to abolish the slave trade in the British Empire ended, with the passage of the Foreign Slave Trade Act in 1807. As the filmmakers point out, however, many of the social problems Wilberforce sought to address, including cruelty to animals, are still with us.

Produced by Bristol Bay Productions and directed by Michael Apted, *Amazing Grace* stars Ioan Gruffudd as Wilberforce, with Albert Finney, Romola Garai, Michael Gambon, Benedict Cumberbatch, Rufus Sewell, Ciaran Hinds, and Youssou N'Dour in supporting roles.

William Wilberforce

For two decades, William Wilberforce (1759-1833) led the struggle in the English Parliament to abolish slavery, and it was his principal concern as a politician and a reformer. But he did not limit his vision of a better world solely to his fellow human beings. Wilberforce was also a founding figure of the animal protection movement, helping to found the first society for the prevention of cruelty to animals and providing essential support for the first modern laws on the subject.

A man of intense personal piety and one of the outstanding lay Christians of his era, Wilberforce was a central figure in the Clapham Evangelicals, a group whose humanitarian sensibility expressed itself in support for a number of social causes, anti-slavery the most important. From the late 1780s to his retirement in 1825, in the British Parliament and in public life, Wilberforce worked to curb and eliminate slavery. After three attempts and twenty years, he and his colleagues secured the Foreign Slave Trade Act (1806-07), the decisive legislation outlawing the participation of British vessels in the slave trade. Although this legislation did not end slavery, it struck a serious blow to the institution throughout the world.

Even as the slavery issue dominated his personal and political life, Wilberforce found time to champion the cause of animal protection from the moment it first surfaced. He was present for and involved with every Parliamentary debate on cruelty issues, from the first failed proposal by Sir William Pultney in 1800 to the watershed breakthrough of Martin's Act in 1822. Over those 22 years, moreover, Wilberforce remained faithful to the cause, against objections that the subject of cruelty to animals was not suited to the dignity of a legislature.

The debate over cruelty was never confined solely to Parliament, of course. In his popular work, *A Practical View of the Prevailing Religious System of Professed Christians* (1797), Wilberforce had castigated field sports designed "to fill up the void of a listless and languid age." But as the eighteenth century drew to a close, controversy settled on the issue of bullbaiting, one variant of a host of sporting activities in which animals were set to fight against one another. Every community had a bullring, and the ritual took place in more or less the same form all over.

As one historian describes it, "A bull, securely tethered to a stake in the ground by a rope long enough to allow him freedom of movement, was set upon by dogs, often specially bred for the sport. While the enraged bull defended himself—tossing, shaking, goring unlucky attackers—the dogs tried to slip and claim the bull's sensitive lips or nostrils in their vise-like jaws. The skill of the attackers, the tenacity of the bull, his bellows of anguish, dogs hurtling through the air with their bellies ripped open, gallons of beer and the clink of silver all blinded in a fevered heat of uproar and excitement."

In the first weeks of the year 1800, a group of citizens journeyed to London from the countryside to speak with Wilberforce about the cruelties of bullbaiting. They were determined to ask Parliament to suppress it. Already involved with dozens of reforms, Wilberforce declined to lead their cause, but promised to support them and to sponsor the legislation if they didn't find anyone else willing to do so.

As it turned out, they did. In April 1800, Pulteney introduced his bill to prohibit bullbaiting. Unfortunately the bill never got to a second reading. Along with Richard Martin and others who would step forward whenever animal welfare legislation arose, Wilberforce supported it. He remarked that the usual summonses for attendance were not sent out to supporters of the bill, and he felt that it had not received the proper stewardship.

Wilberforce thought bullbaiting "cruel and inhuman," and the fact that such events profaned the Sabbath in his mind made them still worse. Wilberforce called bullbaiting one of the "multiplied plague spots" on England's complexion, "sure indicatives" of a "falling state." He felt sure, he told his colleagues, that if the principal opponent to the legislation, Windham, "or any other member, had inquired into the subject minutely, he would no longer defend a practice which degraded human nature."

Pulteney tried again in 1802 and Wilberforce, Richard Martin, and Richard Brinsley Sheridan supported his bill.

Wilberforce spoke in its favor, cautioning his colleagues that the subject ought not to be treated with levity. Countering the argument that baiting was a source of great amusement for "the people," Wilberforce observed that the condition of the people "must be wretched indeed" if this were the case. This bill made it through the House of Lords, but was rejected in the House of Commons.

The next benchmark came on May 15, 1809, when Lord Erskine rose to introduce his bill on cruelty to animals, and delivered the first protracted discussion of the question in any legislative body. Erskine designed his legislation not to abolish a single pastime but to "suppress willful and wanton" cruelty to all domestic animals. The bill's scope was eventually limited to beasts of draught and burden. Along with Samuel Romilly and James Stephen, Wilberforce again spoke in favor. Erskine's bill passed the Lords but failed in the Commons by a few votes. By the time he introduced it again the following year, opposition had stiffened, and the subject would not gain further parliamentary discussion for more than a decade.

The public campaign against cruelty to animals did not end during this hiatus of legislative activity, however. Even without the benefit of anti-cruelty law, Wilberforce and others confronted cruelty in public where and when they could. Once in Bath, Wilberforce got out of his carriage to stop a cart driver from beating and kicking a fallen horse. As the man prepared to turn upon him, another driver stepped up and whispered "Wilberforce" in the driver's ear.

By 1821, the Irish M.P. Richard Martin had emerged as the most ardent champion of anti-cruelty legislation in Parliament. Martin's bill "to prevent cruel and improper treatment of cattle" was introduced in the House of Commons. Wilberforce and Fowell Buxton were amongst its sponsors. In its second introduction, in 1822 the bill sailed through both houses and received Royal Assent on July 22.

Less than two years later, on June 16, 1824, Wilberforce was present with Martin, Buxton, and others, at old Slaughter's Pub, where the Society for the Prevention of Cruelty to Animals was formed. The era of formal advocacy for animals had begun.

*—**Bernard Unti, Ph.D.** is senior policy adviser and special assistant to the CEO of The HSUS. He is the author of Protecting All Animals: A Fifty-Year History of The Humane Society of the United States , and is currently writing a book on the 19th-century animal protection movement.*

For more information, including educational resources and related products, visit the *Amazing Grace* official movie website at: http://www.amazinggracemovie.com/

How You Can Help

Humane Backyard—Ideas for outdoor projects to celebrate God's creation. Humane Backyard is about humane, sustainable ideas for helping local wildlife and habitats. Humane Backyard online includes ideas for projects from birdseed ornaments to repurposing Christmas trees for wildlife. Find ideas for projects all year round that can be created through your faith group at your place of worship or at home. Humane Backyards are peaceful havens for all of God's creatures. They are habitats that shelter and feed native wildlife while bringing natural beauty and spiritual nourishment to the community. Consider transforming your outdoor space at your place of worship into a Humane Backyard. Whether you live and worship in an urban, suburban or rural area, you can create a Humane Backyard.

Visit the website at: http://www.humanesociety.org/humanehaven

Fill the Bowl Project—A pet food collection toolkit to help families with pets and animal shelters in need, right in your own community. Every day, families struggle to keep food on the table for their children and food in the bowl for their pets. Some must give up their pets because they simply can't feed them. Through the Fill the Bowl Project, faith communities can help by collecting pet food and partnering with local food pantries for distribution to families in need. Animal shelters and rescue groups strive to feed the growing number of cats, dogs and other homeless pets in their care, as well. This project encourages faith communities to build relationships with local food banks and animal shelters. Fill the Bowl Project is inspirational and fulfilling for youth groups, service projects, seasonal outreach and more.

Visit the website at: http://www.humanesociety.org/fillthebowl

"Eating Mercifully" documentary—Christian perspectives on factory-farming issues, plus questions for reflection. Twenty-six minutes may forever change the way you look at food and faith.

"Eating Mercifully" examines critical findings of a Pew Commission report on U.S. industrial animal agriculture and considers factory-farming practices from several Christian viewpoints.

Online questions for reflection are provided by Dr. Norman Wirzba of Duke Divinity School. This film is designed for group screenings and discussion of humane farming practices and associated issues.

View the documentary at: http://www.humanesociety.org/eatingmercifully

St. Francis Day in a Box—Celebrate the season of St. Francis, the patron saint of animals, with animal protection projects in your community. Plan a pet food collection, film screening, small group discussion, youth group event and more. This seasonal toolkit is offered for a limited time from late summer through mid-October. Special offers may include discount coupons for the latest books in Christian nonfiction, as well as many HSUS resources to launch animal protection projects in your faith community.

Visit the website at: http://www.humanesociety.org/stfrancis

Join Our Team

Become a member! For just $25 a year, you can join millions of other compassionate people, whose generous support enables us to protect dogs, cats, seals, horses and other animals at home and worldwide. As a member, you'll receive a one-year subscription to our award-winning bimonthly magazine, *All Animals*. Plus, we'll send you updates and action alerts so you can take quick, simple actions for animals each week. Make a difference for animals today.

Join us at: http://www.humanesociety.org/countmein

Volunteer. Advocate for animal rights where you live! Volunteer with HSUS Faith Outreach and become a part of our team. Faith Outreach volunteers learn more about the intersection between religion and animal protection while strengthening important skills such as networking, critical thinking and community outreach. Volunteers have the opportunity to work directly with faith leaders and animal welfare experts as part of a prominent animal protection organization.

Sign up at: http://www.humanesociety.org/faithvolunteers

Explore other opportunities at The HSUS

Do you have a passion for a particular animal protection issue? Find your niche by becoming an HSUS Ally! Allies are encouraged to use outreach skills including letter-writing, phone banking and participate in special events to advocate for animals.

Become an ally at: http://www.humanesociety.org/faithally

Stay connected

Get the latest news and information through *The Humane Steward*, the monthly newsletter of The HSUS Faith Outreach program. Sign up at: http://bit.ly/1JrXYwP

Join us on Facebook at https://www.facebook.com/HSUSFaith

—***Karen L. Allanach*** *is Communications Manager for State Affairs at The Humane Society of the United States. For the past eight years, she helped create community programs and outreach materials for The HSUS Faith Outreach program, including* The Fill the Bowl Project, Eating Mercifully, Humane Backyard, *and the seasonal* St. Francis Day in a Box! *Since joining The HSUS in 1999, Mrs. Allanach has held a number of communications roles at The HSUS, helping to connect the public with animal protection issues and build relationships with press nationwide. Mrs. Allanach received her master's degree from The University of Maryland Philip Merrill College of Journalism, in College Park, MD. Prior to launching into a public relations career, Mrs. Allanach worked as a community newspaper reporter, which she credits as her most valuable professional experience that continues to influence her work today.*

Appendix 2

Animals in World Religions

- Gross, Aaron. *The Question of the Animal and Religion: Theoretical Stakes, Practical Implications.* Columbia University Press, 2014.
- Kemmerer, Lisa. *Animals and World Religions.* Oxford University Press, 2012.
- Perlo, Katherine Wills. *Kinship and Killing: The Animal in World Religions.* Columbia University Press, 2009.
- Waldau, Paul and Patton, Kimberly. *A Communion of Subjects: Animals in Religions, Science & Ethics.* Columbia University Press, 2009.

CPSIA information can be obtained
at www.ICGtesting.com
Printed in the USA
LVHW04s2147260418
575002LV00001B/35/P